The
Torah Mosaic

The
Torah Mosaic

INTRODUCING THE PENTATEUCH IN ITS COMPLEX UNITY

TRACY J. McKENZIE

Baker Academic

a division of Baker Publishing Group

Grand Rapids, Michigan

© 2025 by Tracy J. McKenzie

Published by Baker Academic
a division of Baker Publishing Group
Grand Rapids, Michigan
BakerAcademic.com

Printed in the United States of America

Library of Congress Cataloging-in-Publication Data
Names: McKenzie, Tracy J. (Tracy Joel), 1968– author
Title: The Torah mosaic : introducing the Pentateuch in its complex unity / Tracy J. McKenzie.
Description: Grand Rapids, Michigan : Baker Academic, [2025] | Includes bibliographical
    references and index.
Identifiers: LCCN 2025014267 | ISBN 9781540969095 paperback | ISBN 9781540969606 hardcover |
    ISBN 9781493451845 ebook | ISBN 9781493451852 pdf
Subjects: LCSH: Bible. Pentateuch—Criticism, interpretation, etc. | Bible. Old Testament—
    Criticism, interpretation, etc.
Classification: LCC BS1225.52 .M34 2008 | DDC 222/.106—dc23/eng/20250603
LC record available at https://lccn.loc.gov/2025014267

Unless otherwise indicated, Scripture translations are the author's.

Cover design by Paula Gibson

Baker Publishing Group publications use paper produced from sustainable forestry practices and postconsumer waste whenever possible.

25   26   27   28   29   30   31   7   6   5   4   3   2   1

Contents

Figures

Preface

I have taught aspiring pastors and missionaries for twenty years now in hopes that the beauty and truth of the Hebrew Scriptures might make their way into the pulpit, to the congregations, and among the nations. Although I hope this book might still shape the pulpit, it is an effort to speak directly to those in the pew and to the nations. Here I take my research and class lectures, which stem from an academically informed vantage point, and situate them for a more general audience that is interested in the content but has not had the opportunity to sit in my Old Testament and Hebrew classes. In keeping with that purpose, I left out many of the footnotes that could have pointed to the material that shaped my thinking, including scholars such as John Sailhamer, whom I depend on greatly. Another scholar who deserves particular attention, one of John's many gifted students, is Vernon J. Steiner. Vern left the institutional academy to launch an institute of learning in a church I attended as a young believer. During those formative years, I eagerly learned Hebrew and hermeneutics from him, thus bridging the academy and church, the very thing I attempt to do in this book.

In some ways, this type of endeavor may seem flawed from the start: It may appear overly reductionistic to scholars and far too complex for those outside the academy. But I believe that there is too great a disconnect between the phenomena in the text of the Old Testament—important details that influence a text's meaning—and what one might hear in a sermon on Sunday morning. Hopefully, this book will serve as a bridge and sharpen the way the church reads and understands her foundational Scripture.

Besides the many conversation partners among my students and colleagues at Southeastern Baptist Theological Seminary, whom I wish to thank, I also offer gratitude to the encouraging, courteous, and professional editorial staff at Baker Academic. From the initial conversations with Brandy Scritchfield, my acquisitions editor, to senior project editor Wells Turner and many others in between, the process has been a delight, and their involvement has made this a better product at every turn. What is more, this book and the material therein would have never come to fruition without the thoughtful dialogue, constant encouragement, and unwavering support of my wife, Beth, who took some of those same classes at the Miqra Institute some thirty years ago. Words are not adequate to express the debt of gratitude I owe her.

The Torah Mosaic is dedicated to Vernon J. Steiner and his efforts at The Miqra Institute, which fanned into flame our love for the Bible and for the Lion King who has come and will come again.

Abbreviations

General and Bibliographic

[ ]	encloses alternate versification when different from English Bible verse numbering (e.g., Joel 2:28–32 [3:1–5 MT])
ANF	*The Ante-Nicene Fathers*. Edited by Alexander Roberts and James Donaldson. 10 vols. New York: Christian Literature, 1885–96. Reprint, Grand Rapids: Eerdmans, 1950–51.
anniv.	anniversary
BHS	*Biblia Hebraica Stuttgartensia*. Edited by Karl Elliger and Wilhelm Rudolph. Stuttgart: Deutsche Bibelgesellschaft, 1983.
ca.	*circa*, approximately
cent.	century
cf.	compare
ed.	edition, edited by
e.g.	*exempli gratia*, for example
ESV	English Standard Version (2001)
ET	English text
exp.	expanded
HALOT	*The Hebrew and Aramaic Lexicon of the Old Testament*. Ludwig Koehler and Walter Baumgartner. Study ed. 2 vols. Leiden: Brill, 2001.
i.e.	*id est*, that is
MT	Masoretic Text of the Hebrew Bible
NASB	New American Standard Version (2020)
NIV	New International Version (2011)
NPNF[2]	*A Select Library of Nicene and Post-Nicene Fathers of the Christian Church*. Edited by Philip Schaff and Henry Wace. 2nd series. 14 vols. New York: Christian Literature, 1890–1900. Reprint, Grand Rapids: Eerdmans, 1952.
NRSV	New Revised Standard Version (1989)
NT	New Testament
OT	Old Testament
rev.	revised

TDNT   *Theological Dictionary of the New Testament.* Edited by Gerhard Kittel and
        Gerhard Friedrich. Translated by Geoffrey W. Bromiley. 10 vols. Grand Rap-
        ids: Eerdmans, 1964–76.
v(v).   verse(s)

Old Testament

Gen.	Genesis	Song	Song of Songs
Exod.	Exodus	Isa.	Isaiah
Lev.	Leviticus	Jer.	Jeremiah
Num.	Numbers	Lam.	Lamentations
Deut.	Deuteronomy	Ezek.	Ezekiel
Josh.	Joshua	Dan.	Daniel
Judg.	Judges	Hosea	Hosea
Ruth	Ruth	Joel	Joel
1–2 Sam.	1–2 Samuel	Amos	Amos
1–2 Kings	1–2 Kings	Obad.	Obadiah
1–2 Chron.	1–2 Chronicles	Jon.	Jonah
Ezra	Ezra	Mic.	Micah
Neh.	Nehemiah	Nah.	Nahum
Esther	Esther	Hab.	Habakkuk
Job	Job	Zeph.	Zephaniah
Ps(s).	Psalm(s)	Hag.	Haggai
Prov.	Proverbs	Zech.	Zechariah
Eccles.	Ecclesiastes	Mal.	Malachi

New Testament

Matt.	Matthew	1–2 Thess.	1–2 Thessalonians
Mark	Mark	1–2 Tim.	1–2 Timothy
Luke	Luke	Titus	Titus
John	John	Philem.	Philemon
Acts	Acts of the Apostles	Heb.	Hebrews
Rom.	Romans	James	James
1–2 Cor.	1–2 Corinthians	1–2 Pet.	1–2 Peter
Gal.	Galatians	1–3 John	1–3 John
Eph.	Ephesians	Jude	Jude
Phil.	Philippians	Rev.	Revelation
Col.	Colossians		

Introduction

*Sharpening Our Approach
to Old Testament Interpretation*

The Old Testament (OT) is a complex collection of "books" unified through literary and historical processes.[1] Each book also constitutes a unity, albeit one that developed from distinct parts and complex literary activity. To most Western readers of the OT, however, this complexity has been concealed. This is true for a few reasons. For most, this complexity is less noticeable because we read the text in a translation. Although translation makes these texts more accessible to us, the process of rendering these texts into a different language tends to mask complexities within the original. We also tend to overlook these complexities because we have adopted others' interpretations of the OT prior to engaging the texts ourselves. If you grew up in the Christian church, you have already had some exposure to the OT and an idea of what it's about. Perhaps this exposure came through hearing Bible stories in Sunday school and sermons or from reading a children's storybook Bible. Even if you did not grow up in the church, you may have been exposed to the OT through movies such as *The Prince of Egypt* or *The Ten Commandments*. For many, the stories of Cain and Abel or David and Goliath are part of our cultural memory, shaping how we think about the OT. As these stories are passed down, many

---

1. I use the language of "books" here and throughout although technically speaking the concept of a bound collection of pages (i.e., a book) came much later. These complex textual units were composed on scrolls. This distinction is important when one considers how a textual unit materialized, how these units became documents to form a canon, and what they are and how they function.

church traditions also pass along teachings that deal with and make sense of potential problems in the text, making its complexities seem less apparent. This encultured way of reading can increase our understanding of the OT, but it can also blind us to the preconceptions and interpretive decisions we have subconsciously adopted over time.

In this book, I hope to sharpen our conception of and comprehension of OT texts by attending more closely to the phenomena that occur there and asking questions about what we find. For example, why does Gen. 2 seem to go backward in time and repeat the story of God's creation of humans, and how does the second story relate to the first? Or what do the Table of Nations, the genealogy of Seth, and the tower of Babel have to do with Abraham and the story of Israel? Or why does the author say nothing about the nearly four hundred years of activity between the end of Genesis and the beginning of Exodus? To answer these types of questions, we must engage these texts in a manner that better aligns with how they were produced—as episodes that an author collected and incorporated into a unified text.[2] Understanding the origin and purpose of these texts can reduce the number of interpretive blunders along the way. Knowing, for example, that the first large unit of the OT, the Pentateuch, was intended with a message for future audiences and not primarily to recount the past will shift our expectation of how the Pentateuch conveys its very important messages. Moreover, because the OT provides a foundation for the second part of the Christian canon, the New Testament (NT), this method of reading can also improve our understanding of NT texts and NT theology. In Luke 24 Jesus explains to his disciples that the "Law of Moses and the Prophets and the Psalms" are about him, which is why the church, from the very beginning, has studied the OT to understand the person of Christ and the essential doctrines of Christianity. Christians today must do the same, and to do this, we must begin by learning to interpret OT texts faithfully.

The Book's Purpose and Plan

My aim in this book is to sharpen the way we read the OT Scriptures using the Pentateuch as a case study. I accomplish this in two ways. In the first two chapters, I explain why understanding the *composite* literary character of the Pentateuch is important and how this should inform the way we read it. The word "composite" is meant to describe how an author selects and

---

2. Our modern conception of "author" is not necessarily equivalent to that of the ancient world. I will use the term for now and explain it more precisely later.

arranges various episodes—narratives, poems, genealogies, and more—and integrates content to generate the larger composition.[3] By examining how these episodes are arranged, we can discern the author's purpose to express a unified theological message for the people of God. The second way I hope to hone our interpretive expertise is to provide detailed explanations of each textual subunit in the Pentateuch. In each of the contexts where the author splices texts together, I will clarify what is transpiring at the textual level while also addressing larger interpretive matters. At the end of each chapter, I draw conclusions for how intentions in the text have implications for interpretation, theology, and practical concerns.

The book unfolds in two parts, corresponding to the two ways I engage the interpretation of Scripture. Part 1 sets the stage for how I will interpret textual subunits in part 2. Chapter 1 addresses the essence of Scripture based on Paul's statement in 2 Tim. 3:16–17 and its implications for how we engage Scripture. Even though Scripture is a word from God, it is bound up with human communication and therefore requires us to engage it as written communication. In chapter 2 we will explore how ancient authors used contemporary genres and produced texts to make meaning. We will also address the important notion of intentionality and how, as modern readers, recognizing genre and our own preconceptions of the Pentateuch's literature will enable us to hear its message more clearly.

Part 2 provides two paths through the Pentateuch's material. Chapters 3 and 4 present a panorama of the Pentateuch extending from Genesis to Deuteronomy. In chapter 3, we discover why the first Hebrew word of the Pentateuch, translated by the phrase "In the beginning," anticipates an end. It finds its first "end" in Gen. 49 and the allusive poetry of the blessing to Judah. In chapter 4, we examine the repetition and reuse of words, phrases, and poetic images in the poetry of Num. 23 and 24 and Moses's blessing in Deut. 33. The interpretive reuse of key literary elements yields a message about a *YHWH*-like king, portrayed as a lion, coming at the end of days.[4] The king will inherit the cosmos, his temple palace.

Chapters 5–12 progress through each individual subunit of the Pentateuch. In chapter 5, we analyze Gen. 1:1–2:3 and discover how the chapter's attention rests on the creation of humanity on the sixth day, indicating special roles for man and woman in God's land, which God fashions for their sustenance and

---

3. Although many OT books are anonymous, all available evidence indicates that the authors were men, so I use the masculine pronoun for "author" throughout.

4. Except in cases where it is necessary to draw out the significance of the name, I will normally observe the traditional practice of translating the tetragrammaton (the four Hebrew letters) *YHWH* with "Lord."

stewardship. Chapter 6 juxtaposes Gen. 2:4–3:24 with Gen. 1, demonstrating how this placement highlights the role of man and woman's union in God's plan for the land. Relational harmony between God, humanity, animals, and the land gives way to disharmony. Even so, God ensures the execution of his plan.

Chapters 7–9 survey God's interactions with three individuals: Noah, Abraham, and Moses. In chapter 7 we examine God's grace to one man, Noah, whose family inaugurates the reversing of the curse from Gen. 3. Chapter 8 clarifies God's choice of Abraham and reveals how every tongue, family, nation, and land that emerges in the dispersion of Noah's sons in the earth will find blessing through the seed of Abraham. In chapter 9 we leave Genesis behind to investigate Moses and his role as mediator in Israel's relationship with the LORD. The LORD's power and determination to dwell among his people emphasizes to Israel and the nations that he alone is God, who will bring his people into his presence.

In chapter 10 we confront a well-known difficulty within the Pentateuch: What should we do with the legal codes from Exod. 20 through Num. 10? Narratives framing the blocks of legal code show the layers of cultic ritual that seem to broaden the separation between the LORD and Israel, requiring Moses's role as a mediator so that God can sanctify and dwell among his people. In chapter 11 we address Deuteronomy, which is expressed as a long sermon in which Moses offers his own "explanation of this law" (Deut. 1:5). Toward the end of his sermon (Deut. 30), Moses proclaims the good news of God's future salvation and enjoins his audience to cross into this new covenant. Moses's song to Israel (Deut. 32) unfolds in chapter 12. Although the Israelites are poised to enter the land, Moses's anticipation of their idolatry forebodes trouble, and yet the last chapter of the Pentateuch hints at the LORD's infinite resolve to relate to his people. The concluding chapter assesses Deut. 34 as an interesting test case for this book. Taken as a later transitional piece to the Former and Latter Prophets, this final subunit casts a vision of a Moses-like prophet, a rule-making king, who will know the LORD "face to face" and do similar signs and wonders.

PART 1

Approaching Scripture

Holy Writ, Human Writing

The Implications of Each for Interpreting the Old Testament

The Scriptures are both a word from God and a word from man. While the latter derives from the former, both origins have significant implications for the interpretive task. Later we will examine how a close reading of textual details reveals what the OT's human authors intended to communicate, but first we turn to the Scriptures' divine origin.[1]

A Divine Word

Above all, readers of the OT ought to treat these texts in a way that emerges from Scripture's own view of itself: as God-breathed. Although the OT has its own way of communicating its divine origin, the apostle Paul succinctly articulates the nature of the OT in 2 Tim. 3:16–17. He writes, "All Scripture is God-breathed and profitable for teaching, for reproof, for correction, for training in righteousness, so that the man of God should be complete, equipped for every good work."[2] While every word in these verses provides important context for our discussion, three specific words have special significance for us.

---

1. I will have much more to say about authorship below, but I point out again that ancient writers do not conform to our modern view of authorship.
2. All Scripture translations are the author's unless otherwise noted.

The first word that has significance for us is a compound word that English versions sometimes translate as "God-breathed" (NIV) or "inspired by God" (NASB). The first element in the compound is *theos* [θεός], the Greek word for God. You may be familiar with this word because of its use in the English word "theology," which indicates the study of the nature of God. The second part of the compound is related to the common Greek noun *pneuma* [πνεῦμα], meaning breath or spirit, as well as the Greek verb *pneō* [πνέω], which means to blow or breathe. While English translations commonly render this compound word to indicate that God inspired or breathed out Scripture, the process is not explained.[3] Nevertheless, one thing is clear: God is ultimately the one behind the production of the Scriptures. Their existence is not merely a man-made product. Paul continues, explaining that the Scriptures are useful for teaching, reproof, correction, and training in righteousness in order that the person of God would be perfected for good works. From the outset, then, we can assert that these Scriptures, which originate from God, are true in what they affirm, and are the material the church needs to teach, to reprove, to improve, and to train God's people.

A Human Writing

The second word to consider from this verse is what English versions translate as "Scripture." The Greek word Paul uses here is *graphē* (γραφή). The *Theological Dictionary of the New Testament* offers two glosses for this word, each with several nuances. First, in Greek culture, the word meant a writing, such as a letter or a written statement, or written characters. In other words, *graphē* was simply a text. Second, by the time of the writing of the NT, it also became a term to indicate the Scriptures of Israel.[4] Even though it had become a technical term for "Scripture," according to these uses, *graphē* had at one point referred to merely a writing or text, something as simple as words written on a page. Does it seem odd to you that in spite of all the opposition that Paul and Timothy faced, Paul exhorted his young protégé to focus on a collection of texts?

In light of the entirety of Paul's comments in 2 Timothy, it is clear that Paul wants to encourage his disciple Timothy to stay the course and help the fledgling church move forward. Many refer to this letter as Paul's "last words." Having suffered a great deal in his ministry and knowing that Timothy will

---

3. For a classic articulation of the implications of this view, see B. B. Warfield, *Revelation and Inspiration* (London: Oxford University Press, 1927), 229–59.

4. G. Schrenk, "γραφή," *TDNT*, 1:749–55.

encounter similar challenges, Paul exhorts Timothy to build his ministry on the one foundation that will keep the church on course: these texts that we now call the OT.

Students are often surprised by this. Most have never considered the fact that when Paul directs Timothy to the Scriptures, he refers first and foremost to the OT. Remembering the original occasion of Paul's letter, however, this becomes clear. Consider what Paul mentions in 2 Tim. 3:15: Timothy had been made wise unto salvation through the "sacred writings." These "writings," as well as the "Scripture" Paul speaks of in verse 16, must be the body of religious texts that existed at the time he wrote the letter. They could not have referred to the NT, as this corpus had not yet been written. Paul's use of "all" in 2 Tim. 3:16 also suggests that his readers are familiar with the texts he is discussing. Paul is primarily referring here to the body of texts we know as the OT.[5] This is not to diminish the importance of the NT or to suggest that its texts are not also God-breathed. I am simply highlighting the fact that at the time of writing 2 Timothy, Paul could only have had the OT Scriptures in mind, for at that point in time, the NT as a corpus did not exist. Only later were Paul's letters collected along with the rest of the books of the NT and associated with the Scriptures of the OT.

For Paul and the early church, the OT was of central importance. It is understandable that today, Christians tend to focus on the NT, but we do well to remember that in Paul's parting words to Timothy, he speaks of the OT as both deeply relevant and immensely valuable. These OT texts, Paul explains, contain material useful for teaching truth, correcting error, and training the fledgling church. Immediately following these verses, in 2 Tim. 4:1–4, Paul offers a solemn warning about the gravity of Timothy's task. He commands Timothy to "preach the word" because people's itching ears will cause them to obtain teachers who will tell them only what they want to hear. To guard against falsehood, Timothy must focus on the *graphē*—that is, the *writings*, the *texts*. While I do not want to diminish our pursuit of doctrine and practice from the NT, 2 Tim. 3:16 requires that we ground our theology and practice in the Scriptures of the OT. As we do so, we should keep in mind three ideas about the use of the word *graphē*.

---

5. I am not trying to make a case for whether texts from the OT Apocrypha and Pseudepigrapha should be included or to present a full-fledged defense for the shape and order of the OT canon. Paul was likely familiar with some of these other texts, but given references to "the Law and the Prophets" in the Gospels and Paul—as well as verbal links between the Pentateuch, Prophets, and Writings—I can affirm that Paul's "all Scripture" reflects a collection similar to our OT.

The Focal Point of Paul's Use of Graphē Is a Writing

The word Paul uses to describe the Scriptures most basically means a *writing*. Given Paul's education, ethnicity, culture, faith, and purpose, what other words or ideas could he have used here in his exhortation to Timothy? A brief inquiry into these hypothetical alternatives may highlight the significance of Paul's choice to use *graphē*.

Perhaps it would be helpful to think about this from your own personal experience in the church. If you had been in Paul's position, what would you have told Timothy to focus on in order to edify the church? What would best prepare church members for ministry? Better yet, if someone decided to visit your church one Sunday in order to learn what Christians value and believe, what would they take away from their experience? If they observed your church for several consecutive Sundays, what would they conclude is essential? This observer might watch members share testimonies, participate in singing, sit in a big auditorium with stage lights, and listen to a speech from a charismatic speaker. Would they conclude that this *writing* is the one thing that is essential for the church, as Paul insists in his letter to Timothy?

Having considered this from our modern perspective, how would the answers change if we ask these questions from the apostle Paul's perspective, keeping in mind his Jewish heritage as well as first-century language and culture? Wanting to equip Timothy to lead the church, what other plausible options might Paul have used in this letter? What other words, or ideas, could he have included here? Considering these options will help us grasp the significance of Paul's choice to use this precise term.

Given Paul's first-century context, one likely alternative would be the Jewish law. Imagine if Paul had said, "All the legal codes of Moses are breathed out by God and profitable for teaching, reproof, and correction." After all, Paul's desire was for Timothy to train members of the church in righteousness and equip them for every good work. Choosing the word "law," then, would align with the sense of morality sometimes conveyed in Judaism and Christianity, as well as the Jewish concept of adherence to God's law in order to please him and identify as his people. Furthermore, an emphasis on the law would make sense given Paul's Jewish background. Paul could have told Timothy to isolate the legal codes from their context, examine them closely, study the morality of each command, and carefully obey them so as not to stray from a God-honoring path. However, this is not what Paul does.

Or imagine if Paul had said, "All God's mighty acts of salvation in the history of Israel were God-breathed and profitable . . . so that the man of God should be complete, equipped for every good work." This alternative is plausible, especially considering how many biblical theologians in recent history have focused on these mighty acts to build an OT theology.[6] In this scenario, Paul's admonition would be to focus on the historical events that God had accomplished for Israel. Whether the creation, the exodus, the destruction of Jericho, or some other historical event, the church could attempt to stay the course by reflecting on God's actions in the world. They could dig into archaeology, analyze historical backgrounds, reflect on the actions of God's people, and hypothesize about why God acted in the ways he did. They could use the Bible as a sort of springboard into the past, using the texts to imagine or perceive what *really* happened to Abraham, Moses, and other biblical figures.

The reality is, unfortunately, that Christians often do just this with these texts. We mistakenly think that their primary purpose is to tell us what happened in history so that we can learn from it and modify our behavior. Particularly for evangelicals, who have had to contend for the Bible's veracity, Christians often treat these texts as windows through which they can look onto the "scenes of history" in order to ponder why God, or biblical figures, acted the way they did. And because their so-called window is a biblical text rather than some other writing, they are convinced that this type of interpretation is "biblical." However, this use of the Bible is "biblical" in only a shallow sense of the word. Typically, this mode of interpretation becomes a projection of the reader's own ideas based on personal experience and some rudimentary knowledge of ancient times. This method is also problematic because these texts, while certainly historical in some sense, are not merely historical. They do not reflect modern historiography. They offer us something more than mere records of the past.

Another sensible alternative to *graphē* might be Jesus's spoken words or teachings. Imagine if Paul had said, "All the traditions regarding Jesus and his teachings are inspired by God and useful." Wouldn't it make sense for people to focus on the life, the stories, and the teachings of Christ? Many think so, which is why red-letter Bibles, which print the words spoken by Jesus in red ink, are so popular. Do the red letters in these Bible translations carry more importance or significance than the black letters? Of course not, at least not according to Paul. "*All* Scripture is God breathed," Paul insists. Valuing red-letter words in the Bible more than others suggests that Jesus's teachings, parables, and conversations recorded in the text are "God-breathed" but not the rest of this writing. Red letter editions reveal something about the translators' perspectives on what deserves our attention.

6. G. E. Wright, *God Who Acts: Biblical Theology as Recital* (London: SCM, 1952).

Certainly, God specially revealed himself in the person of Christ during his time on earth, but we do not have "recordings" of those moments. Jesus's words surely carry special significance, but it is not those words alone that Paul calls "God-breathed." He refers to the writings of the OT. Indeed, the entirety of these works have been breathed out by God in order to guide his people into truth and maturity. This confession ought to invigorate our efforts to understand these texts and how the biblical authors convey meaning through them.

Paul Does Not Use a Specific Title for Graphē

Another important point to note is that Paul uses a generic term, rather than a specific title, to refer to this body of texts. Though Christians today refer to this collection as the OT, the NT nowhere does. On eleven occasions, the NT identifies this body of texts as "the Law and the Prophets," and on four occasions it refers to them as "Moses and the Prophets."[7] In one well-known passage, Luke 24:44, Jesus refers to these texts as "the Law of Moses and the Prophets and Psalms." We cannot be certain about the extent of the material to which the term "Psalms" refers. Some have suggested that it refers to the entire third section of the Hebrew Bible, based on the Jewish practice of using the "first word[s]" of a text to refer to its entirety.[8] If so, "Psalms" would here be synonymous with "the Writings," the final section of the *TaNaK*.[9] Although Psalms may refer to the entire section, manuscripts vary in the order of books, so there is not enough evidence to draw a firm conclusion.[10]

Before we explore why Christians have called this group of texts the "Old Testament," perhaps we should also consider how the title influences our perception of this section of the canon. What comes to mind when we hear "Old Testament" and how does this title fare when compared to "New Testament"? Many regard the OT as "outdated," "worn out," "tired," and "in the

7. For the nomenclature "the Law . . . and the Prophets," see Matt. 5:17; 7:12; 11:13 (order reversed); 22:40; Luke 16:16; 24:44; John 1:45; Acts 13:15; 24:14; 28:23; Rom. 3:21. For "Moses and the Prophets," see Luke 16:29, 31; 24:27; Acts 26:22 (order reversed).

8. For the various positions and scholarship, see Lee M. McDonald, *The Formation of the Christian Biblical Canon*, rev. and exp. ed. (Peabody, MA: Hendrickson, 2005), 43–46.

9. *TaNaK* is an acronym for *Torah* (Instruction), *Nevi'im* (Prophets), and *Ketuvim* (Writings). Thus the *TaNaK* is a collection of works that contains the Law (five books of Moses), the Prophets (Joshua, Judges, Samuel, Kings, Isaiah, Jeremiah, Ezekiel, and the Book of the Twelve [Minor Prophets]), and the Writings (Psalms, Job, Proverbs, Ruth, Song of Songs, Ecclesiastes, Lamentations, Esther, Daniel, Ezra-Nehemiah, Chronicles).

10. The Lukan Gospel may refer to Chronicles as the final book in the third section, given his statement "from the blood of Abel to the blood of Zechariah" in Luke 11:51. This statement could be a reference to the final martyr in the canon in 2 Chron. 24:20–22. Contra McDonald, *Formation*, 46–47.

past."[11] Because in today's world titles generally convey a short summary of what a book is about, the title "Old Testament" suggests that this portion of the canon teaches the old covenant. In other words, the mere title of this group of texts colors our perception of what the books mean.

But where did this title come from? According to the writings of Eusebius, it emerged with Melito of Sardis (2nd cent.), who provides a list of books from the "old covenant."[12] In the sentences before offering this list, Melito speaks about the "word" and the "book" from the "Law and Prophets."[13] He then identifies the books "of the old covenant."[14] It is quite likely that Melito gets the term from the apostle Paul's reference to the old covenant in 2 Cor. 3:14. There Paul calls this covenant a "ministry of death" and refers to "letters engraved on stone," likely an allusion to the Ten Commandments. However, Paul does not equate the old covenant with the Scriptures of Israel; nor does he make a statement about what these Scriptures mean. His point is simply that when Moses, or the old covenant, is read, minds and hearts are hardened. Although the Pentateuch contains and refers to an older covenant, it does not mean that this older covenant is an absolute or eternal means for how God relates to his people. We will return to this idea in the ensuing chapters.

Irenaeus employs the description "old covenant" in *Against Heresies*, his defense of the Christian faith written in the second century AD, mainly surviving in Latin manuscripts.[15] While discussing Moses's precepts from the Pentateuch, Irenaeus refers to the "old covenant/testament," or in Latin, *vetus testamentum* (4.15.2). Irenaeus compares Israel's situation under the "old covenant" with that of Paul and his audience under the "new covenant" (*novum testamentum*). Could he be referring here to the texts of the "Old Testament" and the "New Testament," in essence giving these sections of the canon the titles we use today? The confusion results from the Latin word *testamentum*, from which the English word "testament" comes, but this Latin word can also mean "covenant." Later in *Against Heresies* (4.32.2), Irenaeus again speaks of "two covenants" (*duo testamenta*) for two peoples but one God who arranged both. Irenaeus explains that the old covenant had its various purposes, one of which was to express "images of those things that

---

11. Christopher Seitz discusses this issue in his *The Elder Testament: Canon, Theology, Trinity* (Waco: Baylor University Press, 2018), 13–19. See also Daniel Block's opinion in his book *Covenant: The Framework of God's Grand Plan of Redemption* (Grand Rapids: Baker Academic, 2021), xvi.

12. Eusebius, *Ecclesiastical History* 4.26.14. Translations taken from NPNF², vol. 1.

13. Eusebius, *Ecclesiastical History* 4.26.13.

14. Greek: τῆς παλαιᾶς διαθήκης.

15. Irenaeus, *Against Heresies* 4.15.2. Translations taken from ANF, vol. 1.

now exist in the church" through the new covenant. Irenaeus had explained earlier that the prophets preached the *novum testamentum* (new covenant), using *testamentum* to refer to a covenant, not a corpus of writings (4.9.3). Indeed, in all of these instances, *testamentum* refers not to two canons of Scripture but to two contractual administrations in God's relationship to his people—that is, his covenants.

An early Latin edition of the Bible furthered the confusion surrounding these terms. When the well-known scholar St. Jerome (born ca. 342–347, died 420) translated much of the Hebrew Scriptures into Latin, he gave them the title *Vetus Testamentum* (Old Testament or old covenant). Latin translations of the Gospels and other books from Greek manuscripts eventually appeared alongside the *Vetus Testamentum* in a section called *Novum Testamentum* (New Testament).[16] Today we know this translation of the Bible as Jerome's Vulgate, and the designations for the two parts of the canon now appear in the most notable manuscript of the Vulgate, Codex Amiatinus from AD 716.[17] Like Melito and Irenaeus, Jerome translated the Hebrew word for "covenant" using the Latin word *testamentum*, and then he used it as his title for the two sections of the canon, *Vetus Testamentum* and *Novum Testamentum*. Later English Bible translations followed suit, simply transliterating the Latin *testamentum* as "testament," and the longstanding tradition for titling the two parts of the Christian canon took hold along with the resulting misunderstanding.

Modern Christians often assume that the Old Testament's title is indicative of its content, without stopping to consider how this collection of texts received this title in the first place. Believing that the Old Testament is about the old covenant, many Christians relegate it to the past and fail to recognize the relevance and applicability of these texts for Christian faith and practice.

This subconscious starting point shapes our reading of these texts. Modern philosophers of literature have shown that the process of reading begins with a preconceived understanding of what a text means. This preconception may be based on a title, a presumption about the meaning, or an expectation about the genre of the work. Regardless of how the preunderstanding develops, we read the text through this lens, and it shapes how we process its meaning. The text's literary details either affirm or invalidate our preunderstanding of the text. In *Validity in Interpretation*, E. D. Hirsch explains this phenomenon from the perspective of discourse:

16. See the recent edition of the Vulgate, *Biblia Sacra*, Iuxta Vulgatam Versionem, 2 vols. (Stuttgart: Württembergische Bibelanstalt, 1969).

17. Bruce Metzger, *The Text of the New Testament*, 4th ed. (Oxford: Oxford University Press, 2005), 106.

Such experiences, in which a misunderstanding is recognized during the process of interpretation, illuminate an extremely important aspect of speech that usually remains hidden. They show that, quite aside from the speaker's choice of words, and, even more remarkably, quite aside from the context in which the utterance occurs, the details of meaning that an interpreter understands are powerfully determined and constituted *by his meaning expectations*. And these expectations arise *from the interpreter's conception* of the type of meaning that is being expressed.[18]

The interpreter's preconceptions about what a text means powerfully launches and constrains understanding. Hirsch goes on to say, "Such expectations are always necessary to understanding, because only by virtue of them can the interpreter make sense of the words he experiences along the way."[19] Once an interpreter expects a genre with its accompanying meaning, only details in the reading can alter that conception.

Hirsch makes his case with numerous examples. In one story, his own students read the title of a poem and refuse to give up their interpretation of it despite later details that negate their interpretation. The details of the poem were not challenging enough to their understanding to compel them to abandon their preconceptions.[20] In the case of the OT, readers begin with the assumption that it is old or about a past covenant and interpret it according to this preconceived understanding.

Paul's Use of Graphē Highlights That It Is a Human Writing

Third, Paul's description of the OT as a "writing" compels us to focus on the fact that it is a human writing. As we have already affirmed, it is a divine word that has been breathed out by God, true and profitable to equip God's people for good works. However, its divine origin does not make it any less human in its composition. In other words, the human author was not in a vision-like trance, was not blindly recording what was going on around him, and was not merely transcribing what God dictated. He was using the same human facilities to produce a text that are typically required. Because the OT is a human word, we must consider the various facets of human communication and the human process of writing. Although much about our culture is different from that of ancient Israel, the human brain's way of processing

18. E. D. Hirsch Jr., *Validity in Interpretation* (New Haven: Yale University Press, 1967), 71 (my emphasis).

19. Hirsch, *Validity*, 71.

20. Hirsch, *Validity*, 71, 129. See also his story of a scholar who deciphered an ancient tablet (165).

and conveying a message is largely the same. Despite different cultures, tech-nologies, and worldviews—all of which affect our thinking—the brain still functions in a similar manner. To understand these texts, then, we need to perceive and appreciate the many factors affecting human communication, including language, syntax, semantics, genre, historical and cultural forces, and technology involved in text-making, to name a few.

In the next chapter, we will examine a few of these factors in order to im-prove our understanding of these ancient writings. In particular, we will focus on genre and methods of composition. We will also address the important but sometimes misunderstood issue of intentionality within these texts. We often fail to consider the biblical authors' intentions because we misunderstand genre, but we also fail to recognize our own preconceptions.

The Human Production
of Scripture

Having begun with the assertion that Scripture is a word from God and a word from man, we will now explore the implications of viewing Scripture as a human product. If we intend to sharpen our understanding of these "writings" *because* they are a word from God, then we must consider carefully *how* it is that an individual composes a written text. In doing so, we must be willing to adjust our assumptions and attend to the distinct place and time in which the texts were written.

This chapter begins with two challenges associated with interpreting written texts. First, we will explore the significance of genre for author and reader, and then we will examine why words can be elusive even though they convey semantic content. The second part of the chapter pertains to issues of textual production, the way a text is brought together. We often fail to consider textual production, but once we recognize the importance of genre, we realize that the way an author "makes" a text has implications for its interpretation. Third, I introduce the notion of intentionality and explain why we must discern Scripture's intention in accordance with these factors of human production. Finally, we will examine the sometimes overlooked role that we as readers play in interpretation and discovering or, in a sense, recreating meaning.

Challenges of Interpreting Written Texts

Genre

Genre can describe different types of speech or writing that humans use to construct a text or message and to comprehend and interpret a text or message. Some examples include poetry, narrative, and biography. We are more intuitive readers than we might think. In fact, we often switch back and forth between our culture's different genres without realizing it. We treat text messages from friends differently than emails from an employer, and we draw different conclusions from an animated film than we do from a documentary. But we often perform these acts subconsciously based on the medium of the communication, the font and word choice, the writer's tone, and so on.

To illustrate the point, let's consider publications such as *The Onion* or *The Babylon Bee,* which publish satirical news articles. Using humor, exaggeration, and irony, these publications poke fun at various current events, public figures, political parties, and viewpoints. You would not want to read these stories in a hyperliteral fashion. If you did, serious problems would result! Though these satirical pieces seem similar to traditional news articles, they belong to an entirely different genre, and their authors expect them to be read and interpreted as such. However subtle or obvious the differences between genres may be, correctly identifying the genre of a writing helps us grasp its meaning and purpose. We unconsciously use our reading ability to interpret texts by their genre, but not all genres are as sharply distinct as the *Onion* and *Babylon Bee* are from standard news articles. When we encounter a new genre, we must try to understand the function for which it was intended.

This task is complicated by the lack of any absolute, pure, or consistent genre form. All genres are extensions and assimilations of other genres and tend to overlap somewhat in their characteristics.[1] Writers adopt a particular genre from their culture and experience to convey their message, but they may do so without rigidly adhering to every facet of that genre. They may adapt and extend a genre by assimilating characteristics from other genres.[2] Modern authors writing within a particular discipline typically use stable forms of communication that dictate even the tone and word choice. However, individual creativity, knowledge, and experience can take over as artists produce their works. They may utilize elements of one genre while innovatively borrowing words, phrases, or stylistic elements from another genre. This is

---

1. Alastair Fowler, *Kinds of Literature* (Cambridge, MA: Harvard University Press, 1982), 27, 156–212.
2. Fowler, *Kinds of Literature*, 18, 24.

how humans have created and communicated throughout the centuries, and it's what makes the study and practice of writing and literature so interesting. An interpreter coming to such works must embrace the expectations appropriate to that genre, but because these literary categories are from another period and constantly developing, the interpreter may not always be able to recognize all the genre's forms, expectations, and parameters. This is true for those within similar cultures and time periods, but the problem becomes even more pronounced as time passes and historical distance grows between the original message and later interpreters.

Both writers and interpreters use genres emerging from their own culture and subcultures. This obvious truth has significant implications for interpretation. For one, it exacerbates the complexity of cross-cultural communication. When communication occurs between an author from an ancient culture that no longer exists and a modern reader, the genres used by one will likely seem foreign to the other. This makes comprehension more difficult, and the danger of misinterpretation increases. Greater historical distance between the author and reader makes the diachronic aspect of genre more pronounced and makes engaging with the actual literary artifact more necessary and important.

Because of these challenges, we must strive to understand how a writer has constructed a particular scriptural text and its purpose. Otherwise, we will misidentify the genre and misinterpret the text. Considering the many facets associated with the production of a scriptural text is essential to proper interpretation. Even if we affirm that the Holy Spirit "carried along" the writers of Scripture (2 Pet. 1:21), the reality of the human element in communication should compel us to seek to understand the processes by which they produced their texts.[3]

Language

Perhaps the most basic element of communication, which we tend to overlook because it is so obvious, is language.[4] Old Testament authors assume that

---

3. The Chicago Statement on Biblical Inerrancy says,

Article VIII

We affirm that God in His Work of inspiration utilized the distinctive personalities and literary styles of the writers whom He had chosen and prepared.

We deny that God, in causing these writers to use the very words that He chose, overrode their personalities. (https://etsjets.org/wp-content/uploads/2010/03/files_documents _Chicago_Statement.pdf)

4. For an explanation of the issue of language and texts, see Kevin Vanhoozer, *Is There a Meaning in This Text? The Bible, the Reader, and the Morality of Literary Knowledge*, anniv. ed. (Grand Rapids: Zondervan, 2009). For a helpful introduction to the history of literary

a reader knows Hebrew. Translations allow modern readers to encounter and study these ancient texts, but they can also make interpretation more difficult by increasing the distance between us and the Hebrew text. Because there is no one-to-one correspondence between languages, a translation inevitably puts an additional step between the Hebrew text and English readers and represents the Hebrew text in a distinct manner. Proper interpretation requires awareness of differences between languages.

Even when speaking the same language, words can make meaning elusive, as anyone who has had trouble communicating with a close friend understands. Sometimes, when I communicate with my wife, it feels like we are speaking in code. Though we have been married for more than twenty-five years, and she is the person I am closest to in the world, we still talk past one another on occasion. Why? Because we sometimes apply different meanings to the same sets of words, even commonly used words. Despite all we have in common, the content with which we mentally fill up our words can vary significantly. Though words convey information, they do not do so in an immediate or absolute sense.

Let me demonstrate using the word *cat*. Do the letters C-A-T immediately or necessarily indicate the living thing in the external world? Of course not. English speakers have simply agreed to assign the meaning "feline animal" to these three letters. Other languages use a different set of letters to refer to cats, which indicates that using C-A-T to refer to feline animals is not an ontological necessity. We could just as easily have agreed to use some other word.

Moreover, the referents of certain words have changed over time, as in the case of the English word *ass*. This fluidity of meaning makes clear that there is no necessary connection between a specific set of letters and a concrete thing in the material world. Words convey meaning within a culture's language system at a particular point in time by mutual agreement and not because of an immediate, ontological relationship between a word and its meaning.

Now let's approach the concept of elusiveness from a different angle. Is a certain set of letters necessarily, directly, and ontologically bound up with a particular mental concept? We might assume that the mental image would be somewhat stable for certain words, but there is no reason to think that my mental image of a cat is exactly the same as yours. If we both had in mind a house cat as opposed to a lion, our mental concepts would be similar, but they could still differ in details such as age, breed, and coloring. The problem

theory in the modern period, including how some literary theories have influenced our understanding of language and words, see Terry Eagleton, *Literary Theory: An Introduction*, anniv. ed. (Maldon, MA: Blackwell, 2008).

becomes even more complex when we consider abstract nouns such as love, capacity, thought, or imagination, which do not identify concrete objects we can point to. Lacking corresponding physical properties, mental images of these nouns can vary significantly from person to person. Most users of a shared language may refer to a general conception with a commonly accepted word and abide by the conventional understanding of that word within a particular time period. However, the potential for ambiguity remains.

Despite these communication challenges, language is still generally adequate to convey messages and meanings. The alphabet was a brilliant invention! The ability to repeat a combination of letters to convey semantic meaning and to put multiple words into an accepted order to communicate a message was a huge leap forward for human culture. So, while we must be aware of the limitations and pitfalls of language when seeking to communicate or interpret a message, we can still affirm its remarkable usefulness.

Textual Production and Interpretation

Consider how many written texts there are in today's world. From books and magazines to emails and flyers, to text messages and social media, we are inundated with written texts in a myriad of forms. This is a remarkable achievement of the modern world, and it stands in stark contrast to the ancient world. The first printing press, which could machine produce a few thousand pages per day for the first time in history, wasn't invented until the fifteenth century. Prior to this, rudimentary manual printing could produce only about 1 percent of that amount per day. Compare this to the ancient period, when scribes copied texts by hand, and production was limited to a few pages per day. Even our commonplace practice of jotting down notes did not exist in this period. We tend to take the proliferation of texts for granted, but it is important to remember that the mass production of texts is a recent phenomenon.

Imagine a world without texts! For authors of Scripture, however, it was their reality. There were no smartphones, no newspapers, and no typewriters. In fact, there wasn't even paper in the region at that time, and what we know as the modern book did not exist. Writers composed their works on animal skins or, at an earlier time, papyrus, which was made by hammering together the inner substance of a papyrus plant. The writing material was formed into rolls, or scrolls. The Pentateuch was too long to fit on a single scroll, so it was divided into five scrolls based on the form and function of the content (i.e., Genesis contains the stories of the patriarchs, and the story of Moses covers Exodus through Numbers).

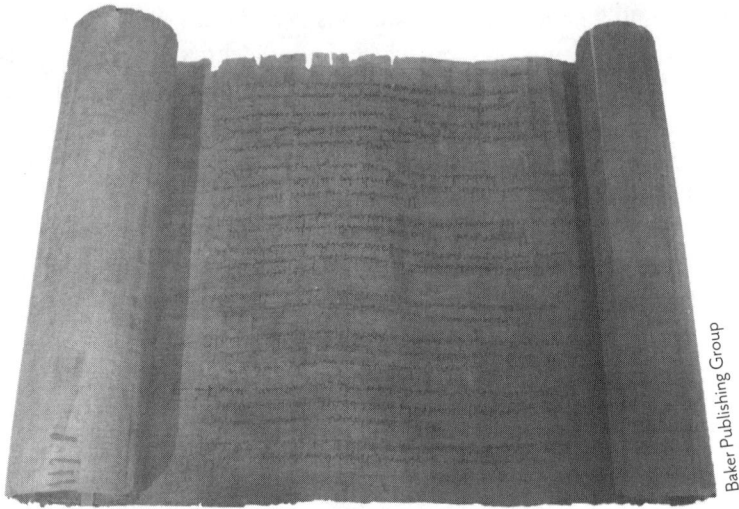

FIGURE 2.1. **An Ancient Scroll**

In our modern conception of authorship, someone generates an article or book over a relatively short period of time and has the right to their intellectual property. Ancient writers, unable to type or even write on consecutive pages and without the protection of modern copyright laws, resorted to other measures to select content and create unity in their literary works. The textual pieces of a scroll may have varied in both origin and genre, but an "author" brought them together into a unity. If an author incorporated an already existing episode, whether written or oral, into a composition, the episode's word choice could differ from original material created by the author. The interpretation of ancient texts encompasses much more than merely distinguishing poetry from narrative. We must also consider textual styles, genres, and production techniques. Taking all these factors into consideration—genre extension and assimilation, the nature of language, the elusiveness of word meanings, and the limitations of text production in the ancient world—can make the task of interpretation daunting. Yet each factor plays an important role in shaping our understanding of the biblical text and makes each text as unique as a fingerprint.

Critiquing Our Insufficient Models

Let's examine some of the most common approaches to the Bible and discuss how most people expect genre to work in Scripture. Based on my own experience growing up reading OT stories and from countless conversations with students, I've found that most people in our culture engage the Scriptures through two general models.

The first model views the Bible as a personal letter. Because much of the NT is letters, many of us bring the same genre expectations to the rest of Scripture. A personal letter is occasional, with a specific occasion, situation, and purpose behind its production. For example, figure 2.2 is the letter my

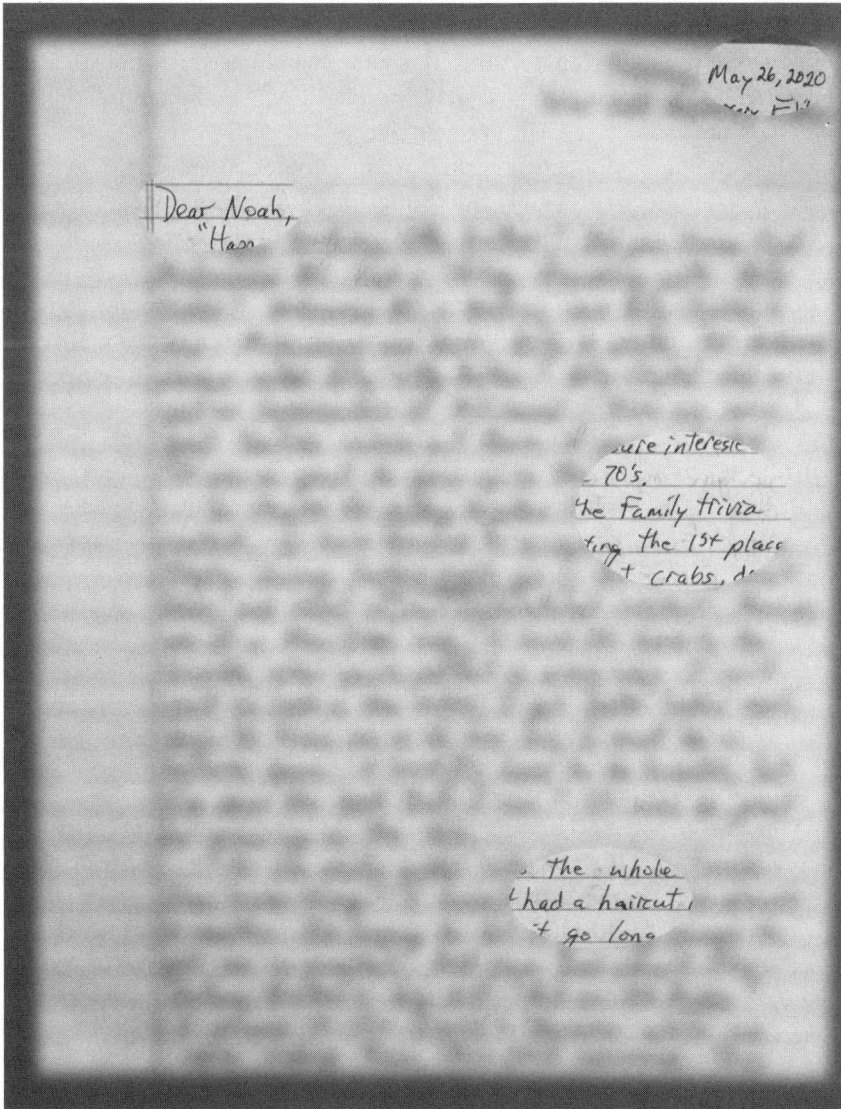

FIGURE 2.2. **A Personal Letter**

brother-in-law wrote to my son for a particular occasion, my son's birthday. The personal nature of a letter also means that the author has certain expectations of the reader, as my brother-in-law had of my son.

As you can see, this letter assumes a great deal of shared knowledge between my brother-in-law and my son. In it my brother-in-law mentions a family trivia game that my son put together for my wife's family during a beach vacation. To fully understand the letter, the reader needs to be aware of this shared experience. My brother-in-law also mentions his haircut. To properly understand the significance of this, the reader would need to know that this letter arrived during an international pandemic, when nonessential matters like haircuts frequently went undone. Because of this, my brother-in-law's hair had grown very long, making his haircut a notable event. All this to say, in occasional letters, writers and readers often presume the knowledge of shared experiences. These are sometimes called presupposition pools, and for occasional letters, they are quite important. If we approach Scripture as if it were a personal letter, then we must consider what knowledge the author assumes we have in common. However, what if these texts are not occasional? How would this change what knowledge the author expects the reader to possess? If the author presumes that readers have little knowledge of his world, or share little of his presupposition pool, it will affect how much research a specific historical context will require in order for a modern reader to understand the author's meaning. I'll return to the idea of a presupposition pool below.

The second primary model approaches Scripture as a type of recorded history. This is how I engaged Scripture when I first entered seminary. I viewed these texts as one would a newspaper, as pieces of literature conveying the essential facts about the who, what, when, where, why, and how of an incident or event. I thought that Scripture's purpose was to tell us what *really* happened. Many of my students today have a similar perspective, as if the biblical author used a video camera to capture the action and preserve the details for posterity.

When we consider other examples of ancient historiography, we find a mix of eyewitness accounts, imaginative storytelling, and an underlying framework woven together to convey their view of the world to an audience. Herodotus (5th cent. BC), often considered the father of history, weaves his own experiences together with other traditions and stories to create a narrative of the battles between the Greeks and Persians. I am not saying that the Pentateuch belongs to the same genre as Herodotus; I am merely pointing out the varied motivations and techniques of ancient writers. Although Scripture contains historical texts, the author's composition of these texts involves additional purposes. To view this genre as a mere recording of bare events is not quite accurate. While we can certainly affirm Scripture's historical veracity, these texts are more than just ancient historiography.

Scripture conveys a theological message and reflects human concerns. Narratives reveal characters' internal thoughts, omit details, jump backward or forward chronologically, retell stories that appear elsewhere, connect material through verbal splicing, and use literary patterns and formulas. An informed reader should understand not merely what is taking place but why the author selected this material and juxtaposed one piece of text with another. In other words, appropriate reading of Scripture depends on a correct understanding of its genre.

Having demonstrated that personal letters and modern historical records do not epitomize the genres in which Scripture is written, are there more appropriate genres or models of text production we can turn to? As authors write, they produce texts in genres emerging from their own culture, genres that they've learned from personal education or experiences. They then develop their work in ways that are uniquely their own. Because of this variety, we cannot say that one specific genre is *the* genre of all Scripture. Likewise, there is no reason to think that one specific model of text production lies behind every sacred text. Each text possesses a uniqueness that requires particular examination and consideration. However, there are some text models we can use to understand these literary works, as well as some general elements of production that provide a place to begin. Armed with this knowledge, we can better discern unaccustomed genres and text models and illuminate their manner and purpose of writing.[5]

Developing Better Models

To better understand the genres that make up the OT, let us consider two examples from contemporary culture that illustrate how authors make texts. Although these examples do not give us an exact understanding of how OT texts were composed, they provide an analogy to sharpen our understanding of genre and text production in the OT.

The first is a ransom note, a type of communication often featured on contemporary detective shows. By composing a message using letters clipped from various newspapers and magazines, a kidnapper communicates his intent without using any recognizable handwriting and thus disguises his identity. While the purpose of a ransom note is different from that of Scripture, we

---

5. I use "genre" here to indicate a literary category with a general purpose. I am using "textual production" to indicate a particular way that authors incorporate other texts into their own literary work.

Clara Pratt

FIGURE 2.3. **A Mosaic**

will see that the production technique—cutting and pasting textual pieces to create a unified text or message—is analogous. Authors of Scripture often select and arrange diverse pieces of textual material, both short and long, and incorporate them with other pieces of textual material. The result is a complex, yet coherent, message.

A photo mosaic is a second example from contemporary culture that helps us picture how an ancient author might make a text. Figure 2.3 is an artist's rendition of Moses using thumbnails of images from Moses's life.

The picture clearly portrays a unified image, but we see greater complexity within the image when we zoom in. The artist has carefully arranged hundreds of photographs from Moses's life to create the overall intended effect. From a distance, we see the unified image of Moses, but upon closer examination, we can see the smaller units that make up the larger image. Up close, the details of Moses's overall figure begin to fade, while the dozens of pictures from his life that compose the image come into view.

The authors of Scripture pieced together their works in a similar way, though the analogy begins to break down when we acknowledge that authors used consonants, words, clauses, and texts rather than photographs to create their works. By selecting, arranging, adapting, and writing texts, OT authors produced structured and purposeful compositions.[6] Also, the demarcations between textual units is seldom as clear as in this mosaic. This makes interpretation even more challenging, especially when using translations, in which the textual seams are less visible. Nevertheless, the ransom note and the mosaic are far better models than the personal letter or modern historiography for understanding how ancient texts developed. Recognizing this mode of textual production will help us discern intentionality in the text and avoid making genre errors as we interpret Scripture.

First and Second Kings as a Model of Textual Production

Many instances of this sort of composition exist in the OT, but one example is 1 and 2 Kings, constituting a larger textual unit in Hebrew. The introductory story in Kings concerns the death of David and the successor to his throne, Solomon. David died in approximately 970 BC, and then his son Solomon took over. From this initial story, we know that this unit originates from this period at the earliest. On the other hand, the final narrative of Kings tells the story of King Jehoiachin, the king of Judah, who was exiled in 598/7 BC. Then, in the last few verses of Kings, the reader learns that Jehoiachin is released from prison in 562/1 BC, when the Babylonian ruler's successor comes to the throne. The text says that the Babylonian king gave Jehoiachin sustenance all the days that he lived, but it falls short of saying how many additional years this was (2 Kings 25:30). The inclusion of this story pushes the date of Kings even farther into the future and gives us the earliest date that this literary work could have been completed. The author of Kings could have created both narratives at an even later period than these dates indicate, but these dates establish at least a 410-year interval between the first and the last story in the composition. This means that the author could not have been an eyewitness to all of the events mentioned in these accounts, but then where did he get his information?

Jewish tradition identifies Jeremiah as the author, but there is little evidence for this beyond the common language between Kings and Jeremiah, and if the author constructed his work from a variety of textual pieces, the evidence of

6. Tracy J. McKenzie, *Idolatry in the Pentateuch* (Eugene, OR: Pickwick, 2010), 47.

FIGURE 2.4. **The Composition of Kings**

common language becomes less compelling. However, since the genre of Kings is not a personal letter, we do not need to know the author's name or identity in order to discern the work's intended effect. Nor does not knowing the author's name affect its status as Scripture. In fact, the 410-year time span confirms that the individual stories in Kings were not written by only one eyewitness. The author was not merely recording events and situations occurring around him at the time, so the genre is dissimilar to a newspaper or a video recording. He selected and arranged the episodes for specific reasons, and he was interested in more than just compiling a chronological history of what *really* happened.

Interestingly, the author tells us where he got his information. Thirty-four times he mentions various records, sometimes translated as "chronicles," and he specifically refers the reader to the records of the Chronicles of the Kings of Israel (or Judah) as well as the Chronicles of Solomon for more information about a particular king. He apparently draws from these annals to compose his work, but he is selective in his use of these records. For example, his account of the reign of King Omri of Israel is a scant thirteen verses even though biblical and extrabiblical accounts indicate that Omri was a powerful ruler in the area, who established Samaria as his capital, expanded the borders of Israel, and made treaties with nearby kingdoms, including Judah. In contrast to the meager amount on Omri, the author devotes sixteen chapters to the prophet Elijah. The inclusion of stories about Elijah and Elisha as well as other prophets indicates that the author's purposes went beyond simply reporting the deeds of the monarchs. What these prophets portend becomes a central aspect of Kings.

The author's method—and in part, his purpose—emerge as these details come into focus. He lived after all these events had transpired. He selected stories of kings and juxtaposed them in a dovetail fashion. His perspective is of someone standing at the end of the entire process of textual production, after the stories had been written down by various court chroniclers. He already knows what has transpired in Israel and Judah, but he expresses his intention by selecting and situating these past episodes for readers.

We often presuppose that the scriptural writers are somehow in the story itself, experiencing the very events of Scripture and recording them as they happen. However, this is not the case here. The author looks back at the events in retrospect, arranging the episodes in a particular manner in order to convey a message about these events and about the course of history. The first part of his work highlights Solomon's failure to be the promised Davidic king. The second part tells the stories of the divided kingdoms, Israel and Judah, and their repeated failure to serve only the LORD. The author selects a narrative concerning a king of Israel, followed by one concerning a king of Judah, repeating this structure until Israel and eventually Judah are destroyed. This arrangement of simultaneous storytelling divulges another aspect of his message: none of the kings measure up to King David. They all die, and consequently we still await *the* Davidic king, who will come after the prophesied destruction of Jerusalem.

The composition of Kings provides a glimpse into the production of Scripture. An author selects texts that he wants to use, arranging them in a way that accomplishes his purposes, sometimes adapting them to better fit his message, and writing additional material as needed to contribute to a unified and purposeful text.[7] In all of this, authors intend to communicate to the reader their divinely inspired message.

Intentionality and Human Production

Because God breathed out a *written* word, we as readers must seek to understand the various conventions, features, and nuances of human writing. It is intuitive to us that humans write to communicate a message, and while the process is more complex than we realize, we can still seek to discover the

---

7. The writing of Kings is complex, containing multiple levels of "authorship." Originally, a court scribe wrote each chronicle, presumably authoring the text with a particular intentionality. Second, someone gathered these texts into a composite whole in order to express a different intention. Scholars sometimes call the person who compiles or reworks the literary work an editor, but I prefer the term "author" for anyone who carefully arranges the pieces into a literary whole.

intended message of each text. Although literary theory has helped us see the complexity in language—that language by its nature has inadequacies, and that absolute certainty in interpretation is not humanly possible—it has overplayed the inadequacies, overstated its conclusions, and eroded our confidence in what we can understand. God was gracious in giving us something as stable as a writing to know his purposes and plans.

While many features of human written communication are important, perhaps the most significant, when it comes to interpretation, is the notion of intentionality. Authors intend to communicate through their works, and readers can pursue their intended messages by understanding the production of the text. However, we sometimes fail to understand our own starting point and misinterpret the purpose of a text. We can also misunderstand genre and thereby miss the text's purpose.

Although authorial intention is more complex than normally assumed, the notion of intentionality is particularly compelling for those who believe that God moved humans to write Scripture. As article 8 of the Chicago Statement on Biblical Inerrancy affirms, "God in His work of inspiration utilized the distinctive personalities and literary styles of the writers whom He had chosen and prepared." This same article also denies that "God, in causing these writers to use the very words that He chose, overrode their personalities." It is significant that God not only inspired these texts but made use of human communication and human intentionality to speak to us. Readers can discern this intentionality in several ways: noting where the author has stated his intention; recognizing the reworking of a text; observing repetition, structure, and wordplay; and understanding other literary devices. We will explore some of these practices in the following chapters.

Our Role in Interpretation as Readers

As I explained above, all readers approach a text, including Scripture, with a preconception of what it is about. If you had to articulate in a few words what the Pentateuch—Genesis, Exodus, Leviticus, Numbers, Deuteronomy —is about, what would you say? Is the Pentateuch about the history of Israel? The law? The covenant? While there may be validity in these ideas, any answer reveals your preconception of the text's meaning, and this influences how you will interpret its stories.

Preconceptions are not in and of themselves negative. In fact, because our brains need a generalized idea as a starting point when processing and organizing information, preconceptions are an essential and necessary element for understanding. However basic it may be—such as an educated guess about a text's genre or meaning—this preconception furnishes the building blocks through which understanding is built. We can also think of preconceptions as the prescription lenses through which we understand a text. As we move through a text, we encounter new information that helps us redirect our preconceptions toward a more appropriate or accurate understanding.

For example, if we preconceive the Pentateuch to be about the law, we will organize our initial understanding through that lens. Then as we encounter details in the text, we may decide to alter or refine our conception of what the Pentateuch is about. If the Pentateuch is about law, then why are the legal codes set in a narrative context? Why does it take so long—seventy chapters combined of Genesis and Exodus, to be exact—to get to the bulk of the legal codes? And why does the author introduce other stories into this context that are not about the legal codes at all? These textual details raise questions that reshape our conclusions regarding what the text is about. Ultimately, they suggest that something other than the law is consequential to what the author is communicating. The goal is to modify our conception as best we can to match the text's presentation, and to achieve this, we must read and reread the text.

So, can you sum up your preconception of the Pentateuch in one word? In the next two chapters, I begin my account of the theology of the Pentateuch with an explanation that starts with the first word of Gen. 1 and extends to the end of Deut. 33. Although the theme I detect is not mentioned as many times as "law" or "covenant," it is placed in prominent positions and is distributed from the beginning to the end of this literary work we know as the Pentateuch. Don't miss the details!

PART 2

Engaging Scripture

The Beginning and the End

The Lion from Judah

The author of the Pentateuch composed his text with a few central concerns in mind, one of which was a king who would command obedience from the nations in "the end of the days." The author draws these concerns together in three lengthy poems (Gen. 49; Num. 24; Deut. 33), each of which involves a major figure commanding an audience to gather together so he can tell them what will transpire "in the end of the days."[1] In this and the following chapter I show how this concern emerges as the author of the Pentateuch incorporates different texts and draws contexts together, alluding, patterning, rewriting, and drawing out meaning in various ways. That the author returns

---

1. John Sailhamer recognizes the significance of this "thematization" and its underlying relationship of texts in the Pentateuch. See his various works, including *The Pentateuch as Narrative* (Grand Rapids: Zondervan, 1992), 235, 405–9, 477; *Introduction to Old Testament Theology: A Canonical Approach* (Grand Rapids: Zondervan, 1995), 277; *The Meaning of the Pentateuch: Revelation, Composition, and Interpretation* (Downers Grove, IL: IVP Academic, 2009), 342–43; "Hosea 11:1 and Matthew 2:15," *Westminster Theological Journal* 63 (2001): 87–96 (for "thematized," see p. 91). Interestingly, he is not the first to detect the common terminology between the poems, an observation that can be traced as far back as the scrolls from Qumran: Johannes Zimmerman, *Messianische Texte aus Qumran*, Wissenschaftliche Untersuchungen zum Neuen Testament 2/104 (Tübingen: Mohr Siebeck, 1998), 58, 98, 442. In the next chapter, I show in detail how Num. 24 rewrites phrases from Num. 23 and how Deut. 33 draws on other texts with various implications.

to his central concern throughout his work and develops it at the end of the composition indicates his intent to focus on this very point. Discerning this central concern will also help us recognize and prioritize other emphases of his work.

Composition Techniques and Influences

The Pentateuch's author had only the Hebrew language available to him to affect his readers and communicate a message. Compared to modern genres of cinema or music, with a vast array of visual and audio effects, written language can seem very limited. However, biblical authors had more tools at their disposal than we might realize, and with these tools they create nuance and emphasis. A simple way to show emphasis, for example, is to repeat the main point throughout the text from start to finish.[2] Authors who are bringing together many pieces of text rather than writing something from scratch often repeat these main points within smaller pieces of text.[3] In the Pentateuch, the author not only returns to the same linguistic details in the poems of Gen. 49, Num. 24, and Deut. 33, but he poetically draws on the preceding narratives in each poem and develops the repeated language in the later poems. This creates coherence in the larger literary work and unifies it.

When we fail to recognize such devices, we may think the author has no communication strategy other than simply telling us what happened. But if an idea concerned an author a great deal, would he have expressed it only in passing, leaving to chance that the reader would catch it the first time? Surely he would return to that point often and incorporate it in a variety of ways. We cannot be sure that every author was so clear in their intent, but a close reading of the Pentateuch shows us that its author used language in this way, and because we can demonstrate this, we can look for similar techniques in other passages.

Repetition was not the only technique ancient authors used to draw readers' attention to their main point. They used and reused rare words or loaded terms, poetic images, and particular Hebrew grammatical constructions; rewrote

---

2. James Muilenburg, "A Study in Hebrew Rhetoric: Repetition and Style," in *Congress Volume: Copenhagen 1953*, ed. G. W. Anderson, Supplements to Vetus Testamentum 1 (Leiden: Brill, 1953), 97–111; Moshe Kline, "Structure Is Theology: The Composition of Leviticus," in *Current Issues in Priestly and Related Literature: The Legacy of Jacob Milgrom and Beyond*, ed. Roy Gane and Ada Taggar-Cohen (Atlanta: SBL Press, 2015), 225–64.

3. Consider how the recurring assessment of whether a Davidic king did or did not do what was "upright in the eyes of the LORD like David did" creates coherence and unity across the various episodes in Kings.

clauses with minor alterations; and employed certain narrative techniques to draw in readers and compel them to ask questions. They also employed or broke patterns to lead the reader in a particular direction. In chapters 7 and 8, we will see how the author of the Pentateuch creatively uses something as mundane as a genealogy to highlight characters and concepts. Realizing that ancient writers used these and other techniques can alter our preconceptions and shift our anticipation of how their texts will influence us. Just as the director of a play might turn the spotlight on a particular actor or employ shrill music to build tension, so ancient authors worked through the limitations of language and manipulated textual pieces to communicate their message.

As we consider how the author of the Pentateuch used literary techniques, we should also think about why Genesis, or the entire Pentateuch for that matter, is considered a single literary work. In what ways are ancient texts such as the Pentateuch a unity? This unity is brought about in part because its subunits—shorter pieces of text—work in harmony with one another. Consider, for example, how the story of the tower of Babel is next to the genealogy in Gen. 11. The tower of Babel narrative could be independent, as could the genealogy, but in addition to being linked through particular words, they also work together to move the story along. Or think of how the story of the exodus (Exod. 1–14) follows the story of Joseph (Gen. 37–50). We will see how the author has intentionally put the two stories next to one another, for it is not as though one happened right after the other. Have you ever considered why the author does this? As we will see in chapter 9, the author merges the stories to achieve greater coherence.

However, ancient writing techniques and styles do not display the same sort of coherence that we are accustomed to in modern stories. Modern technology allows for more advanced writing techniques than were available in the ancient Near East. Even so, the Pentateuch's author wanted the subunits of his work to move toward a coherent whole. The author also had to ensure that the subunits worked together to reinforce his main points. Unity in these texts may not always be as apparent as in a modern novel, but it can still be demonstrated despite the Pentateuch's complexity. In order to understand how the author generated this complex literary work, we will consider what coherence is and how it is brought about.

The Pentateuch's author created unity in ways other than simply placing textual subunits next to one another. He also used wordplays and consonance to bring together texts and concepts.[4] The author's theology was another

---

4. *Consonance* is the repetition of consonant sounds to create an association between words or concepts.

important influence that shaped his work. There were certain theological ideas that the author wanted to convey to his readers. He also used exegetical measures to draw out meaning and focus attention on his central concerns, which gives the overall work its unity and coherence. As we will see, the author draws meaning out of a textual subunit by commenting and further developing its content.

The Time of the Lion King

The Author's Perspective, Genre, and Textual Production

Let's start with the first word of the Pentateuch, *bere'shit*, which most English translations render as "in the beginning." As we begin here, we should not make the mistake of thinking that the author begins his work on the book *only* from the perspective of Gen. 1. Rather, we must consider the entire perspective of the author as he begins this composition.[5] As the author is "carried along" by the Holy Spirit (2 Pet. 1:21), he has authority to shape its contents and strategy. Though we don't often consider this point when reading the Bible, the author put the so-called final touches on his book *after* the events therein took place, and he composed it after many of the textual pieces had been completed. Just as the author of Kings used excerpts from the annals, so the author of the Pentateuch, living long after the events took place, used many textual subunits that had already been completed, including the account of the golden calf in Exod. 32, the instructions for the Passover in Exod. 12, and the Ten Commandments in Deut. 5, to name a few. "In the beginning" may start his *book*, but he himself starts from the perspective of its end.[6]

The Pentateuch concludes with Deuteronomy, most of which is Moses's farewell speech to the second generation of the Israelites who had come out of Egypt. Deuteronomy 1:1–5 frames the speech by stating that the people are poised to enter the land that God had promised to Abraham, Isaac, and Jacob, which we hear about in Gen. 12–50. The first generation of those who had come out of Egypt had passed away in the wilderness, and they never read the book that we now consider the Pentateuch. Of course, neither did

5. Up to this point I have avoided using the word "book" because its modern meaning does not suit our discussion of scrolls and ancient writing, but to reduce the repetition of cumbersome words such as "literary work" and "composition," I will use it going forward to convey the idea of a coherent and unified literary composition.

6. Franz Delitzsch, *Commentar über die Genesis* (Leipzig: Dörffling & Franke, 1860), 91; Otto Procksch, *Die Genesis: Übersetzt und erklärt* (Leipzig: Deichert: 1913), 265; Sailhamer, *Meaning of the Pentateuch*, 342–43.

Adam, Abraham, Isaac, and Jacob. We have no reason to think that any of the figures within the stories had an early form of the Scriptures. Even if they did have some short textual piece, they did not have the Pentateuch in the shape and order that the author would eventually present it. We should also not assume that the author intended the book exclusively, or even primarily, for the second generation of Israelites who came out of Egypt. The book is about the future, not merely the past. In fact, most scholars think that the Pentateuch stems from a hand later than Moses.[7] If this is correct, then the book was obviously not intended for an audience at that early period. However, even if Moses *did* complete the book, it seems evident that he intended the book to communicate to a later, general audience.

Because it is beyond the purposes of this book, I will not attempt to prove or disprove who completed the Pentateuch. If we are interested in learning about the genre and intended message of the text, searching for the precise time or person involved in the text's completion is unnecessary. Indeed, OT books are typically anonymous, and wrong assumptions about authorship could lead us to misinterpret the text. I am more interested in discerning the structure, design, or author's presumption of particular content, which often sheds light on the author's communication strategy or intentions. We often think that the first steps in interpretation are determining the author's audience and societal background and acquiring a general historical knowledge of the time. We assume that this helps us discern what an author presumes of his readers and even what the author himself experienced. But this view assumes a particular genre of writing and a modern view of authorship. This information can certainly be helpful, especially when we discern within the text some historical perspective that stems from a period later than the events in the narrative, such as God's covenant with David, the restoration to Jerusalem, or the monarchy. Without such information, however, I prefer to remain open-minded about the time frame of the author and look for evidence of design or structure. From there, I ask what question the author may be grappling with.

Why do I prefer this approach? Because the author *does* have an issue that he is grappling with and a point to make. As I mentioned above, we typically approach these texts in ways we have inherited from our upbringing or culture. Many of us grew up treating these texts as if they were virtual reality headsets giving us an actual view of the events the texts describe. We treat the narratives like a history lesson and try to draw good or bad morals from

7. Although the final author may be later than Moses, he is certainly not earlier than Moses. My point here is simply that we must recognize that the first readers of the Pentateuch were not those characters within the story itself.

it. We ask questions such as "How can we be like Abraham and have faith or obey in the face of a trial?" If the author were merely writing a history lesson to tell us what happened, then this sort of moralizing might be appropriate and lead us in the right direction. But the genre the author uses in the Pentateuch conveys much more than this. He composed the Pentateuch with hindsight, using many textual pieces in order to produce his book, such as historical traditions, genealogies, poems, blocks of legal codes, episodes, and theological influences. Three of the textual pieces that this author uses are poems, all of which concern events that transpire at "the end of the days," and it is to these poems that we will soon turn our attention. How does the author use these poems to communicate his central concerns, and how are these three poems connected to the opening of his book, "In the beginning"?

The Beginning That Assumes the End

The Pentateuch begins with "in the beginning," but beginnings are not all that the author intends to highlight with this word! He uses this phrase knowing full well the primeval history, the patriarchal stories, Moses the lawgiver, the wilderness wanderings, and Israel's complicated relationship with the LORD. But his use of "in the beginning" is not only a signal that he is aware of the whole story or that this is its beginning. It also signals an intentional connection to the word's opposite, the "end" (*'acharit*), a word that occurs in the three large poems. To put it another way, the first word of Genesis has a relationship with at least two textual units. On the one hand, it relates to Gen. 1:1–2:3 because of the sequence of "days" in this subunit, but it also has a relationship with the entire Pentateuch through the word pair "beginning" (*re'shit*) and "end" (*'acharit*).

This word pair appears in the three large poems of Gen. 49, Num. 24, and Deut. 33. Each poem's imagery draws upon the narrative that precedes it, exhibiting a structure within the larger literary work. Genesis 49 reflects language and motifs in Gen. 1–48, acting as a synthesis before the next section begins, with Gen. 50 serving as a fulcrum between the stories of the patriarchs and the beginning of Exodus. Numbers 24 likewise incorporates language and motifs from Exod. 1 to Num. 22, and from the poetry in Num. 23. It also comments again on several themes from Gen. 49, including "the end of the days," "the lion king," and God's relationship to Israel and the nations. This second section of the Pentateuch concludes with Num. 25–36, which connects its material to the beginning of Deuteronomy and the material in Joshua. Similarly, Deut. 33 draws from Gen. 1 through Deut. 31 in order to theologize about the lion king.

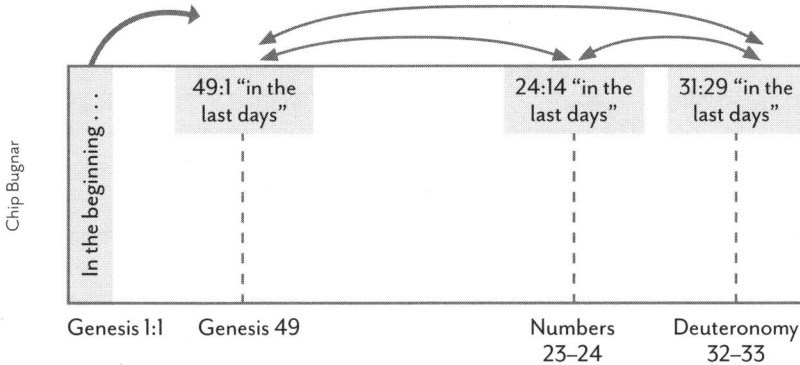

FIGURE 3.1. **The Placement of Poems**

Because of the structural importance of these three poems, the word pair is activated as a component of the author's strategy. "Beginning" (*re'shit*) describes different figures in the long poems in Gen. 49:3 and Num. 24:20 and draws upon Gen. 1.1 in a unique way in Deut. 33.21.[8] The author also associates each poem with the word's opposite in the phrase "in the end of the days" [*be'acharit*]. The recurrence of this phrase in Gen. 49:1, Num. 24:14, and Deut. 31:29 is the first thing we recognize in a panoramic view of the Pentateuch. The poems contain other significant repetitions related both to each other and to the time and person of a coming king, but "in the beginning" and "in the end" indicate that the author has a significant interest in this future time.

The first word in Gen. 1:1, "beginning," might seem like a natural choice since we are accustomed to understanding it in the context of Gen. 1, but the author's selection of this Hebrew word proves to be surprising. If the author had *merely* wanted to refer to a point in time, a "beginning" or a "first" in a series of days, other Hebrew words were available to him. The Hebrew synonyms *techillah* (beginning) and *ri'shon* (first) are often used in Scripture to indicate a temporal beginning, with *re'shit* (beginning) having a slight nuance. It appears eighteen times in the Pentateuch, *ri'shon* (first) fifty-five times, and *techillah* (beginning) four times. Figure 3.2 illustrates the overlapping connotation of these words (see next page).

A Hebrew lexicon indicates the different nuances in each word. *Ri'shon* indicates the first in a series of items; the first in relation to a second; a temporally related period, such as "in the first month" or "in the first day"; or some other ordinal concept.[9] *Ri'shon* can also refer to a period, whether an early

8. In chapter 5 I will explain more about this word's relationship to Gen. 1:1–2:3, and in the next chapter I will discuss its occurrence in Deut. 33.21.

9. *HALOT*, 2:1168–69.

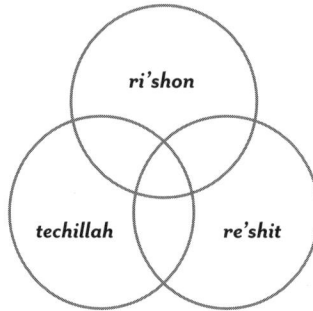

FIGURE 3.2. **Overlapping Synonyms**

time in relationship to a later one or even to a beginning time, as in Gen. 13:4: "at the place of the altar where he had made it at *first*." *Techillah*, a much rarer word in the Pentateuch, can indicate a beginning, a start of something, or a specific time when an activity begins.[10] Interestingly, the meaning of *techillah* (beginning) would seem to fit the most common understanding of Gen. 1 as the beginning of time or creation. *Re'shit*, on the other hand, conveys a peculiar meaning in its other uses in the Pentateuch, often referring to the first of a thing in contrast to something later, such as firstfruits (in contrast to the rest of the harvest) of an offering or tithe, which were dedicated to the Lord.[11] Similarly in Gen. 10:10, the author uses *re'shit* to indicate that the "beginning" of Nimrod's kingdom included four cities, and then he later went on to Assyria and built other great cities. In other uses, *re'shit* indicates a *first* in relationship to an *end* (*'acharit*), the same word pairing that appears in the three poems. For example, Deut. 11:12 describes a land watched over by God "from the *beginning* [*re'shit*] of the year and unto the *end* [*'acharit*] of the year." Other passages pair the words similarly:

Isa. 46:10: "Declaring from the *beginning*, an *end*, and from ancient times, things which have not been done."

Job 8:7: "Your *beginning* was always small, but your *end* will increase greatly."

Job 42:12: "The Lord blessed Job's *end* more than his *beginning*."

Eccles. 7:8: "A matter's *end* is better than its *beginning*."

10. *HALOT*, 2:1717.
11. *HALOT*, 2:1169–70.

These usages suggest that "beginning" (*re'shit*) and "end" (*'acharit*) were often formulated together.

Taking these uses of *re'shit* into consideration, we ought to ask if there is more to its usage in Gen. 1:1. We generally understand it in Gen. 1:1 as the temporal beginning of creation because of its relationship to the rest of Gen. 1. But could it also be a "beginning" that expects an "end"? If the author wanted primarily, specifically, or only to indicate "beginning" as a temporal frame of reference, he could have chosen *techillah* or the far more frequent *ri'shon*.

This is not to say that we should translate *re'shit* with a word other than "beginning," but it raises an important question: Why did the author choose *re'shit* here in Gen. 1 instead of one of the other synonyms? If the author wanted to draw attention to something later—a later time, an end—this is the precise word he would use. To put it another way, the author wants the reader to understand Gen. 1:1 as the beginning (*re'shit*) of God's appearance and activity in a way that evokes his appearance and activity "in the end" (*'acharit*).[12]

The End of the Days

This nuance to "beginning" in Gen. 1:1 is brought out by the introductory phrase of the three large poems: "in the end [*be'acharit*] of the days" (Gen. 49:1; Num. 24:14; Deut. 31:29). Besides this introductory phrase, a significant amount of repetition in these three poems makes their connection impossible to ignore. As John Sailhamer points out, in addition to *re'shit* (beginning) and *'acharit* (end) appearing in each context, a narrative figure commands an audience so that he can tell them what will transpire "in the end of the days" (Gen. 49:1; Num. 24:14; and Deut. 31:29).[13] In each context, a long narrative introduces the figure, a poem follows, and a short narrative concludes the recurring pattern.

In Genesis, the narratives about Abraham, Isaac, and Jacob come to an end with a long narrative in Gen. 37–48 featuring Jacob's son Joseph. The first long poem then emerges in Gen. 49, when Jacob commands his sons to gather around so that he can tell them what will happen to them "in the end of the days." After the poem, a short narrative concludes the story of Joseph and the other sons, and Genesis ends.

---

12. Not only are these two words antonyms, but they also conclude with the same grammatical ending and contribute to consonance and assonance in the poetry of the passages in which they appear.

13. Much of this initial information stems from John Sailhamer's works, including "Genesis," in *The Expositor's Bible Commentary*, vol. 2 (Grand Rapids: Zondervan, 1990), 322–27.

The pattern recurs in Numbers when the narrative about Balaam the prophet emerges in Num. 22. Numbers 23 and 24 recount four poetic visions followed by a narrative about Israel's idolatry in Num. 25. The third and fourth of these visions contain messianic imagery as well as Balaam's command to gather an audience so that he can tell them what will happen to them "in the end of the days." Numbers concludes with an extended account of census reports, legal instructions, battle narratives, and travel itineraries.

The pattern in Deut. 33 differs slightly from the previous two. What precedes the poem is not so much a narrative as a sort of farewell speech from Moses. He berates the Israelites for their idolatry and toward the end of his speech commands them to come together so that he can tell them the disaster that they will experience "in the end of the days" (Deut. 31:29). Two poems follow that give important indications of what will happen in the future. The second of the two poems is especially relevant because it draws upon Gen. 1:1, Gen. 22, and poetic images from Gen. 49 and Num. 24 and illustrates how the author develops imagery from elsewhere in the Pentateuch. As was the pattern for the other two poems, a short narrative that concludes Deuteronomy indicates a connection to subsequent material and expects a future figure.

The Description of the Lion King in Genesis 49

When we come to the poem in Gen. 49, much of the imagery in the blessing comes from the stories of Jacob and his sons in Gen. 29–48. Genesis 12–28 leads into these narratives by means of God's promise to Abraham that he would bless him and his descendants, one of whom is his grandson Jacob. The blessings for Jacob's older sons—Reuben, Simeon, and Levi—allude to their questionable behaviors recounted in the preceding narratives, whereas the blessings for less prominent children contain very little information. Joseph, the hero of the long story in Gen. 37–50, naturally receives a longer blessing from his father. Together these blessings seem to make up an independent poem about the twelve brothers who would eventually become the tribes of Israel.

Judah's Blessing (Gen. 49:8–12)

In contrast to the blessings for his brothers, Judah's blessing in Gen. 49:8–12 merits special attention.

> [8]Judah, you, your brothers will praise you.
>   Your hands are on the neck of your enemies.
>   Your father's sons will bow down to you.

⁹Judah is a cub of a lion.
>   From the prey, my son, you have gone up.
He kneels down. He crouches like a lion,
>   and like a lioness, who will rouse him?
¹⁰The scepter will not depart from Judah,
>   nor the making of rules from between his feet,
until he comes to whom it belongs,
>   and to him will be the obedience of the peoples,
¹¹tying his foal to the vine,
>   and his donkey's colt to the choice vine.
He washes his garments in wine,
>   and his robe in the blood of grapes.
¹²His eyes are darker than wine,
>   and his teeth whiter than milk.

As with the other brothers' blessings, Judah's begins with a wordplay on his name. This pun on the words "Judah" and "praise" first occurs in his birth story in Gen. 29:35, but here in Gen. 49:8, Judah's brothers are praising him. This seems odd since in the story leading up to this blessing chapter, Joseph was the one his brothers honored as second-in-command in Egypt. In Jacob's blessing, Judah's hands will be on the neck of his enemies, an image evoking subjugation. Further emphasizing his superior status is the statement that "your father's sons shall bow down to you." In Joseph's story, the brothers describe themselves as "sons of one father" (Gen. 42:32) and bow down to Joseph both in his dreams (Gen. 37) and on the several occasions when they encounter him in person (Gen. 42:6; 43:26, 28). In the poem, the author borrows this imagery from Joseph's narrative and applies it to Judah, portraying him with the authority that Joseph earned in Gen. 37–48.

Lion Imagery

Images of lions and lionesses fill the poem in verse 9. The first clause describes Judah as the "cub of a lion." This exact phrase shows up again in the poem of Deut. 33. While "lion" occurs often in the OT (forty-seven times), this phrase occurs only three times: here, in Deut. 33:22, and in Nah. 2:12. The next clause portrays Judah arising from his "prey," an image shared with the poems in Num. 23:24 and Deut. 33:20.[14] The second half of Gen. 49:9

---

14. I am using the Hebrew wording to follow these descriptions throughout my explanation. The lion imagery in Num. 24, the poem I will address shortly, borrows its imagery from Num. 23:24. Whereas Num. 23 concerns the people of Israel, Num. 24 concerns an individual.

presses the lion imagery further, stating, "He kneels down. He crouches like a lion." Numbers 24:9 repeats the first verbal action with its own picture of a lion, while shifting the second clause slightly to "lies down like a lion." Indeed, each of these poems makes the comparison "like a lion." Genesis 49:9 concludes, "Like a lioness, who arouses him?" This correlation to a lioness is repeated in Deut. 33:20, and the entire question appears a second time in Num. 24:9. Numbers 23:24, on the other hand, includes it as a statement. It is obvious that these poems share the poetic imagery of a lion, but what is not so obvious is how Num. 24 takes up lion imagery from Num. 23 and how the writer in Deut. 33 must add to that poem in order to make his point about the imagery's significance. These are all points I will return to in the next chapter.

Royal Imagery

The poem introduces another significant image in Gen. 49:10, "The scepter will not depart from Judah." Within this stanza, the author not only employs parallelism, a literary device characteristic of Hebrew poetry, but also makes use of metonymy, a figure of speech in which a particular item refers to something related to it. In this case, the scepter—a king's staff—refers to a king and his authority. To put it simply, the line declares that Judah will never lose the authority to rule. Like the lion imagery, "scepter" also appears again in the poetry of Num. 24:17.

The second line of Gen. 49:10 conjures up another royal image: "the making of rules from between his feet." This statement parallels the first by comparing "scepter" to "the making of rules." This second line assumes the verb "will not depart" from the first line, and parallels "from Judah" with "from between his feet." Poetry can have an evocative power, and in the vague portrayals and terse description here, the poet intends the reader to wonder and meditate. Who and what kind of ruler will this be? Notably, the parallelism is not exact. Although "Judah" and "between his feet" are parallel (both introduced by "from"), they are not equivalent. Somewhat suddenly, the author shifts the imagery from the tribe of Judah to a masculine singular figure (note the pronoun "his"). While the poetic imagery should not be taken hyper-literally, we should at least pause to consider this shift. Would the author use the imagery of "between his feet" to refer to an entire people? This shift from collective people to singular ruler is even more obvious in Num. 24's description of a masculine singular king, shifting the reference from Israel camped below Balaam in Num. 23 to the king likened to the LORD in Num. 24.

The Lawgiver

The unassuming phrase "the making of rules" offers yet another clarification. In Hebrew, the phrase is just one word—a rare verb in participial form. This form occurs only three times in the Pentateuch, one of which is Deut. 33:21 to explain the lion imagery of 33:20 and 22.[15] Because of the Pentateuch's portrayal of Moses as the unparalleled lawgiver, its use here suggests that this figure will be Moses-like and will administer laws. In other words, this figure is not just a sovereign but one whose decrees will result in legislation—an administration that will presumably be as morally just as it is supreme in power. The concluding clause in Gen. 49:10 reinforces all that we have seen up to this point in the blessing. It repeats the masculine pronoun "to him" and declares that he will have the "obedience of the peoples." The context of the line suggests that this "Judah" figure will be a sovereign who will make rules and command obedience among multiple peoples.[16]

Repeated Themes

in the last days
major character within the narrative
narrative, poetry, concluding narrative
lion imagery
king imagery, "ruler," or one making rules
scepter
a command to "come"
imagery of judgment in "hands on neck"
obedience of peoples
scepter will "not depart"
from Judah
third-person masculine singular figure

So far we have learned that the lion king—portrayed with the authority of a scepter, controlling his enemies, and making rules—will come from the tribe of Judah in the end of the days and command obedience from the

---

15. The third occurrence is in Num. 21:18, which refers to who was present and what they used to dig the well when Moses struck the rock, causing water to come out in Num. 20; see also Exod. 17.

16. The remainder of Judah's description depicts this sovereign with rather vague language that does not reappear in the other poems, so I will not comment on it here. Nonetheless, the language appears to evoke a positive image of the ruler.

peoples. The poem of Num. 24 is where the author next introduces the reader to another major figure and his instruction about "the end of the days," repeating language and imagery from Gen. 49 while also drawing upon stories from Exod. 1 to Num. 22 and the poem from Num. 23 to say more about this king. In the next chapter, we will begin by examining the well-known story of the prophet Balaam, who risks the ire of Balak, king of Moab, who hired Balaam to curse Israel. Bound by God's will, Balaam could only bless Israel.

4

The Lion King

A Panorama of the Pentateuch

The Pentateuch's panorama of a lionlike king reigning in the end of the days is launched in Gen. 1:1, gaining significance in the poem in Gen. 49 as we saw in chapter 3. This significance continues to take shape in the poems in Num. 24 before it culminates in the poem in Deut. 33. In this chapter, we will focus on these poems in Num. 24 and Deut. 33. Were it not for the peculiar use of *re'shit* (beginning) in Gen. 1:1 and its antonym, *'acharit* (end), in the opening of Jacob's blessing in Gen. 49:1, the use of *'acharit* in Num. 24 might not give us pause. But the repetition of an entire phrase ("in the *end* of the days"), similar patterning, and other repeated words and imagery make obvious that the author has incorporated these poems to liken this lion king to the LORD himself who delivered Israel from Egypt. The poem in Deut. 33 capitalizes on its own lion imagery to describe the king who enlarges Gad, provides the *re'shit*, and is likened to a temple-like rule maker who will come in the end of the days.

The *YHWH*-Like Lion King from Jacob (Num. 24)

Balak Tries to Curse Israel (Num. 22–24)

Just as the poem in Gen. 49 borrows from the patriarchal narratives and the story of Joseph for its imagery, so Balak's story and Balaam's poetic announcements and visions in Num. 24 depend on Israel's story from Exod. 1 to Num. 21. Pharaoh fretted that "the people of the sons of Israel are too many and too numerous," and if "war should break out . . . they would fight against us," which is why the Egyptians "loathed the sons of Israel" (Exod. 1:9, 10, 12). So Pharaoh oppressed the Israelites, saying, "Come, let us deal shrewdly with them" (1:10). Portrayed in the same language, Balak, king of Moab, "loathed the sons of Israel" because "the people were many" (Num. 22:3). Referring specifically to the exodus, Balak says to Balaam, "The people came out of Egypt. . . . Now, come curse this people for me because they are too numerous for me. . . . Perhaps I am able to fight against them" (22:6, 11). As Pharaoh sought to destroy burgeoning Israel three different ways in Exod. 1, so Balak seeks to curse Israel three times in Num. 22–24.[1]

Additionally, poetic lines in Num. 24 riff on Num. 23's poetry concerning the LORD's deliverance from Egypt, while the narrative of Balaam and Balak draws from Israel's defeat of surrounding nations as they traversed the wilderness (Num. 21). Seeing what Israel did to the Amorites, Balak summons Balaam to curse Israel as they dwell in their tents on the plains of Moab. The people of Moab were very worried because Israel "covered the face of the earth" (22:5, 11; 23:9–10). Balaam, however, refuses to curse Israel—not because of their vast number, as Balak assumes, but because God will not allow it. In a statement that the author alludes to later (24:9), God announces to Balaam, "You will not curse this people; they are blessed" (22:12).[2] Balak takes Balaam to different vantage points, hoping that if Balaam sees fewer and fewer of Israel's encampments, he will finally curse Israel (22:41; 23:13, 27). Balaam refuses each time, however, and "the LORD puts a word in his mouth," so that Balaam "lifted his proverb and he said . . ." (23:5, 7, 18). The announcements that follow these "proverbs" reflect God's commitment to bless Israel and descriptions of Israel's vast numbers and strength.

Balaam Sees, Hears, and Worships the King (Num. 24)

Compared with Num. 23, the poetic vision announcements in Num. 24 contain significant differences. In contrast to the other times, Balaam does not go out to look for omens with which to curse Israel or to hear from God. Rather, this time the "Spirit of God" comes upon him (Num. 24:1–2). This

---

1. John Sailhamer, *The Pentateuch as Narrative* (Grand Rapids: Zondervan, 1992), 406–7.
2. Genesis 12:3 reflects the expression in Num. 24:9. However, rather than repeating the lexeme for "curse" ("The one who curses you, I will curse"), the writer of Gen. 12:3 utilizes a separate verb for "curse" ("The one who dishonors you, I will curse"). The lexeme glossed as "dishonor" is taken from the flood narrative rather than from Num. 24:9.

fact alone alerts us that something special is about to transpire. Even though the prophetic announcements begin the same way as Num. 23, they contain additional descriptions.

Duplicate introductions to the visions appear in Num. 24:3–4 and again in verses 15–16, saying,

> The utterance of Balaam the son of Beor,
>   and the utterance of the man whose eye is opened.
> An utterance of one hearing the words of God,
>   who sees the vision of the Almighty,
>   falling down, eyes uncovered.[3]

Unlike the previous announcements, these visions proclaim that Balaam hears the words of "God" (*'El*) and sees a vision of the "Almighty" (*Shadday*). We might be tempted to think that this merely describes God's impersonal word coming to Balaam as with the other prophets, such as Ezekiel, but this account is clearly different. Balaam not only hears God's words; he has a vision of the Almighty. This particular Hebrew construction for "words of God" appears only three times in the Hebrew Bible—Num. 24:4, 16, and Ps. 107:11, which alludes to Exodus–Numbers—highlighting the rarity of these divine words. Moreover, the Hebrew root *ch-z-h* (related to having a vision) occurs two times in the clause "sees the vision of the Almighty" and for the first time here in the Balaam story. Furthermore, in the second vision announcement in Num. 24, the writer adds the phrase "having knowledge of the Most High."[4] The epithet "Most High" is combined with "God" (*'El*) in the story of Abraham's interaction with Melchizedek in Gen. 14:18–22 and is used as a title for the LORD in Deut. 32:8–9. Clearly, whatever Balaam sees, he considers it to be God.

Yet another change is Balaam's posture in the descriptions of Num. 24. Numbers 22:31 describes how the LORD "uncovered his eyes," and Balaam fell down in worship once he recognized the angel of the LORD standing in the road. By contrast, no such acts of reverence accompany the announcements that follow in Num. 23. However, both visions of Num. 24 depict Balaam as "falling down" when he has his eyes uncovered. He sees something that produces reverence. Three times in each announcement, Balaam describes

---

3. Numbers 24:16 contains the additional clause "and having knowledge of the Most High." See discussion below.

4. This takes the place of the relative pronoun in the explanatory clause "who sees a vision of the Almighty." That clause becomes an independent clause in Num. 24:16, highlighting the inclusion of "Most High."

himself as having "utterances," a genre indication that he is conveying a word of divine matters. This prophetic classification is yet one more indication that Balaam saw a special word from Almighty God.[5]

The King's Sudden Appearance

Balaam's first vision characterizes Israel's vast assembly that had worried Balak in Num. 22 and that Balaam "sees" in Num. 24:2: "How beautiful are your tents, Jacob, your dwelling places, Israel" (Num. 24:5). This refers to a myriad of Israelites camped on the plains below him. In parallel imagery, verse 6 portrays Israel's assembly as plants sprouting up along a water source. One might think that verse 7 merely expands on this portrait of the people, but a shift in reference is about to take place.

Numbers 24:7 begins "Water will flow from his buckets and his seed is in many waters." Notice the shift in person from "*your* dwelling places" and "*your* tents" to "*his* buckets" and "*his* seed." "His" could refer to Jacob/Israel, since the people are treated as a singular entity in verse 5 ("your [sing.] tents"; see also 23:24),[6] but the shift from second to third person suggests a different referent. Whatever decision one makes about the third-person pronouns in verse 7a, the following clause removes any question about the poem's point: "His *king* will be higher than Agag" (Num. 24:7b). No matter how one translates the singular pronoun "his" modifying the king, "king" cannot refer to the people Israel.[7] This introduction of the "king" who will exercise dominion over nations jolts the reader.[8] Is more said about this king?

The next clause expresses at least two facts about this king. First, not only will this king be higher than Agag, but his kingdom will also be exalted. The notion of a kingdom seems out of place in the Pentateuch, but another passage may help. In 1 Sam. 15, Agag is king of the Amalekites, a people who first arise as Israel's enemies in Exod. 17. Israel's first king, Saul, fails to obey the Lord's command to kill all Amalekites. As a result, the Lord rejects Saul from being king, taking the kingdom from Saul and giving it to David (1 Sam. 15:26–28).

---

5. On each occasion, Balaam modifies one of the utterances as an "utterance of the man," a description used only in this passage, 2 Sam. 23:1, and Prov. 30:1—each of which has implications for the Davidic son of God. See Tracy J. McKenzie and Jonathan Shelton, "From Proverb to Prophecy: Textual Production and Theology in Proverbs 30:1–6," *Southeastern Theological Review* 11, no. 1 (2020): 3–30.

6. The NIV's consistent rendering of the masculine singular pronoun as a plural throughout Num. 24 reflects this interpretation. Compare, e.g., the NIV's "Water will flow from their buckets, / their seed will have abundant water" with the ESV's "Water shall flow from his buckets, / and his seed shall be in many waters."

7. I will describe the relationship to Num. 23:22 below.

8. Though see Num. 23:21, where "king" is parallel to "Lord God."

Later, 2 Sam. 5:12 uses the exact language of Num. 24:7b when speaking of David's "exalted kingdom," some four hundred years after Balaam's vision. The similar language has compelled some scholars to interpret Num. 24:7 as emerging in the time of the monarchy and referring to a Davidic king. Regardless of the time period, there can be no doubt that the passage indicates a future king whose kingdom the LORD will establish and exalt.

Second, and even more important for our understanding of the king, is the pronoun modifying kingdom: "*His* kingdom will be exalted." This pronoun unmistakably refers not to Israel or to the LORD but to the king mentioned in the previous clause. Why is this important? Numbers 24:8a contains the same pronoun with another reference to the king, "God brings *him* out of Egypt." Remarkably, this verse restates Num. 23:22 ("God brought *them* out of Egypt") but changes one Hebrew letter! The plural pronoun in Num. 23:22 refers to Israel's pilgrimage from Egypt, so why does Num. 24:8 rewrite it with a masculine singular "his"? Because the writer does not intend this clause to refer to the people of Israel but instead looks forward to a king whom God will bring out of Egypt or an Egypt-like situation.

The second clause in Num. 24:8a also incorporates a clause from Num. 23:22 and repeats it exactly! "He is like the horns of a wild ox." In the poem of Num. 23, there is little question about its meaning. The LORD has brought his people from Egypt, delivering them from Pharaoh with great wonders, power, and mighty acts. In Num. 23's poetic imagery, Balaam portrays how the LORD brought them out, "like the horns of a wild ox." God acted in the exodus, committed to blessing Israel, and no divination could change that. Like the proverbial bull in a China shop, the LORD had pushed and gored anyone and anything that got in Israel's way. But how is this clause used in Num. 24:8a?

Because Num. 24:7 introduces a "king," with corresponding masculine singular pronouns, the same pronoun in Num. 24:8a now refers to this king! When God brings him from Egypt, he will be like the horns of wild ox. The reader must wait until Num. 24:9, 14 to know more about the identity and time of this king. But using the reference to the LORD and his activity in the exodus in Num. 23:22, the writer portrays the king in Num. 24:8 as having the same power! And just like the LORD defeated Egypt in the exodus, the king of Num. 24 will wreak havoc on his enemies. Numbers 24:8b reads, "He will consume the nations, his adversaries, / and their bones, he will gnaw. / And with his arrows will he shatter." The king in Num. 24:8 is likened to the LORD from Num. 23:22. In the plague narratives, the LORD had delivered his people from slavery and displayed his power over nature, darkness, death, and the Pharaoh. This king in Num. 24:8 will also have victory over these and other enemies.

The Lion King

Numbers 24:9 also selects and adapts material from elsewhere in Scripture, using the lion imagery from the poem in Gen. 49:9 and adapting it with the lion imagery from Num. 23:24.

Numbers 24:9	Numbers 23:24
	Behold, a people, like a lioness it will arise. And like a young lion lifts himself,
He kneels down, he lies down like a young lion, and like a lioness, who will arouse him?	he will not lie down until he consumes the prey and the blood of the slain, he will drink.

Numbers 24:9	Genesis 49:9
	Judah is a cub of a lion. From the prey, my son, you have come up.
He kneels down, he lies down like a young lion, and like a lioness, who will arouse him?	He kneels down. He hunches down like a lion and like a lioness, who will arouse him?

The first verb in Num. 24:9 ("He kneels down") is drawn from Gen. 49:9b exactly, but the continuation of Num. 24:9 ("He lies down like a young lion") shares a noun ("young lion") and verb ("lie down") with Num. 23:24. Although the final phrase of Num. 24:9a ("And like a lioness, who will arouse him?") also occurs in Gen. 49:9b, it is more likely adapted from Num. 23:24 ("Behold, a people, like a lioness, it will arise"). There the lioness refers not to a singular figure but to the "people." The logic of Num. 23 relates to Balaam's insistence that God will not allow Israel to be harmed and that they will most certainly rise up and consume their enemies. The masculine singular pronoun ("arouse him") at the end of the clause in Num. 24:9a mirrors the one in Gen. 49:9b to ask who would cause him to rise and to establish the king's authority, the king who will come out of Egypt and consume his enemies.

The King Is the Seed of Abraham

The final clause of Num. 24:9b likewise integrates material from other literary contexts. Balaam's narrative, preceding the poem, focuses heavily on "blessing" (occurring fourteen times) and "cursing" (occurring seven times). Balak turns in fear to divination and sorcery to curse Israel, but Balaam does nothing but bless them. So when Num. 24:9b says "The ones blessing you will be blessed / and the ones cursing you will be cursed," the themes of blessing and cursing fit neatly with the context. God had earlier told Balaam "You will not curse this people; indeed, they are blessed" (Num. 22:12). However, a notable shift at this point draws in another context altogether. After consistently using third-person forms in 24:7–9a, the author suddenly uses a second-person singular pronoun ("you") twice in 24:9b. In this case the shift in person results from the author incorporating material from another passage, from Jacob's blessing in Gen. 27:29.[9] This blessing corresponds precisely to the grammatical forms in Num. 24:9, but the writer has inverted the order: "Cursed are those who curse you and blessed are those who bless you."[10] In the patriarchal narratives, Jacob obtains Isaac's blessing through trickery. By integrating this clause at the conclusion of Balaam's vision, the author associates this blessing concerning Abraham's seed with the king depicted as a lion who would come in the end of the days (Num. 24:14).[11]

Numbers 24:13–14 links to the same timeframe as Jacob's blessing in Gen. 49:1. Balaam says, "If Balak would give me his house full of silver and gold, I would not be able to transgress the command of the LORD, to do good or bad of my own will. Whatever the LORD says, that I will say. And now, behold, I am going to my people. Come, let me tell you what this people will do to your people *in the end of the days.*" Like the pattern in Gen. 49, the central figure of the narrative commands an audience to come together so that he can tell them what will happen to them in the "in the end of the days."

The King Is the Most High

Numbers 24:15–16 is the preamble to the second vision. Here, in addition to "words of God" and "vision of the Almighty," the author adds a third depiction of the one Balaam sees: "the Most High." Speaking about the Most High, Balaam says in verse 17 "I see him, but not now; / I behold him, but not near," using a masculine singular pronoun. Does this pronoun refer back to the "people" of Israel as it did in Num. 23:24?

In this instance, it cannot refer to Israel. Balaam knows that his vision concerns the future, "the end of the days" (Num. 24:14). He sees him "but not *now*; he beholds him but not *near*" (24:17). Balaam cannot be referring to the people of Israel whom he saw encamped before him (24:2). Numbers 23:9

---

9. See also Num. 22:6, although variations occur there.

10. Scholars call inverted constructions like this Seidel's Law; it points to a clause's composition from other material.

11. The similar promise in Gen. 12:3 relates Abraham's seed that would bring blessing to the earth's families. There the author incorporates the clause from Num. 24:9/Gen. 27:29 but adapts the wording to correspond to the different words for "curse" both in the garden and from the flood. Thus the reader knows this lion from Judah and Jacob is associated with Abraham's promised seed.

uses the same verbs—seeing and beholding—to depict Balaam's panorama of Israel "from the top of the rocks" and "from the hills," but in the vision of Num. 24:17, these verbs refer to a time that is not now and a place that is not near. Who, then, is Balaam talking about?

The answer comes when we consider how Balaam expands on the earlier preamble—"hearing the words of God" and "seeing a vision of the Almighty"—by adding the clause "having knowledge of the Most High" to his description. Across these three clauses, the Most High parallels God and, in particular, the Almighty. After referring to the "vision of the Almighty," Balaam immediately says in verse 17 "I see him . . . and I behold him!" Balaam considers this "him" to be God himself, the Almighty, the Most High! The next sentence in verse 17 turns our attention to the king who holds the scepter in Gen. 49:10, making the referent even more obvious.[12]

This masculine figure that Balaam refers to cannot be Israel because he says next in Num. 24:17b: "A star marches from Jacob; a scepter will arise from Israel." This figure marches *from* Jacob and arises *from* Israel, indicating it is not the entire people of Israel encamped in the valleys below him.[13] In this important context, "scepter" emerges again, as it did in Gen. 49:10, to refer to a king. Parallel to "scepter" in Num. 24:17 is the figure of a "star." While the star's explicit connotation is not obvious from the context, other uses within the Pentateuch are suggestive. A "star" was one of the lights intended to "rule the night" (Gen. 1:16–18), much like a king rules a kingdom. Therefore, a star is a fitting description of one who marches and rises with a scepter. The end of verse 17 tells us this marching ruler—not the nation of Israel—will "crush the foreheads of Moab" and "break down the sons of Seth."

The King's Dominion over His Enemies

An even more likely reason for the author to use "star" emerges from the repeated promise that Abraham's seed would be as many as the "stars of the heaven" and would "possess the gates of their enemies."[14] One of these stars coming from Jacob makes sense given the promise to Abraham and

12. This shows the shift in *who* the writer refers to and *how* he uses the poetry of Num. 23:9 toward a different referent in his poem in Num. 24:17. These subtle uses and changes in content reveal the author's intentions. He is not merely arranging material but adapting it to convey his point.
13. Nothing grammatically prohibits it from referring to Judah's tribe, but tribal Judah has not been mentioned since Num. 13. Also, upcoming clarifications negate this possibility.
14. See the various formulations in Gen. 15:5; 22:17; 24:60; 26:4; Exod. 32:13; Deut. 1:10; 10:22; 28:62. See also Gen. 37:9. The only other meaning for "star" in the Pentateuch is in the warning to Israel not to worship the sun, moon, and stars (Deut. 4:19).

The Poems' Shared Theme:
A future king from the tribe of Judah will appear,
to whom the obedience of the nations belongs.

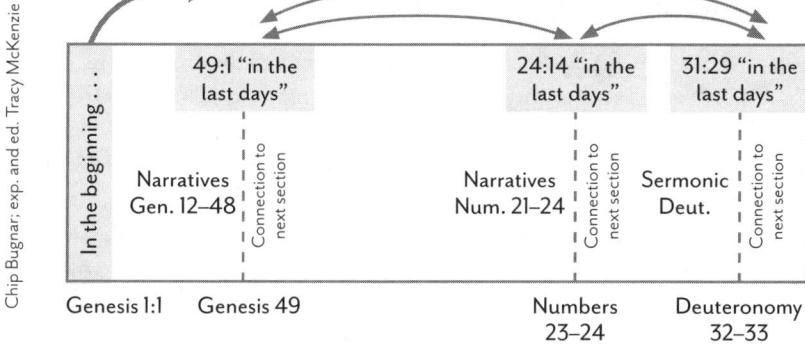

FIGURE 4.1. **The Layout of the Lion King Poems in the Pentateuch**

the other patriarchs. The poetry in Num. 24:18 also mirrors the language of this promise. The noun "possession" appears twice, "enemies" appears once, and a pun on the word "gate" (*sha'ar*)—the name "Seir"—provides yet another connection to the promise. Seir and Edom, two monikers for Esau's progeny, are Jacob/Israel's perennial enemies who appear in the very narratives that contain the promise. This star from Jacob/Israel will help Israel to "do valiantly," verse 18 adds, while Num. 24:19 concludes the vision, "He will have dominion from Jacob and will destroy the survivor from the city." The second vision equates the Most High with a single royal descendant of Jacob and Judah who will dispossess Israel's enemies in the end of the days.

The Temple-Like Royal Rule Maker (Deut. 33)

The final occurrence of "in the end of the days" in Deut. 31:29 segues into the final poems of Deut. 32–33. Deuteronomy is set as Moses's final speech to the Israelites before they enter the promised land. At the end of his long sermon, Moses calls an audience together to tell them what will happen "in the end of the days." In a similar threefold pattern of narrative/poetry/concluding narrative like Gen. 49 and Num. 24, Deut. 34 reports Moses's death. In his sermon, Moses is aware that his fellow Israelites will not obey the LORD but will instead provoke him with idols, so he calls heaven and earth to witness against them before warning what will befall them "in the end of the days" (Deut. 31:29).

The Poem Blesses the Lion King

The poem of Deut. 33 contains Moses's blessing to each of the tribes. The poem's difficult style and grammar leave us with many questions. Moses's role as the one who gathered the people and gave them God's law is restated at the beginning (33:4), along with the LORD's own care for Israel (33:2–3). Verse 5 ambiguously states that "a king was in Jeshurun" but without the same royal elements and context that occur in Gen. 49 and Num. 24.[15] Deuteronomy 33:7 conveys a short blessing for Judah, but it contains none of the repetitions we might expect and nothing significant other than Moses's request that the LORD "bring him to his people"—as if there is a future "Judah" to come. Moses also requests that the LORD be a help over Judah's "adversaries," a word occurring in Num. 24:8. A few other notable poetic images are repeated in the ensuing blessings,[16] but only when the poem turns to Gad do borrowed images and words elicit explanation.

Notably, the blessing is not to Gad at all. Rather, Moses says, "Blessed is he who enlarges Gad" (Deut. 33:20a). And the next clause indicates this one is "like a lioness," echoing portraits of a lion we have encountered already in Gen. 49 and Num. 24. This lioness "sits, tears the arm, indeed, the crown of the head." While it is possible that it originally referred to Gad, considering the repetition of the lion imagery and the contents of 33:21, this clause must refer to the one who enlarges Gad. This imagery of the lion sitting and tearing its prey associates this blessing with the same root word occurring in Gen. 49:9a and Num. 23:24b and 24:9. Moreover, the "star" and "scepter" in Num. 24:17 will "smash the forehead" of his enemies, mirroring what the lioness does here.[17] A similar trope appears in Dan's blessing: "To Dan he says, Dan is the cub of a lion; he leaps from Bashan" (Deut. 33:22). The clause depicts a

15. Readers often take the nameless king to be Moses or the LORD, but interestingly, the Septuagint contains a future tense verb rather than the past tense verb found in *BHS*, indicating that they still awaited the king. See Seth D. Postell, "Messianism in Light of Literary Strategy," *Bibliotheca Sacra* 177 (July–September 2020): 329–50. Significantly, Moses is never given the title of king. While the LORD could be considered king, grammatically it does not fit because there has been no reference to him since 33:3. And we still have the question of when the LORD was called king. Deuteronomy 33:2b is notoriously difficult, as the text-critical apparatus indicates. The introductory verses contain a variety of pronouns (i.e., third-person singular and plural, second-person masculine singular, and even first-person common), making the interpretation challenging.
16. E.g., "smash" (33:11), "kneeling down" (33:13), and horns of a "wild ox" (33:17).
17. The same Hebrew noun glossed as "crown of the head" in Deut. 33:20b occurs in Num. 24:17 in the Samaritan Pentateuch (as well as a similar construction in the Masoretic text of

lion preparing to apprehend its prey, and one who leaps from Bashan, the land of King Og, whom the Israelites defeated in Num. 21. The exact expression "cub of a lion" also occurs in Gen. 49:9, providing yet another connection between the poems.[18] But what should we make of the fact that these statements appear in the verses related to Gad and Dan?

More details from Deut. 33:21 make apparent that Deut. 33 is an adaptation of an independent piece of literature. The reference to Bashan in Deut. 33:22 suggests that the text originally blessed Dan and Gad because of their lionlike activities in the battle against Og (Num. 21).[19] Like the adaptations we examined in Num. 24, the writer uses narratives from Exodus through Numbers to portray the lion king who would come. The writer composes similarly here, elaborating the poem and splicing Deut. 33:21 in between the poetic lion imagery.

The Complexity and Origins of Deuteronomy 33:21

The significance of this splicing will become clear, but first we must address the complexity of Deut. 33:21. Many have noted that the verse is unusual and difficult and has given rise to a great variety of English translations. Its grammar (particular verb types, syntax, and style) is distinct from the poetic style of the surrounding verses. The two narrative clauses in Deut. 33:21 suggest that the verse has been moved from earlier in the chapter.[20]

> Then he provided the re'shit [beginning] for himself,
> For there was the portion of the temple-like rule maker;
> And he came with the leaders of the people;
> He executed the justice of the LORD,
> And His ordinances with Israel.

Jer. 48:45), at the least suggesting that others have understood an association between the two clauses.

18. The only other occurrence is in Nah. 2:12.

19. See Num. 32:33; Deut. 3:1–13.

20. Frank M. Cross Jr. and David Noel Freedman, "The Blessing of Moses," *Journal of Biblical Literature* 67, no. 3 (1948): 191–210, specifically 202–3. Concerning verse 20 and the verses related to Gad, we are told that the Masoretic Text (the tradition that underlies our modern Hebrew Bible) "is suspicious, as the only instance in which the blessing is applied to *YHWH* instead of the tribe." In regard to the second colon of verse 20, they say that "there is no connection between the first colon and those which follow, however the words are interpreted." In a later article, Freedman explicitly rewrites the poem so that verse 21 relates to the content in verses 5–10. He says, "In my view, vs. 21 has nothing to do with the Blessing of Gad." See David Noel Freedman, "The Poetic Structure of the Framework of Deuteronomy 33," in *The Bible World: Essays in Honor of Cyrus H. Gordon*, ed. Gary Rendsburg et al. (New York: Ktav, 1980), 25–46, in particular 33–35.

The verse's beginning narrative verb grammatically connects to Deut. 33:2–5 before the poetry begins.[21] Verse 2 depicts *YHWH* "*coming* with ten thousand from his holy ones," the same verb that describes the rule maker in verse 21. Verse 4 indicates that Moses had provided law as a possession before verse 5 describes a king gathering with the heads of the people. Why would the author transpose some of the content to Deut. 33:21?

Verse 21's genre can best be described as pastiche, a literary technique in which words or phrases from various passages are stitched together to give Scripture an authoritative voice. Writers select these words based on what they desire to say in the new location. The author in Deut. 33:21 draws upon royal lion imagery and the themes of land, blessing within the Abrahamic line, and a Mosaic lawgiver. He does so not only to explain the lion imagery—the one who enlarges Gad, and the one who leaps from Bashan—but also to create a unified text by drawing from the entirety of his work. Moreover, because the poem itself is a blessing, the writer knows that any blessing passage will connect quite nicely with his theme here. It is not difficult to see, then, why the author draws from passages that focus on blessing, such as Gen. 1, 22, 49, and Num. 24.

The Lion King Provides and Inherits the Re'shit

This blessing in Deut. 33:21 is remarkable in the richness of its theology. The first clause of verse 21 merges key words from two passages in Genesis. First, it integrates a phrase from Gen. 22:8, "God will *provide for himself* a lamb for the burnt offering" (cf. vv. 4, 13, 14). This grammatical construction "provide for oneself" also occurs in 1 Sam. 16:1, when the LORD chooses David to be king (cf. v. 17). The phrase becomes the central idea in Gen. 22 and provides the place with its name, "The LORD will provide" (Gen. 22:14). The author integrates this terminology in Deut. 33:21 to match the provision of a lamb for the burnt offering and provision of a Davidic king. Abraham's obedience amid the LORD's test yields the LORD's strongest affirmation of blessing in Gen. 22:17–18, with blessings of numerous offspring, possession of enemy lands, and blessing of all nations.

Second, the thing "provided for himself" is none other than Gen. 1:1's *re'shit*. Why splice together the LORD's providing for himself and *re'shit*? What does "He will provide the *re'shit* for himself" mean? We noted earlier that *re'shit* has nuances of beginning or first but most often indicates the first of a thing in contrast to its end. The one that Moses blesses in verse 20, "enlarging

---

21. Another grammatical verb does not occur until verse 21, and only one occurs after that (v. 28).

Gad, like a lion sitting and tearing," is now said to have provided this "first" thing in contrast to later things.[22] But if indeed the writer draws this word from Gen. 1:1, he is also associating the one who enlarges Gad, this lion, with the one who created the heavens and the earth in the *re'shit* (beginning), inviting comparisons of the first act of creation to the later acts of creation!

The next clause in Deut. 33:21 stems from two, if not three, passages, and is linked to the previous clause through the causal conjunction "for": "For there was the portion of the temple-like rule maker." Where, we might ask, is "there"? Based on the author's use of the conjunction "for," which links the adverb "there" to the previous clause, the author is pointing to the location of the *re'shit*. In other words, the *re'shit* is the "portion of the rule maker." This word "portion" is used only twice in the Pentateuch, here and in Gen. 33:19, where Jacob buys the "portion of the field where he had pitched his tent." Joshua 24:32 looks back on the purchase of this "portion" and recounts how the Israelites buried the bones of Joseph in this inheritance plot because he told them that God would visit them and deliver them to the land he swore to Abraham, Isaac, and Jacob (Gen. 50:24–25; Exod. 13:19). The word signifies a place, most often a field or plot of land that one purchases or receives as an inheritance. By making "there" point to *re'shit*, which is likewise a "portion," an inheritance, the author indicates that the lion king both provided creation and time and will yet inherit it! Although it raises additional questions, understanding the related passages allows us to interpret in more appropriate ways. The *re'shit* is the rule maker's portion/inheritance!

The Lion King Is the Temple-Like Rule Maker

The author also borrows the description of the rule maker from Gen. 49:10, where it is translated "the making of rules." This rare verb links the two passages and identifies the lion king as one who has authority to make rules. This recalls Moses's status as one who delivered laws and his description in Deut. 33:4. However, its placement here alongside lion imagery leaves no doubt that the description is yet another intentional association between the three poems, pointing to the future king who will come in the end of the days and rule over his people. In this way, the author "types" this future king as someone like Moses. This is particularly fitting given the statement in Deut. 18:15 that God would raise up a prophet like Moses.

22. Because the LORD is the only subject of the verb "bless" in the poetry, he is the subject in 33:20, who "enlarges Gad." This blessing would include the remainder of the verse, "Like a lion, he dwells, he tears the arm, indeed, the crown of the head." Despite English translations that have added the tribal name, Gad is not the explicit subject of pouncing and tearing like a lion.

Scholars have struggled to understand one more word in Deut. 33:21. I translated the clause as "For there was the portion of the temple-like rule maker." Modern English versions have translated this word "temple-like" in various ways, typically as "was reserved" or "was kept." In the abstract to his article on this word, scholar Gary Rendsberg says, "The meaning of the word *sāfûn* in Deuteronomy 33:21 has defied scholars for millennia. The ancient versions and rabbinic interpretations, which typically point to an understanding 'hidden, buried,' reflect more eisegesis than any real awareness of the word's actual meaning."[23] The term occurs five other times in the Hebrew Bible, with most of the uses occurring in 1 Kings 6–7, an account of the construction of the temple and Solomon's house, which he had *paneled* with fine wood. If the verb normally means "to cover a surface with wood paneling," we must ask, as Rendsburg puts it, "What would a paneled ruler be?"[24]

The writer in Deut. 33:21 describes this rule maker in the same manner as the ornate woodworking of the LORD's temple and royal palace. Here the author explains that the "one making rules," decorated as temple and palace, has a "portion." While we might at first think the *re'shit* is merely a piece of land because of its association with "portion," this would be a misunderstanding of how the author is connecting these terms. The *re'shit* was the first act in creating time and space—that is, God's creation of the heavens and the earth. The one making rules provided it and will inherit that portion. This one making rules is described in temple and palace imagery, we could say. He is sovereign over creation and time, is priest for it, and is himself involved in its "first act," now awaiting its last act.

The author composes the verse's final three clauses in similar fashion, clarifying several ambiguities. Verse 21's second narrative clause, "And he came with the heads of the people," integrates the rare verb from Deut. 33:2 in which the LORD "came" (*'atah*) and the phrase "the heads of people" in 33:5. The phrase "gathered among the heads of people" in 33:5 describes the congregation of the king. If indeed the author draws the clause from that context, it suggests that it originally described Moses as king but now indicates the one who provided the *re'shit* for himself, the temple-like rule maker, who "came with the heads of the people." In this way, we can clarify the ambiguity regarding the king in Deut. 33:5: it is no longer a reference to

23. Gary Rendsburg, "ספן: Deuteronomy 33:21," *Hebrew Union College Annual* 81 (2010): 17–42. Rendsburg goes on to say that the reading of the Greek translation of the OT is impossible because it assumes a form that occurs nowhere else within or outside of the Hebrew Bible. Moreover, our oldest manuscript, found in the environs of the Dead Sea, witnesses to the Hebrew text that we have in the Hebrew Bible, making it likely that the word was part of the original text.
24. Rendsburg, "Deuteronomy 33:21," 31.

Moses but to the lion king from Judah, the star from Jacob. He is the one making rules, and according to the next clause in verse 21, "he does the righteousness of the LORD." The final clause of the verse reminds the reader that "his judgments are with Israel"—yet another instance where "his" is clearly distinct from Israel. It also cannot refer to Moses. As great as Moses was, he was not the king that they waited for, and his time was not the end of the days. Finally, the pairing of the roots "righteousness" (*tsedaqah*) and "justice" (*mishpat*) suggests that none but the LORD and the LORD's king could enact these virtues.[25] The king who makes rules, adorned like palace and temple, inherits the entire cosmos, and does the righteousness of the LORD himself.

Summarizing Deuteronomy 33's Contribution to the Pentateuch's Panorama

The author of the Pentateuch has found within this old poem about Moses and the tribes a way to formulate and clarify a message about the last days and this so-called lion king. Although originally a reference to Gad, the author has "exegeted" the imagery about the royal lion from Gen. 49 and Num. 24 to speak of a future king. He has drawn new associations to the rule maker's provision and inheritance of the re'shit, the heavens and the earth—the entire cosmos—describing him in royal and temple imagery as one who enacts the LORD's righteousness and justice.

Conclusion

Interpretation

I want to conclude this chapter with a word about interpretation and a word about theology. This type of textual production—authorship, I would say, because of his intent to draw in the entirety of the work—might be unfamiliar to us modern readers. We must remember that the ancient world differed greatly from ours. To better read Scripture, we must grapple with its textual production, genre, and purpose. While there's much we can say about the Pentateuch's purpose, one thing is clear: the author wanted to say something about the "end of the days." He had a message about this future period and

---

25. 2 Sam. 8:15; Isa. 9:7 (9:6 MT); 11:4; Jer. 23:5; 33:15. The Dead Sea scroll 4Q252, which contains a midrash of Gen. 49:10, makes a similar juxtaposition. It reads, "A ruler will not depart from the tribe of Judah . . . there will not be cut off a king in it belonging to David for the ruler's staff is the royal covenant . . . until the righteous messiah comes." See Martin G. Abegg Jr., "Messiah at Qumran: Are We Still Seeing Double?," *Dead Sea Discoveries* 2, no. 2 (1995): 125–44, in particular 134.

used texts from the past to communicate it. He selected, arranged, adapted, and incorporated portions of text from other places in Scripture, rewriting lines to say something about this future period. Additionally, his literary methods—drawing together "the end of the days" language and lion imagery from the poems and associating them with *re'shit*—coalesce to give us a unified work. For this reason, we can understand the Pentateuch as one text and this writer as an author, even though the unity we find is different from that of a modern book.

Before we can interpret a text, we must understand its boundaries. If we don't, we won't have the proper context in which the author expresses himself, and we will not fully grasp the author's ideas and purposes. The way to determine the boundaries is to discern where the author has stopped talking about his central concerns. While we have not exhausted his concerns, by observing the prominence the author has placed on the end of the days and this lion king, and by tracing the way he has adapted and integrated texts to explain their coherence within his work, we can understand the boundaries of the Pentateuch and see its unity, which allows us to interpret the book more appropriately.

Theology

What message, then, is the author trying to communicate? Starting from his last adaptation in Deut. 33:21, we see the conquering lion king "sitting and tearing the arm and the forehead." He provided the *re'shit* for himself; it is his portion from which his just and righteous rule was and will extend to the peoples. This lion king is a son of Judah, a seed of Abraham, meaning he is human. Perhaps that seems like an odd place to begin, but it is no small thing to say one man will rule the cosmos with the righteousness and justice of the LORD. Numbers 24:8 likens him to the LORD, who delivered Israel from slavery, for he too will deliver his people from slavery. Like the LORD, he also is like the horns of a wild ox. In Num. 24:16–17, Balaam beholds him as the "Most High," equating him with God Almighty! Later in Scripture, the son of David is himself called God Almighty (Isa. 9:6), so this should not surprise us. What is perhaps more interesting is that this lion king is said to have "provided the *re'shit* for himself." In other words, he gave us time and creation! Everything we see in the so-called creation account of Gen. 1:1–2:3, he was involved in bringing it about. If this is so, he must be like God himself, because Gen. 1:1 declares that God created the heavens and the earth "in the *re'shit*."

And what about "the end of the days"? Is the first word in the Hebrew Bible associated with the "end of the days" and the work of the lion king from the tribe of Judah? If in conjunction with each of these three poems the author has used *re'shit* (beginning) because it intentionally evokes the *'acharit* (end), then we must recognize that the very first word of the Bible is not merely about the past. What happens during "the end of the days"? The lion from the tribe of Judah, the star of Jacob, the Most High king, rules and judges quite ferociously. He was not merely present during the exodus from Egypt, because as Balaam says, "I see him, but not now; / I behold him, but not near." From the perspective of the author, he would come, and nations would be his "possession." Balaam calls him "the Most High" as well as "Almighty," names used of the God of Israel throughout the OT. The lion king is *'El Shadday*. He rules and all peoples obey his authority because all of time and the cosmos is his inheritance. The first word in the Bible points us to the divine son of Judah who will rule over the nations in the last days. It is this son of Judah that the entire Pentateuch is about.

Are their others who have understood this message? John 1:1–3 says, "In the beginning was the Word, and the Word was with God, and the Word was God. He was in the beginning with God. All things were made through him, and without him nothing was made that was made." Consider also how Paul interprets Gen. 1:1 in Col. 1:15–20:

He is the *image* of the invisible *God*, the *firstborn* of all *creation*. For by him all things were *created*, in *heaven and on earth*, visible and invisible, whether thrones or dominions or rulers or authorities—all things were *created* through him and for him. And he is *before all things*, and in him *all things* hold together. And he is the *head* of the body, the church. He is the *beginning*, the *firstborn* from the dead, that in everything he might be *first place*. For in him all the fullness of God was pleased to dwell, and through him to reconcile to himself *all things*, whether on *earth or in heaven*, making peace by the blood of his cross.[26]

The lion king's kingdom has begun. As one scholar puts it, "Already in Gen. 1:1 the concept of 'the last days' fills the mind of the reader."[27] The Pentateuch, the first larger text in the Bible, asserts with its first word something about its end. It speaks of the end of the days when the lion from the tribe of Judah comes in judgment and salvation, ruling over time, the cosmos, and its peoples. Is this your understanding of Jesus? John writes in his revelation, "And one of the elders said to me, 'Weep no more; behold, the Lion of the tribe of Judah, the Root of David, has conquered, so that he can open the scroll and its seven seals'" (Rev. 5:5).

26. I have italicized words Paul seems to use based on an understanding of Gen. 1.
27. Otto Procksch, *Die Genesis: Übersetzt und erklärt* (Leipzig: Deichert: 1913), 425.

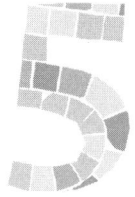

God's House and His Viceroys
(Gen. 1:1–2:3)

Taking Our Cue from the Larger Text

The previous chapters showed that the lion king, the rule maker, the Most High, provided the *re'shit* for himself, will inherit time and the cosmos, and will rule over it in righteousness in the end of the days, obtaining obedience from all nations. Each of these elements—the last days, a king from Judah, an international kingdom, obedience—will receive more emphasis in the coming chapters. The author of the Pentateuch looked forward to the last days and the Most High King from Judah. He would have loved to see our time.

Repetition plays a key role in the author's strategy in the poems of the Pentateuch. Even more, the interpretive nature of Deut. 33:20–22 and the final occurrence of "the end of the days" indicate that the boundaries of the author's work are Gen. 1 to Deut. 33/34. Other factors also suggest the unity of the book, such as the pursuit of a land promise from Gen. 12 forward, a "land" that we will also trace back to Gen. 1. Moreover, Moses's death before entry into that land likewise indicates the author's conclusion to his work. Moses, the key figure since Exodus, receives legal codes from the LORD and becomes his appointed mediator, tasked to bring the Israelites into the land promised to

FIGURE 5.1. **The Author's Location in Relation to Events**

Abraham. These factors show that as complex and diverse as the Pentateuch is, it is still one great text made up of smaller writings.

Even so, from our modern perspective, the unity may seem rather strange. We could state the matter another way. We can discern intentionality in the text—what we could call intelligent design—through repetition and connected words, phrases, and concepts, as well as style. Because it is impossible that the author was unaware of these connections, they show us something of the *modus operandi* of this author. He does not merely record what he has seen, nor has he merely taken dictation. He uses sophisticated literary techniques to craft his text.

How does seeing the text's panorama inform our understanding of the selection and arrangement of smaller texts? If the announcement of the lion king theme is important to the author, how does he use smaller texts to buttress this theme? From a reader's perspective, we can expect smaller units to somehow fit with a main concern and to develop that theme as well as any other central concerns. Writing from the end and with it in view, the author selects and arranges smaller units to move his point along (see fig. 5.1).

Whereas the last two chapters considered the Pentateuch from the perspective of the entire unit, we now turn our attention to the smaller units in order to discern how these units cohere with the panorama. The first of these smaller units is Gen. 1:1–2:3, which is marked by distinct repetitions and its pattern of seven days. Although space constraints prevent us from analyzing in detail every subunit in the Pentateuch, we will consider how any prominent material fits into the composition of the entire unit.

Genesis 1

While Gen. 1 obviously has something to say about God's creative act, the chapter is about more than just creation or science. Since its origin, readers have understood that the chapter makes claims about the LORD's involvement with the cosmos. Just to give one example, OT scholars often propose that its author argues against other creation accounts in the ancient Near East. While the chapter could have originally related to other creation stories, we should ask if this explains the author's incorporation of this subunit into Gen. 1–11 and the Pentateuch as a whole. One way to answer this question is to ask how often he polemicizes against other creation narratives in his larger work. The Pentateuch's author apparently does not find the subject important enough to return to often or place these arguments in prominent positions throughout his book. The chapter conveys that God is creator, but can we answer why or how it connects to the larger narrative?

Because of modern concerns with creationism, the chapter and its basic theological statements resulting from God's creative act are familiar to us. Does the author include it merely to say that the God of Israel is creator, or does he begin with creation because it's the chronological beginning, so to speak? And if chronology is the point, does he leave anything out of his description? The answer is yes; Gen. 1 is an abbreviated account of the "week." We do not read of the creation of angels, demons, dinosaurs, or any number of things that would have taken place. Genesis 2:5 also steps backward to a time prior to the creation of man in Gen. 1, suggesting that a mere recounting of events is not the main point. If the author's interest within Gen. 1 is not merely chronology or creationism, what remains, and how does the subunit's structure indicate where the author is heading?

As an introduction to the entire Pentateuch, this first subunit must bear the weight of all that the author will eventually convey. The material in Gen. 1 does not stand alone but has a conspicuous connection to what is in Gen. 2, and we should ask why. Genesis 2:4 demonstrates the strategic placement of the events in Gen. 2 after those of Gen. 1, even though chronologically they occur prior to the sixth creation day. Why this arrangment? If the author intends to say something about the lion king's authority over the cosmos, he must begin with God's creative act and his authority over the heavens and earth. God prepares it for man and woman, whom he will make his viceroys in the land, and for their offspring, who will inhabit the land and eventually possess it. How does the chapter connect with this larger point? We have already seen how the phrase "in the beginning" anticipates an "end" and shows the unity of the Pentateuch as a whole. We must now examine the connections within the subunit itself.

"In the beginning" forms a bond within this subunit for a few reasons. First, in Hebrew it puns with the verb "create," having the first three letters (*br'*) in common. This forms a bond not only with what follows in verse 1 but also with later occurrences of the verb in this chapter (1:26–28).[1] Additionally, the word for "earth" (*'erets*) that ends verse 1 connects with verse 2, which begins with the same word, as the author narrows his focus from the cosmos ("heavens and earth") to this "land" that God will shape in the remainder of the chapter.[2] Speaking of "heavens and earth," the seventh day in Gen. 2:1 begins with this same compound phrase, forming an outer frame around days 1 through 6. Genesis 2:3b forms an additional outer frame to this first subunit by restating God's work of "creating to make," two key verbs in the chapter. Establishing these clear boundaries prepares us to understand the structure of the subunit and recognize where the author's focus lies.

Seeing the tight connection between Gen. 1:1 and 1:2 also dispels a common misconception regarding the first verse of Gen. 1. Many assume that 1:1 is a summary of what the author will report in detail in the remainder of the chapter, but verse 2 tells us that the earth is already there and goes on to assume the existence of the great deep and the waters. Thus what Gen. 1:1 describes is the moment of creation, the "heavens and the earth" coming into existence.[3] The remainder of the chapter tells how God continued to work, shaping the earth and preparing it for the humans God would create on the sixth day to inhabit it. Since God created it, it is his to give to his stewards.

What does the author mean by "heavens and earth [*'erets*]," and how does this help us understand the "land" (*'erets*) in the remainder of the chapter? "Heavens and earth" constitutes a figure of speech called a *merism*, a literary device that indicates a sum total from two contrasting parts. We use a merism when we say, "I am wet from head to toe." In other words, I am drenched.

1. Scholars discuss whether the Hebrew word "beginning" in Gen. 1:1 is definite or indefinite. Because it lacks an article, many consider it indefinite and therefore translate, "When God began to create . . ." But of its fifty-one occurrences, this Hebrew word never has the full definite article *ha* and occurs only once with the preposition *la* (Neh. 12:44), where it functions as a noun within a list of nouns. In Isa. 46:10, the word occurs without an article but is clearly definite based on the context, which allows the possibility that it is also definite in Gen. 1:1. Also, adverbial constructions such as this do not usually take an article in Hebrew, making its absence less significant and thus not evidence that "in the beginning" should be understood as indefinite.

2. A subject followed by a *qatal* verb is a technical verbal construction in Hebrew, and the fact that "was" follows "earth" in Gen. 1:2 signifies an action that is circumstantial to verse 1. See Alviero Nicacci, "An Integrated Verb System for Biblical Hebrew Prose and Poetry," in *Congress Volume: Ljubljana 2007*, ed. André Lemaire, Supplements to Vetus Testamentum 133 (Leiden: Brill, 2010), 99–127, in particular, 105.

3. The basis for many of the Gen. 1 observations stem from John H. Sailhamer, *Genesis Unbound: A Provocative New Look at the Creation Account* (Sisters, OR: Multnomah Books, 1996).

It needn't mean that every square inch of my body is wet but merely that, in general, I am wet from top to bottom. The merism in Gen. 1:1 indicates that the totality of creation is in view. But if God created the totality of creation in Gen. 1:1, what is he doing in the rest of the chapter? God had other preparations to make before humans could inhabit his creation. The rest of the chapter explains the ordering, dividing, and positioning of objects until the sixth day's final act of creation, after which God's work is complete, and he rests.

The land needed work before man and woman could inhabit it. The author uses "create" only at special junctures in this chapter. Genesis 1:2 explains the condition of God's creation. Verse 2's first word shifts the perspective from the merism's comprehensive picture to the "earth," or better yet, "land" ('*erets*).[4] The verse begins "And the land was a waste and a wilderness." English versions sometimes translate that the earth was "formless and void," which to the modern mind may suggest a gaseous, black hole of nothingness, perhaps with the earth not even created yet. This is just one way that modern science or a technological perspective can influence our interpretation. The writer does not use these words with that idea in mind. With one of the words from Gen. 1:2, Deut. 32:10 describes the LORD's discovery of Jacob, saying,

> He found him in a desert land,
>   and in a *wasteland*, the howling of a wilderness,
> he surrounded him, he cared for him,
>   he kept him as the apple of his eye.

The author speaks of Jacob and Israel's journey in a wilderness. Jacob had camped in a place of stones when he met God, and Deut. 32's poem describes it as a "wasteland," like a howling wilderness. Using both words from Gen. 1:2, Isa. 34:11 describes a wasteland where wild animals dwell, and stones and boundary markers are all that is available to measure the otherwise empty land. Although God had created the cosmos, the land was nothing more than an empty wilderness, apparently devoid even of light, which he must now supply. God's Spirit was active in the darkness over the waters as verse 3 begins the chapter's day framework.[5]

Before we begin the account of days in Gen. 1, it may help to consider the larger context and what will become of this "land" after Gen. 1. This first subunit is literarily interwoven with Gen. 2:5–3:24, but for now, it is enough to

---

4. '*Erets* can be translated as either "earth" or "land." Sailhamer points out that translating the word as "earth" obscures the connection that the author is making with the land of promise. See John Sailhamer, *The Pentateuch as Narrative* (Grand Rapids: Zondervan, 1992), 82.

5. Days 1 through 6 each begin with "And God said."

FIGURE 5.2. **The Structure of Creation Days**
Viewed as a Skyscraper's Framework

know that the author connects this land to the garden near Eden, which he later associates with the promised land. At least two of the rivers that flow from Eden to the garden in Gen. 2:10–14 compare with the borders to the land promised to Abraham in Gen. 15:18.[6] Recognizing these connections helps us to understand Gen. 1's purpose and avoid isolating the chapter as an argument for or against creationism or as a mere prooftext for our doctrine of God.

Keeping in mind the author's larger purpose for the land, let's return to Gen. 1's framework of days. Through repeated words and phrases, the chapter's structure escalates in content and significance so that we can see where the author's attention will ultimately rest. Genesis 1:3–5 makes up day 1 and commences the repetitions that the author will use to structure the chapter. Using God's speech, actions, and the evening/morning pattern, the author organizes his outline and cultivates content and meaning. We could think of the outline like a skyscraper (see fig. 5.2).

While the skyscraper is being constructed, we see the steel beams and concrete that make up the skeleton of a building. The building is eventually

6. Sailhamer, *Pentateuch as Narrative*, 99.

filled out and finished with finer details. The author's repeated words and phrases are akin to skeletal features that structure the chapter, which he fills out with words and content until he makes his point.

Repeated Words
And God said . . .

Let . . .

And there was . . .

And God saw that it was good.

And God called . . .

And there was evening and there was morning.

The [first, second, etc.] day . . .

The symmetry of the chapter demonstrates God's orderliness, but what details does the author use to arrive at his point?

Continuing the building metaphor, we can see that the author develops content on each floor ("day"). For example, Gen. 1:3–5 constitutes one day and, though brief, yields several interesting details. The expression "Let there be light" conveys the idea of presence instead of an act of creating. God is bringing light into the presence of his creation. This same verb and a similar word for "light" reappear in verse 14 when God prepares the sun, moon, and stars, and places them in the "expanse of the heavens" to give light and govern their respective spheres. He did not wait until the fourth day to "create" them; if he had, there would have been no morning and evening on days 1–3, and there could have been no plants bearing fruit (Gen. 1:11–12) without the sun. Exodus 10:23 uses the same two words to say that "light was" in the Israelites' dwellings while darkness plagued the Egyptians' camp. It does not explain how there was light amid darkness, just that it was there. In Gen. 1:3 it is as though light has dawned upon creation for the first time and, consequently, brought about evening and morning. In the remainder of the day, God separates light from darkness and names them day and night. We can already see that God is going about the work of organizing, dividing, and naming. Genesis 1:5 provides another interesting detail at the conclusion of the day: "There was evening and there was morning, day 1." Unlike the ordinal numbers he uses for the remainder of the days in this chapter (second, third, fourth, etc.), the Hebrew number in verse 5 is the cardinal number 'echad (i.e., "one," not ri'shon, "first"). Apparently, the author wished to describe it as the day on which the week began but avoids calling it the first day.[7] Day 1 then includes God's configuration of evening and morning and supports the understanding that Gen. 1:1–2 describes creation's unspecified duration prior to the onset of day 1.

The second day (Gen. 1:6–8) involves more separation and naming. Through his formation of an "expanse," God separates the waters below from the waters above and names the waters that are above. In contrast to "create" (bara', 1:1), the verb "make" ('asah) emerges in verse 7 to describe God's formation of the "expanse." This verb appears frequently in the OT and expresses a much more generic kind of action. Even in English, someone can "make" a portrait, "make" an appointment, or "make" a bed. Not unlike the generic English gloss, the underlying Hebrew verb can describe trimming fingernails (Deut. 21:12), washing feet and trimming a beard (2 Sam. 19:24), making a meal, and many other actions. Although some draw too sharp a distinction between these two verbs, generally speaking, "create" is used in a prominent manner in Gen. 1 and usually alongside "blessing." On the other hand, "make" describes God's formation or arrangement in accordance with his intent to separate and fill. Although the account of the second day remains brief, these three verses represent a longer description than the three verses of day 1.

The third day (Gen. 1:9–13) contains two acts, making it the longest description yet and suggesting an escalation. God decrees in verse 9 that the waters be gathered into one place, and he names the resulting land and seas before the description closes with "And it was good." He then decrees that the land sprout plants, resulting in grass and fruit trees and receiving a second commendation, "It was good." The plants yield seed and fruit after their kind, establishing the pattern for the earth's vegetation. Although no "dividing" takes place, the gathering of waters separates seas from dry land, and God keeps naming creation's constituents.

The fourth day (Gen. 1:14–19) continues the trend of an ever-increasing number of verses devoted to each day, creating the sense that the author is purposely building toward something.[8] God does not "create" the luminaries

---

7. It is possible that 'echad is being used here in the sense of "first," but even so, its use here with an indefinite noun is unique. See Bruce K. Waltke and M. O'Conner, An Introduction to Biblical Hebrew Syntax (Winona Lake: Eisenbrauns, 1990), 274. Ultimately, the point is not essential to my larger argument, which is that there is a crescendo leading up to the preparation of the land for human habitation.

8. Day 1 contains a mere thirty-one words, while the second day contains thirty-eight. The third and fourth day each contain sixty-nine words, although the fourth day occupies six verses instead of the five verses of day 3. The fifth day reverts to fifty-seven words, but the sixth day more than doubles any previous day with 139 words as well as several other unique features, prompting us to consider the importance of this day. The seventh day, set apart as it is, contains a multiple of seven at thirty-five words. Genesis 1:1 contains seven words, and 1:2 contains fourteen words.

on day 4 but brings them in "to divide between the day and the night in the expanse of the heavens" (v. 14).[9] Although this arrangement of lights in the skies on the fourth day instead of on day 1 has perplexed readers, the chapter's arrangement into dividing spheres and filling them is consistent.[10] God speaks his intent, which promptly takes place. He then separates, names, and fills that space. The fourth day is no different, given his desire that the luminaries divide between day and night in the expanse of the heavens and give light (Gen. 1:15, 17). What is more, God prepares the skies, seas, and the land on days 1 through 3. In the fourth through sixth days, he fills them with items that regulate, govern, proliferate, and steward the spheres, pronouncing them good at the end of each day's activities.

The fifth day marks new developments in God's creative agency, while maintaining his practice of filling the waters and the expanse of the sky. Genesis 1:20 reports his intention that the waters swarm with "living creatures" and that birds fly in the expanse of the sky. He creates (*bara'*) these sea creatures and the birds in verse 21, both of which proliferate "after their kind" in the same way that plant life did. The verb "create" emerges for the first time since Gen. 1:1 and, along with God's "blessing," suggests increasing emphasis on his activity. Immediately after this creative act, "God saw that it was good." In comparison to day 3's two acts and two "It was good" clauses and day 4's expansive six verses, day 5 ends in brief, perhaps exhibiting a rush to get to the climactic day 6.

FIGURE 5.3.

Narrative Symmetry in Genesis 1

In these days . . .

God separates	God adds
Day 1: Light from darkness	Day 4: The luminaries to govern day and night
Day 2: Sea from sky	Day 5: Fish and fowl
Day 3: Land from sky	Day 6: Land animals and man/woman

9. Wilhelm Gesenius, *Hebrew Grammar*, ed. E. Kautzsch, trans. A. E. Cowley (Oxford: Clarendon, 1910), §114h, p. 348.

10. Old Testament commentators Keil and Delitzsch say that the heavens and the earth were not "completed until the fourth day." C. F. Keil and F. Delitzsch, *Commentary on the Old Testament* (Grand Rapids: Eerdmans, 1986), 1:58–59. Calvin says, "The world was not perfected at its commencement, in the manner in which it is now seen, but that it was created an empty chaos of heaven and earth." See John Calvin, *Genesis*, Geneva Series Commentaries (Edinburgh: Banner of Truth Trust, 1975), 69–70.

FIGURE 5.4.

Parallelism in Genesis 1:27

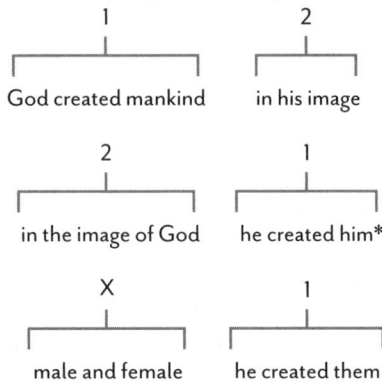

1	2
God created mankind	in his image

2	1
in the image of God	he created him*

X	1
male and female	he created them

* "Mankind" is grammatically masculine singular so I have translated it here
as "him" to distinguish it from the plural pronoun in the following clause.

Literary symmetry demonstrates yet another factor in the chapter's structure and the attention drawn to the sixth day (see fig. 5.3). Day 1's light and
darkness corresponds to the day 4's luminaries, day 2's division of waters
below and above in the expanse of the sky corresponds to day 5's sea creatures
and birds, and day 3's proliferation of plants on the land corresponds to day
6's animals and humankind who consume and steward the earth's fruitfulness. The literary symmetry, the day framework, and repeated formulas all
point to a highly structured and symmetrical work that allows us to discern
where the author's attention finally rests: the sixth day.

Additional indicators emphasize the sixth day's prominence. In chapters 3
and 4 above, we discussed the author's use of poetic images to draw attention
to concepts and content. Although Gen. 1 has not displayed any poetry up
to this point, Gen. 1:27 exhibits parallelism, a feature of Hebrew poetry in
which parallel words indicate relationships within their respective clauses.[11]

The sequence of verb and its constituents + prepositional phrase is reversed
in the second clause of 1:27, and the verb stands alone in the third clause in
relation to an entirely new element, male and female. Another indicator of the
sixth day's prominence is the alliteration between "create" (*bara'*) to "bless"
(*barak*). Although the fifth day's activities also involve God's creative activity followed by blessing, the sixth day's blessing is substantially greater (see
below). The prominence of the verb "create" is additional evidence of the

11. The author uses poetry to feature aspects of his message in Gen. 2–4 and 9.

FIGURE 5.5.

The Culmination of Days in Genesis 1

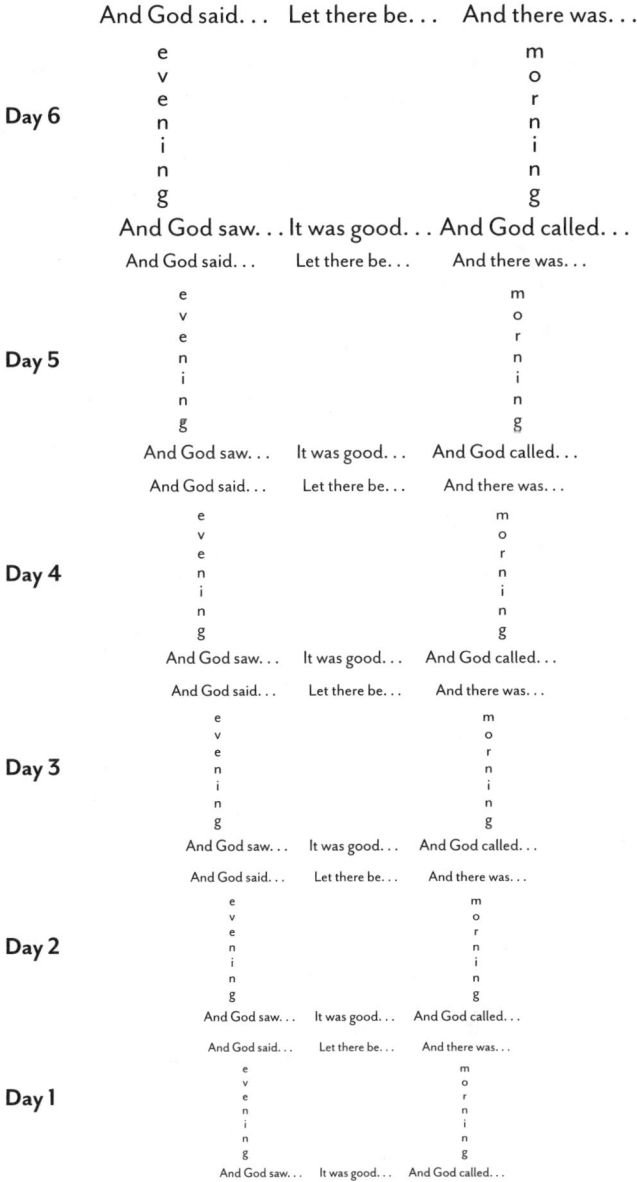

And God said. . . Let there be. . . And there was. . .

Day 6

```
e                          m
v                          o
e                          r
n                          n
i                          i
n                          n
g                          g
```

And God saw. . . It was good. . . And God called. . .

And God said. . . Let there be. . . And there was. . .

Day 5

```
e                          m
v                          o
e                          r
n                          n
i                          i
n                          n
g                          g
```

And God saw. . . It was good. . . And God called. . .

And God said. . . Let there be. . . And there was. . .

Day 4

```
e                          m
v                          o
e                          r
n                          n
i                          i
n                          n
g                          g
```

And God saw. . . It was good. . . And God called. . .

And God said. . . Let there be. . . And there was. . .

Day 3

```
e                          m
v                          o
e                          r
n                          n
i                          i
n                          n
g                          g
```

And God saw. . . It was good. . . And God called. . .

And God said. . . Let there be. . . And there was. . .

Day 2

```
e                          m
v                          o
e                          r
n                          n
i                          i
n                          n
g                          g
```

And God saw. . . It was good. . . And God called. . .

And God said. . . Let there be. . . And there was. . .

Day 1

```
e                          m
v                          o
e                          r
n                          n
i                          i
n                          n
g                          g
```

And God saw. . . It was good. . . And God called. . .

Each day grows greater in the amount of material and builds toward a sense of culmination as one moves from day 1 to day 6, which erupts into prominence and uniqueness.

uniqueness of the sixth day. It appears three times in verse 27, while its only other occurrences are in Gen. 1:1, 1:21, and 2:3. Interestingly, the verb makes its seventh appearance in the transitional verse, 2:4. A final rationale for the sixth day's importance is the conclusion: only on this day do we read, "God saw all that he made, and behold, it was very good" (1:31).

What can we make of the literary symmetry and the chapter's culmination? While the symmetry shows the prominence of the sixth day, its unique content clarifies its purposes.

> And God said, "Let *us* make humankind in *our image* according to *our likeness* and let them *rule* over the fish of the sea and over the birds of the sky and over the beasts and over all the land and over everything which creeps upon the land." And God created humankind in his *image*, in the *image* of God, he created him. *Male* and *female*, he created *them*. And God *blessed* them, and God said *to them*, "Be fruitful, multiply, fill the land, and *subdue* it and *rule* over the fish of the sea, over the birds of the sky, and over every living thing, creeping upon the land." (Gen. 1:26–28)

The Sixth Day's Unique Content

First-Person Deliberation in the Godhead

In all God's actions to separate and fill the earth, only on the sixth day does he deliberate in the first person about what to do.[12] It is here that the godhead strategically plans among himself to make humankind; the previous days provide no other evidence of this divine contemplation. In light of the subsequent sin of the original human couple and of the violence that required a flood to wipe it out, one may be tempted to think that God made a mistake in making humans. But God's premeditation reveals his determination to make humankind, even though redemption would be required. The eternal godhead put thought into the decision to create humankind.

Created in the Image and Likeness of God

Perhaps the most notable aspect of the sixth day is God's creating humankind *in his image*. Instead of humans reproducing "after their kind"

---

12. Although a divine council involving angels is possible (as in Job 1:6), the notion of a diverse godhead is quite plausible, despite the lack of a trinitarian formulation at the time. The Spirit of God hovers over the waters in Gen. 1:2 and Balaam hears "the words of God," has knowledge of the "Most High," and sees a vision of *Shadday*. Also, Deut. 33:21 associates the lion-son of Judah with the one who had provided the *re'shit*.

like other creatures and the vegetation (see 1:11, 12, 21, 24, 25), 1:26–27 repeats four times that God created humankind in his image and likeness.[13] No other living or inanimate thing is created "in his image," only humankind. What exactly it means to bear God's image has prompted a great deal of reflection and discussion, but one thing is certain: only humankind is said to be the recipient of this special design. The remaining unique factors of the sixth day merely clarify what it might mean that we are created in God's image. God's intentional design for humanity gives us a value that is quite distinct from other animals and plants, and all who are human have this value! Even though animals and the earth deserve special care from us as stewards of God's creation, no other creature has this signification. If someone is a human, they are created in God's image and have value because of this design.

God Gives Humanity a Purpose

Humanity's purpose flows out of God's intent to make humankind in his image and likeness: to "have dominion over" the fish, birds, animals, the earth, and everything creeping on it (1:29–31). Although sin and the flood disrupted this dominion, the balance of the six-day symmetry shows that God gave humankind the task to steward land and animals, while using plants and fruit for consumption, ordering all that God had fashioned. The chapter arrangement presumes that humankind has the capacity and responsibility to steward God's creation in accordance with his design for it. God gave humankind a purpose.

Gender Is Made Explicit

Besides being created in the image of God, the next conspicuous element that the sixth day reveals is that humans have gender. Why was nothing said about biological sex distinctions for the birds, sea creatures, and animals, even though such distinctions obviously apply? Could it be that gender has some special significance in relation to the image of God? Consider again the poetry in Gen. 1:27 and how its structure highlights the distinction of male and female (see fig. 5.4 above).

In the poetic lines of 1:27, notice how "male and female" is parallel to "the image of God." Soon gender will become the main theme (Gen. 2:15–25),

---

13. "Image" appears three times and "likeness" once: "God said, 'Let us make humankind in our *image* and in our *likeness*.' . . . God created man in his *image*. In the *image* of God he created him."

but can we discern more significance here? Commenting on this issue, Karl Barth says,

> The only thing that we are told about the creation of man, apart from the fact that it was accomplished by the Word of God in and after the image of God, is that "God created them male and female." Everything else that is said about man, namely, that he is to have dominion over the animal kingdom and the earth, that he is blessed in the exercise of the powers of his species and the exercise of his lordship and that his is to draw nourishment from the plants and trees, has reference to this plural: he is male and female.[14]

Barth rightly notes the distinction that both male and female were given dominion to rule over the animal kingdom and the earth. This fact is worth pausing over. Following God's intent to "make humankind in our image according to our likeness," the subsequent clause relates "And let *them* rule. . . ." In other words, "humankind" (*'adam*) is not the proper name Adam; nor does it indicate merely male humans. Rather, the plural pronoun "them" refers to all humanity, "male and female." Similarly, the poetry in Gen. 1:27 states that God created both male and female in his image. The middle clause reads "In the image of God, he created *him*," but the Hebrew "him" refers not merely to Adam but to humankind, since "humankind" is a masculine singular noun in Hebrew. The last clause makes explicit that God "created *them* male and female." Finally, the imperatives "Be fruitful, multiply, fill the earth, and subdue it" are all plural in number, indicating that both man and woman are given these commands. Both woman and man are created in the image of God, and both are given the task to subdue and rule God's creation. They are equal in value as image bearers of the Creator.

God Speaks "to Them"

Although God regularly speaks in Gen. 1, he only speaks *to* someone on day six. God addresses other creatures when he blesses them in verse 22, but the language of speaking "to them" is unique to verse 28. What does it mean that God spoke only to humanity? The content of God's address to humanity begins in the same manner as the blessing he gives to the sea creatures and birds in 1:22, to "be fruitful, multiply, and fill" their respective spheres. But in addition to these blessings, God instructs humanity to "rule and subdue" and to use the plants and trees for food. Although the statement that he spoke

---

14. Karl Barth, *Church Dogmatics*, vol. III/1, *The Doctrine of Creation*, trans. G. W. Bromiley, ed. T. F. Torrence (London: T&T Clark, 2004), 185–86.

"to them" consists of only a few words, its brevity belies its importance. God spoke to Adam and Eve! At the climax of God's creative activity on the sixth day, God reveals his special plans for humankind. Even so, the seventh day implies that more is to come.

The Seventh Day

On the sixth day, God completes his work and on the seventh day he rests. Genesis 2:3 indicates that he blessed and sanctified day 7, but the author also uses a markedly different style and vocabulary to describe the day. God does not "speak" or "work" as he did on the other days, and, unlike the other days, the seventh day is not described as "good." There is also no concluding "evening and morning" as on the other days. That God did not work is recorded three times, emphasizing the rest that would come after work. Even though there is a different structure, we are obviously still in the same textual unit because of the threefold reference to the "seventh day." The structure and symmetry of the creation account is broken, and the seventh day is unique. The "rest" recorded on the seventh day does not end with "evening and morning" but instead draws to a close with a summary of the week's work that "God created to do" (2:3). This is not the last time we see this language; it is mentioned again in the "rest" that Noah will provide after the flood through an offering on an altar (Gen. 8:20–22). God smells Noah's offering and promises not to curse the earth again on account of humans. As long as the earth remains, "day and night will not rest." Although the sixth day is the climax of Gen. 1, the seventh day's uniqueness, final position, and lack of a concluding structure indicate that God's creative and preparatory acts are not, in the end, for themselves but have as their goal something more, a rest that creation still awaits.

THEOLOGY and PRACTICE

Based on our reading of Gen. 1, there can be no mistake that every individual has value in the eyes of God. God created humankind in his image. Regardless of race or gender, it is hard to overstate the implications of Gen. 1: racism, misogyny, genocide, slavery, abortion, sex trafficking, and any other activity—great or small—that denigrates individual humans are all prohibited. One implication is that we cannot sit idly by while other humans are suffering. Whether they are babies in the womb, those with mental disabilities, immigrants approaching our borders, oppressed peoples in another country, fellow Americans in our own community, or inmates in our prisons, a person made in God's image has value because they are made in the Creator's image. Our rhetoric and actions must underscore this doctrine of the image of God in every human being.

This doctrine also elevates humans above other living things. While animals, fish, insects, trees, vegetation, and all the earth are gifts from a benevolent Creator and deserve our kind care and stewardship, they are not imbued with the same value as humankind. Sometimes I wonder if we treat animals better than we treat humans. That is a problem. Should we really spend exorbitantly on animals while individuals created in God's image suffer want?

Although we may fail to fully live up to these ideals, I cannot help but consider how Gen. 1's worldview differs from philosophical naturalism or even other religions without the Scriptures. Put simply, philosophical naturalism supports atheism, believing nothing exists besides nature. Knowledge is obtained only through scientific investigation into matter. There is no god or supernatural power that created this material world. Everything occurs by chance through a deterministic physical process. No higher power has imbued creation with any particular purpose; life is what we make of it, including our ethical choices and worldly pursuits. Although some individual atheists may have morals, philosophically there can be no claim to morality or purpose except what has come into being by chance through a deterministic process. If there is no Creator who has imbued us with value, how much worth can an individual have, someone who evolved from other matter by mere chance? What is the foundation for the value of an individual human?

These considerations also relate to humanity's purpose. Unlike philosophical naturalism, which disallows any outside purpose other than material things, Gen. 1 expresses that God has given humanity a stewardship over all nature, every living thing, and all the earth. Scripture tells us that humanity's purpose has been given by the one who created everything in the first place. The implication is that as part of humanity, God has made you for a task. Because the Creator made humanity—male and female—to "subdue the land and rule" over its creatures, you can find joy in that task! What does this task look like for you? Don't settle for doing nothing!

Let me return to the issue of biological sex and gender. Because of what is ahead in Gen. 2–3, this will not be our last word on the issue. Although because of its male authors, Scripture assumes a male perspective, we can know for certain that male and female are both created in the image of God. Men are not more valuable in God's eyes than women. Women are not relegated to secondary status. Neither are women more prized than men. We will find out in Gen. 2–3 that this equality is situated within a God-ordained authority structure. The union of man and woman takes center stage in Gen. 2, where the author grounds the marriage of man and woman. Although their union goes astray immediately, its fruit will provide the needed relief from the enemy. Unfortunately, the disobedience of man and woman exacerbates shame and mistrust so that the issues remain difficult to address.

Finally, let me address the issue of revelation between God and man. Only on the sixth day and only to humankind does God speak more than merely a general blessing. From the outset, God communicates to man and woman their responsibility and his provision for them. In other words, God conveys the necessary information to Adam and Eve, granting them authority to do what God, the Creator, has orchestrated them to do in his creation. This exact issue will prove to be Adam's downfall in Gen. 3. Where does humanity locate its basis for authority? Our culture has undergone a fundamental shift in where it finds authority for its decisions. The locus of authority is no longer in any sort of revelation from God, either in the church or the Bible. When Western culture and its institutions no longer see divine revelation as a worthy source of authority, why then would someone submit to the Bible's view of marriage, the home, work, or sexuality? But if not the Bible, where do individuals look for authority? It certainly should not be the culture, which, as we have seen in its views on homosexuality and transgenderism, can shift wildly based on popular opinion. As much as science tends to hold sway, science itself is easily manipulated based on one's perspective, analysis of the data, and choice of which data counts. Science changes as data and perspectives change. If we are to see beyond our humanness, revelation must come from God. Otherwise, we are left to our own subjective experiences and thoughts without an objective word from outside.

6

Marriage and Its Purpose
in the Story (Gen. 2–3)

The author's method of composition has given us two cases, the first stretching throughout this complex and diverse text, Gen. 1:1–Deut. 33, and the second in his inaugural subunit, Gen. 1:1–2:3. The panorama shows his strategic placement of three large poems drawing from smaller narratives and poems to express that a king from Judah would come in the end of the days, obtain obedience from the nations, and eventually inherit and rule the *re'shit*. The second case involves a self-contained subunit, a neatly structured text whose attention rests on the creation of man and woman in God's image. To man and woman, God gives the task of stewarding the earth and proliferating in it. Almost anticlimactically, the subunit ends with God resting from his work of fashioning the heavens and earth while awaiting the evening and morning of the seventh day. How does Gen. 1:1–2:3 fit within the larger panorama? For what reason does the author place Gen. 2:4–3:24 after his first subunit? What issue or problem is the author grappling with, and how does he seek to resolve it with this text?

As we familiarize ourselves with this author's method, we should review how the text exhibits intentionality. Repetition of words and phrases has played an outsized role so far and will continue to be important, but it is not the only tool available to the author. Even through repetition, the author has drawn upon words and phrases, spliced them together with other words, and added new material to draw attention to his point. Poetry, with its image-driven capacity, represents another tool. Because the text is composite, made up of smaller independent subunits, a variety of techniques may emerge through which one can discern intentionality, structure, and nuance. Genesis 2:4–3:24 differs so noticeably from Gen. 1 in its literary makeup, scholars have practically severed the literary bond between them. But such a conclusion reveals more about modern assumptions about textual coherence than any real problem. However, it does provide a forewarning that the textual makeup—and therefore, the author's techniques—may look quite different in this subunit.

Have you ever considered why the subunit Gen. 2:4–3:24 follows the material of 1:1–2:3? Your answer to this question may reveal your assumptions about Genesis's genre. Could the author have put a different narrative next in this position? Did he have the authority and agency, so to speak, to create his text? Recall that even though the text has its origin in God, he used an individual with full human capacities to compose the text. Under the guidance of the Holy Spirit, the author could have chosen a different episode to further his point. Many who read Gen. 2:4–3:24 treat it as if it were simply the next thing to happen rather than recognizing that Gen. 2:5 reverts to a time prior to the sixth day. This shows that the author specifically selected the story to say something more about the emergence of man and woman in the land.

It will take this entire chapter to fully demonstrate why the author chose this narrative, but it may help to consider where the episode closes. Genesis 2–3 is a two-part narrative whose parts mirror one another. Because it is one unit—albeit woven together with diverse parts—Gen. 2 cannot be adequately understood without Gen. 3 and vice versa. In brief, Gen. 2 contains the placement of man in the garden and the giving of harmonious marriage while Gen. 3 mirrors that point with the disruption of harmonious marriage and the surrender of the garden. To put it another way, Gen. 2:5–25 begins in the garden; Gen. 3 ends with humanity kicked out of the garden. Genesis 2:25 ends with the blissful union of man and woman while Gen. 3 opens with its disruption. That the author selects this twofold narrative to develop his story reveals a considerable amount about the issues he is grappling with: God's authority and wisdom to give commands, the role and plight of humanity in a forlorn land, their loss of the place God gave them to inhabit, and the one through whom it will be won back.

Genesis 2:4: The Connection Between Creation and Garden

How do we know the author intentionally selected this garden episode and arranged it next to the seven-day week? In a sense, the author uses a piece of "tape" in the form of words (eight from Gen. 1 and three from elsewhere in Genesis) to show us that he is developing the story with this new narrative. He writes verse 4 as a transition to connect the garden narrative to Gen. 1:1–2:3: "These are the generations of the heavens and the earth when they were created on the day the LORD God made the earth and the heavens." Keywords drawn from Gen. 1 include heavens, earth, created, day, made, and God. The final words of the verse—"the earth and the heavens"—are an inversion of the phrase "heavens and earth" occurring in Gen. 1:1 and 2:1, 4a, showing in another way that he is linking the accounts.[1] Even though these two accounts do not harmonize from the perspective of modern historiography, we can discern from this verse that the author spliced them together and expected readers to follow his lead.

Genesis 2:5–17: The Land and Command

Genesis 2:5–9 assumes information from Gen. 1 but develops material the reader needs for the remainder of Gen. 2–3. Genesis 2:5 says, "And no shrub of the field was yet in the land and no plant of the field had yet sprouted, for the LORD God had not brought rain upon the land and there was no man to cultivate the ground." The twice repeated adverb "yet" sends the reader back to a period before plants had appeared in the descriptions of Gen. 1, while references to "the land" and "ground" throughout these verses show the author's continued interest in the land. The statement "there was no man" indicates a time before God had created humanity and prepares the reader for his action in verse 7. Verse 6 explains how God watered the ground even though rain had not fallen "upon the land." In this way, Gen. 2 briefly backtracks before charting a distinct course related to the emergence of humankind.[2]

New material also prepares the reader for what will transpire in Gen. 3. The shrub and "plant of the field" that had not yet "sprouted" anticipates the "curse on the ground" where thorns and thistles will "sprout" and man will "eat the plant of the field" (Gen. 3:18). In preparation for Adam and Eve's misstep, the LORD God causes to "sprout all the trees of the ground desirable in appearance and good for food. The tree of life was in the midst of the garden and the tree of the knowledge of good and evil" (2:9). These two trees

---

1. This appears to be a case of Seidel's Law, a literary technique by which authors connect two texts.

2. T. Desmond Alexander refers to this as a "zooming in" effect, a helpful perspective; see *From Paradise to the Promised Land*, 3rd ed. (Grand Rapids: Baker Academic, 2012), 120. I prefer to think of Gen. 2:4–3:24 as the author panning the camera, so to speak, to this episode to lead the reader in a particular direction.

are important to the story in Gen. 3. The woman sees that the tree is "good for food" (exact words from 2:9) and a "delight to the eyes, and desirable to make one wise" (also similar to 2:9).

Genesis 2:7–8 relates the forming of man, while verses 10–14 account for rivers and the fine materials in the garden. Verse 7 says, "And the LORD God formed man of dust from the ground and breathed into his nostrils the breath of life and man became a living being." The formation of man from "dust of the ground" anticipates his "return to the ground" in Gen. 3:19, "because from it you were taken, because you are dust and to dust you will return." What is more, God plants a garden in Gen. 2 and places man there, whereas Gen. 3 ends with his banishment from the garden. Verse 10 elaborates on how the garden with its plants and trees was watered from Eden. From there it became four sources, flowing into four rivers (2:10–14). Why is this distinct section about rivers not reflected in Gen. 3? Its integration here shows the author's interest in the land that God promises to Abraham (Gen. 15:18). In addition to showing how the garden was watered, in this way it also links the garden to later content. The precious metals from the river regions will later adorn the tabernacle.[3] Why draw in the tent of meeting at this early point in the Pentateuch?

The tabernacle becomes the place where God dwells among the Israelites, but because of God's holiness, Israel must obey regulations before entering the LORD's presence. The specific language in Gen. 2:15 likens man's place-ment in the garden to that of a holy object in the tabernacle, followed by the regulation that he must obey (2:16). Verse 15 says, "And the LORD God took man and put him in the garden to work it and keep it." The Hebrew verb underlying the English translation "put" means "to cause to rest," and the purpose clause "to work it and keep it" has its origin in the service and charges of the tabernacle. In other words, God's causing the man to rest in the garden reflects God's holy intent for man,[4] while the phrase "for service and charges" stems from regulations involving holiness.[5] Early Hebrew scribes interpreted this clause and passed it along as indicating that man was "to work the garden and keep it" and they are not necessarily wrong.[6] From Gen. 2:5 the reader is

---

3. For "gold," see Exod. 25 throughout, as well as 26:6, 29, 32, 37; 28:11–14, 20–27, 30–33; 30:3–5; see also the description of the temple's construction in Exod. 35–40. For onyx stone, see Exod. 25:7; 28:9, 20; 35:9, 27; 39:6, 13.

4. For man's placement in the garden, see the entry נוח in *HALOT*, 1:679.

5. For his "service," see Exod. 35:21, 24; 36:1, 3, 5; 38:21; 39:32, 40, 42. For the Hebrew root word from which "charges" comes, see Exod. 16:32–34; Lev. 8:35; 18:30; 22:31; Num. 1:53; 3:7–8, 25, 28, 32, 36, 38; 4:27–28, 31–32; 8:26; 9:19; 18:3–5, 7–8; 19:9; 31:30, 47.

6. The Masoretes (early Hebrew scholars) added vowel marks to the consonantal text and gave us diacritical marks indicating this. See also John Sailhamer, *The Pentateuch as Narrative* (Grand Rapids: Zondervan, 1992), 100–101.

already aware that man will eventually "work the ground," and 3:23 reports that after being sent from the garden, man must "work the ground," which Cain promptly does in 4:2. Regardless of the implications—and I cannot say more now—the fact that the LORD's first command comes to the man in Gen. 2:16–17 foreshadows not only Israel's failure at every turn but the failure of all humanity. God commands the man alone that he may eat from all the trees of the garden, but "from the tree of the knowledge of good and evil, you may not eat." That in the narrative the woman has not yet been formed from the man has important consequences, which unfold in Gen. 3. The command itself becomes an object of interest to the snake in Gen. 3, yet another living thing the narrative has not mentioned up to this point. Hopefully, we have seen enough to recognize the textual unity of Gen. 2:5–3:24, even though the author has included other textual pieces as well. We have yet to consider the genesis of woman, which the remainder of Gen. 2 highlights.

Genesis 2:18–25: From Unity to Diversity and Return to Union

Genesis 2:18–25 focuses entirely on the introduction of the woman and the couple's union, both of which play important roles in Gen. 3. God pronounces that it is "not good" that man be by himself (2:18), so he declares, "I will make him a helper corresponding to him." Unlike Gen. 1, in which God pronounced seven times that something was good, his pronouncement of "not good" reveals that something is amiss or lacking: a suitable counterpart for the man is needed. The formation of the "beasts of the field from the ground" (2:19) includes birds and livestock—"living beings" just like man (2:7)—that were previously mentioned in Gen. 1, while the phrase also portends the snake in 3:1, who is more cunning than any "beast of the field." Despite the parade of animals, verse 20 concludes that there was still no one for man, showing the true purpose behind the topic's inclusion in the story. Because man is still missing a counterpart, the LORD puts Adam to sleep to take a rib from him, which he then builds into a woman, bringing her to the man. Adam immediately recognizes Eve's correspondence, but it's his announcement along with the narrator's verdict that reveals the purpose of the episode. When all has been said, the manner in which God formed the pair, and their subsequent union, will chart the new course.

Adam's pronouncement and the narrator's verdict from the story seem to establish marriage just as Gen. 1 established creation. Of primary importance is the episode's incorporation for how humanity will return to God's presence after their banishment from the garden. But for now, the narrator takes the opportunity at the conclusion of Gen. 2 to inaugurate marriage as the foundational institution of humanity. When Adam sees the woman that God has brought to him, he says, "This one at last is bone from my bones and flesh from my flesh. This one will be called woman, because from man, she was taken" (2:23). After inspecting and naming all the animals, Adam finally finds someone like him. In three expressions—each one verbalizing that her members came from him—the man poetically utters how God provided the woman. It was from his bone and from his flesh that she emerged. Like his task of naming the animals, he names this one "woman, because she was taken from the man." Unlike most wordplays in Hebrew, this one comes through in English and the emphasis is clear: she is called *wo*man because she came from man. I stress this detail not only because the narrator's verdict will be drawn from it but also because our theology and practice will likewise flow from the prominence placed on the poetry and the conclusion in 2:24.

The story's plot and poetry evoke the declaration, "For this reason, a man will leave his father and mother and will cling to his wife, and they will be as one flesh." What is the reason alluded to here, and whose father and mother is this, since none have been mentioned thus far in the narrative? "Father and mother" reminds us that the author is writing at a much later point, after the proliferation of humanity. It also suggests that even though the episode serves a purpose within the larger context, the author seizes the moment to highlight society's marriage practices (a point we will return to later in the chapter under "Theology and Practice"). But the justification for his conclusion comes from both the man's poetic exclamation and the logic of the story itself. Man was alone until God took a piece from him and, from that piece, built a woman. From one person came two. In the logic of Gen. 2:18–23, the woman was built from the one; marriage is a reversal of this bifurcation. Man and woman are now individuals—they have diversity—but the *two* will become *one*. Verse 24 concludes, "They [plural] will be one [singular] flesh." Though the math—two as one—doesn't seem to add up, their union will return them to the oneness they had when Adam was one. Though they are distinct individuals—whose identities biologically and personally they will bring into the marriage relationship—marriage returns them to oneness.

Why would the author choose marriage as his second topic? After creation itself, at the commencement of all things, marriage is introduced and instituted. The institution of marriage is not in the middle of the overall story, nor at the end, nor merely hinted at in some narrative along the way, but at the beginning. In the Bible's second chapter, when so many topics could be discussed, so many ideas, concepts, and important factors of life could be set forth, the author sets about to establish marriage. Have you ever asked why?

What other information or narrative could the author have selected in Gen. 2? He could have addressed why God allowed evil or why he created demons and allowed Satan to fall. The author could have told us when God created dinosaurs and how they died. And wouldn't the cure for cancer have been a welcome topic? Or why didn't the author speak about Jesus? Perhaps in his own way, he did, but we mustn't rush ahead.

Why is the notion of marriage in Gen. 2 placed so prominently at the beginning of the Bible? The author connects the sixth-day creation of man and woman in the "image of God" with this episode's formation of woman from man and their subsequent union. This juxtaposition means that we must consider what the union of Adam and Eve will bring about in Gen. 3. What will become of this marriage? Although their diversity will end in trouble, their union will yield an offspring: the woman's son, who will crush the head of the enemy. By the end of Gen. 3, Adam will name his wife a second time, Eve, meaning *living*. "She will be the mother of all of the living," eventually giving birth to the seed who will crush the head of the enemy. So the discussion of marriage in Gen. 2 prepares us for the events of Gen. 3.

Genesis 2:25: The Pivot Between Bliss and Broken

Genesis 2:25 pivots from the couple's unity to the tragedy about to unfold with the serpent, who was "more cunning than any beast of the field" (3:1). The plural verb and pronoun, "They were, the two of them," and the nouns "the man and his wife" from Gen. 2 are coupled with new concepts, "naked but not ashamed." A wordplay between "naked" in 2:25 and "cunning" in 3:1 binds the two episodes together and acts as the pivot between the chapters. The two words are spelled the same and become homonyms because of their lexical forms. The description of the serpent in 3:1 not only hints at the trouble to come with this beast of the field but also signals how the man and woman will attempt to hide and cover their "nakedness" after their disobedience.

Genesis 3: An Unfortunate New Normal

Genesis 3 opens with a suspicious absence—so suspicious that it is conspicuous! Man is nowhere to be found. An animal among the beasts of the field—whom the man had named in Gen. 2:19–20—speaks to the woman about God's command that he gave to man (Gen. 2:17). Woman had not yet been fashioned when God gave him the command, and now he fails to expound its meaning. After the key role Adam played in Gen. 2, his absence here and silence is deafening. Besides the six verses dealing with the trees and rivers in 2:9–14, *'adam* or its pronoun occurs in every verse after his formation in 2:7, the noun itself occurring an incredible fourteen times from 2:7 through 2:25. His complete absence in 3:1–6a is intentional; scholars call this sort of characterization a "minor character," or secondary character, whom the narrator intentionally caricatures as taciturn and aloof.[7] This ploy works here alongside another strategy called a "gap"—intentional omission of a word, character, or other content in order to draw the reader into the plot.[8] In other words, these techniques lead the reader to say, "Wait, where is the man? He was the one given the command!"

No sooner is the serpent described as cunning, than he speaks to the woman about God's command. Using the exact same words that God had used to tell the man he could "eat from any tree of the garden" except for one, he subtly negates the statement and draws the woman's attention to that very tree. Although aware of the command, the woman either confuses or misunderstands the precise formulation of it. God made no mention of touching the fruit. Whether this is a good idea or not, the narrator only hints at, but the imprecision suggests that the woman does not have a good handle on God's command. Where is the man?! The serpent seizes on the misunderstanding and utters a direct contradiction to God's assertion that they would die. He then goes on to slander God himself, saying that God is withholding the knowledge of good and evil from them, a statement that in and of itself was true. They could be like God himself if they had it, "knowing good and evil," and what could be bad about that? In the striking silence of man's direct knowledge of the command as well as his experience of God's generous provision of the garden, animals, birds, and the woman herself, the woman is left to her own senses.

The couple's disobedience will plunge man and woman into an unprecedented and cryptic knowledge. Interestingly, the woman sees the tree for what it is. Genesis 2:9 describes the trees as "good for food" and "desirable in appearance," and she likewise "saw that the tree was good for food" and "a delight to the eyes," the adjective "good" making yet another appearance in our story. What is more, 3:6 applies the adjective "desirable" from 2:9 to her assessment that the tree could "make one wise," suggesting that the serpent's enticement in 3:5 that they would "be like God knowing good and

7. For a discussion of this way of characterizing, see Shimon Bar-Efrat, *Narrative Art in the Bible* (Sheffield: Sheffield Academic, 1997), 86; Robert Alter, *The Art of Biblical Narrative* (New York: Basic Books, 1981), 114–30.

8. Meir Sternberg, *The Poetics of Biblical Narrative: Ideological Literature and the Drama of Reading* (Bloomington: Indiana University Press, 1987), 186–229, 235–39.

evil" had been effective. Without a hint of deliberation between the couple, the woman "took from its fruit, ate, and gave to her husband with her, and he ate." Although the man finally appears at the end of verse 6, the flat characterization is unmistakable as he is merely acted upon by the woman and fails to register the slightest objection. God had given the commandment to him but at the direst hour, he had neglected to defend the commandment or the woman: "and he ate."

Interestingly, the serpent did not fully lie: "their eyes were opened, and they knew that they were naked," trying to cover it up with leaves from the garden. Significantly, their new strange knowledge brings with it a compulsion to cover their nakedness, a sign of their unity in 2:25 now causing them to hide from the very Creator who had brought them together in a productive, watered, and beautiful garden. The trees that were a blessing in Gen. 1 and beautiful and good for food in Gen. 2 now in Gen. 3 become a temptation, a stumbling block, and a place to hide from God. "In the garden" is mentioned twice in 3:8, leaving no doubt about the episode's connection to Gen. 2 and communicating that something serious has happened with their strange new knowledge. What now?

In what ways do the remaining narrative and poetry reveal intentionality? Given the conspicuous absence of the man in Gen. 3:1–6a and the order in which the figures are introduced in Gen. 3, the thoroughgoing reversal of both of these elements indicates God's reorientation of the land. Whom does God approach first? The man. Genesis 3:9 says, "And the LORD God called to the man, and he said, 'Where are you?'" The man and his wife had hidden among the trees when they heard the LORD, and apparently the mere fact that they had done so alerted the LORD that something was wrong. The LORD's question "Where are you?" (one word in Hebrew) addresses Adam alone, the brevity of the inquiry intimating the LORD's despondence over the situation. Adam admits that he heard the LORD God and was afraid because he was naked. What was once happy bliss without shame in 2:25 has now become a reason to hide from the very one who created the situation in the first place. It was "not good" that man should be alone, so God brought man a wife. Now, in light of disobedience, the very thing that symbolized their unity becomes a sign of their bodily awareness. Their nakedness causes their shame, compels them to cover themselves, and sends them into hiding. Genesis 3:11 contains the third occurrence of "naked" in the chapter. Knowing the answer to his question about their discovered nakedness, God immediately questions them about the command not to eat from the tree. Verse 12 is the fourth verse in which 'adam (man) has played a major role: "And the man said, 'The woman, whom you gave to be with me, she gave to me from the tree, and I ate.'" This sad statement anticipates the torn relationships that would result from these chaotic decisions. The man blames God, who gave woman to man to be a blessing, he blames the woman, and he is silent regarding the command. Hiding, blaming, and being unwilling to admit wrong—the implications for broken relationships, lost identity, and insecurity are endless. And the woman doesn't fare any better after her sin. Unfortunately, this destructive portrayal is just the beginning.

In one verse, the entire conversation between God and the woman transpires. God approaches the woman second and asks a three-word question in Hebrew, "What is this you have done?" Her response is also three words in Hebrew: "The serpent deceived me, and I ate." Although not a lie, she likewise fails to accept responsibility for her actions, blaming instead the deceptive serpent. Tellingly, the LORD's inquiry in verse 11 ends with "Did you eat?"; the man's response in verse 12 ends with "and I ate"; and the woman's short statement in verse 13 also ends with "and I ate." They have eaten from the forbidden tree and must now live with the consequences, which are just beginning to unfold.

The LORD approaches the serpent last and, without allowing him a response, begins the pronouncement of judgment. The serpent was the first figure in the episode, the first word of the chapter, and the first figure to talk. The woman was introduced second, spoke second, and was given full range in the six verses in which she and the serpent dialogued. The man, introduced third, never speaks in the first act of the chapter, not uttering a word until responding to the LORD in verse 10. The length of his response is three verses (vv. 10–12), the woman's reply one verse (v. 13), while the serpent is passed over without a word in verse 14. God's judgment is delivered in reverse order: the serpent, then the woman, and finally the man.

There are thus two reversals of order in Gen. 3. The characters are introduced in the narrative in the order serpent-woman-man, but God approaches them in the order man-woman-serpent and pronounces judgment on them in the order serpent-woman-man. In these sequences, we see not only intelligent design and the structure of the chapter but where the author wants to direct our attention. God reorients the order of creation.

The poetry in Gen. 3:14–19 articulates the LORD's judgment on his creatures but also shows signs of his redemption and mercy.[9] The serpent faces the strictest penalty and is the only creature who receives a curse: "The LORD God said to the serpent, 'Because you have done this, cursed are you more than all

9. In Gen. 1, 2, and 3 we have now seen this pattern of narrative, followed by poetic verse, and concluding with a short narrative. We will see it again in Gen. 4 and 9, showing that the author's use of poetry in the Pentateuch's panorama appears in Gen. 1–11 as well.

creatures and more than all beasts of the field.'" "Curse" is not an idle word in the primeval history (Gen. 1–11) but will return at key moments in the story.[10] The serpent is cursed more above all other animals because he beguiled the woman, twisted God's command, and created the tragedy. As a result, he faces an existence of crawling on his belly and eating dust, which, interestingly, is what the man will return to upon his death.

Genesis 3:15 is an important verse in the history of Christian interpretation because of the NT's understanding of "seed": "Enmity I will place between you and the woman and between your seed and her seed. He will bruise you on the head, and you will bruise him on the heel." The word "enmity" is fronted in the clause, apparently for emphasis. With the mention of "seed," the clause envisages not only progeny from the couple's union and from the serpent himself but a war between their offspring, with the victor coming from the woman: "He will bruise your head." The sentiment is ambiguous when viewed in isolation, but from the perspective of an intentional arrangement—episodes stitched together with various narratives, genealogies, poems, and other literary constructions—the verse sounds the first note of the lion king's future vanquishment of the curse of the land. More than a reflection of womanly hatred of snakes, the clause anticipates the importance of the two "seeds," about which the author will have a great deal to say. These two entities—the offspring of the serpent and the offspring of the woman—will be two nations at war with one another, and it should not surprise us to see this battle begin with Cain and Abel.

Speaking of the woman and her offspring, Gen. 3:16 casts her in a highlighted role, even if man still retains his own hierarchy in the passage's structure. Not unlike the symbolism throughout the poem, the author seizes upon the woman's pain in childbearing to express her unique contribution to all humanity and, indeed, to presage the outsized role that Sarah, Rebekah, and Rachel will play, just to name a few. The pain of childbirth will be a reminder of God's promise that victory will come through the seed of woman. The verse ends with a reminder of the trouble already witnessed in the couple's evasive excuses: "Your desire shall be contrary to your husband, but he shall rule over you" (ESV). The knowledge of their nakedness, laid bare by their ill-gotten wisdom, brings with it a battle of its own. And what of the pronouncement upon the man?

Although technically not a curse upon him, his relationship to the ground, which instead receives the curse, is ruined as long as the earth's cycles remain (Gen. 8:21–22). The pronouncement upon the man receives the most attention,

10. Gen. 3:17; 4:11; 5:29; 9:25; 12:3.

the number of words allotted to the man's pronouncement being the combined sum of the words used for the woman's and serpent's judgments.[11] The ground that yielded plants, trees, and fruit after their kind for all the creatures' food, and that 'adam (man) was to serve and have charge over, would still be the source for food, but its cultivation will now be painfully toilsome. Five times the poetry mentions the verb "eat": two times in the LORD's reminder of man's disobedience to the command and three times in the declaration that through toilsome labor he will eat from the ground. It's as if eating will never again be merely an incidental by-product. What is more, man will now return to the ground, his origin from dust being his just end. The curse upon the ground— perhaps what could be called the human or earthly condition—remains with us today, even though the promise of the seed has proved true. With the end of the poetry comes the climax of the chapter. What will happen now to man and woman and the blessing they received on the sixth day? The LORD must now act to clothe the man and the woman and guard the other tree.

Genesis 3 wraps up the story of the garden on a note of hope even though things will never be what they were. The narrative resumes at 3:20 to state a second time that the man named his wife, the clause "call his/her name" now becoming a sign of prominence within the story.[12] He "called his wife's name Eve [ḥawwa] because she was the mother of all the living [ḥay]." The author uses another wordplay to highlight the meaning of Eve's sentence and her role. Kenneth Mathews writes, "Hebrew ḥawwa is phonetically related to the word ḥay ("living"); thus by a phonetic play, Adam explains why she is named Eve. She is the 'mother of all the living,' for all human life will have its source in her body."[13] This woman will give birth to all humanity and, in particular, be mother to that important "seed" who will someday defeat the serpent.

The LORD God responds to the couple's new awareness of their nakedness by making clothes for them and deliberating with himself, stating, "Like one of us, man knows good and evil." Not unlike the holy garments to dress Aaron and his sons in preparation for the priesthood in Exodus and Leviticus, God dresses Adam and Eve in garments in recognition that their new awareness

---

11. Forty-six words in Hebrew comprise his sentence compared to thirteen words for the pronouncement to the woman and thirty-three to the serpent. The narrative introduction to the man and the woman's pronouncement of judgment is coordinated with that of the serpent's through a Hebrew verbal construction; see Bruce K. Waltke and M. O'Conner, *An Introduction to Biblical Hebrew Syntax* (Winona Lake: Eisenbrauns, 1990), 650–51. A better description of this phenomenon is found in John Sailhamer's unpublished "Notes on Biblical Hebrew Syntax," 110–15.

12. Gen. 2:23; 3:20; 4:25, 26; 5:2, 29; 11:9.

13. Kenneth A. Mathews, *Genesis 1–11:26* (Nashville: Broadman & Holman, 1996), 254.

brings with it a need to cover their shame.[14] While God had not originally forbidden man from eating from the tree of life, access is now prevented lest man eat from this tree and live forever in his fallen state. God therefore casts the pair out of the garden to work the ground from which they were taken and stations "cherubim with turning, flaming swords guarding the way to the tree of life." Things have changed. The innocent nakedness of the man and woman has now become their shame, an aspect of their being that they want to hide. Their world has been turned upside down. They had been in a paradisiacal garden but are now banished east of Eden. The ground that once produced food now produces thorns and thistles. Relational harmony between God and man, man and woman, and man and beast has been replaced with tension and enmity. Man is separated from God and from other individuals and animals. This bad news is not the end of the story. 'Adam (man) named his wife "living" as a reminder of the life that would someday flow from her womb. The rest of the biblical story is how man will again dwell with God. God is not defeated; he has reoriented the creation order, provided clothing for humankind, protected the tree of life, and promised the victorious seed who will crush the head of the enemy.

Interpretation

A new subunit brings another genre, one with its own techniques for conveying meaning. What practices or strategies did you notice? For one, repetition still signifies the structure through which the author develops content. The precise words and phrases from Gen. 2:5–17 are picked up in Gen. 3, showing that the story is cut from the same cloth. Also, the repetition in Gen. 3 reverses the introduction of the three figures, creating a chiastic structure: serpent-woman-man, man-woman-serpent, serpent-woman-man. Although varied in style, poetry appears again. The author also uses literary techniques to depict the man as a flat character, aloof and wanting, and the judged serpent as dismissed and confined, in contrast to how he appears at the start of the chapter (3:1–5). Dialogue shows a figure's relative importance within the narrative. As we saw in Gen. 1, so in Gen. 3 the number of words allotted to various sections appears intentional and invites explanation. Finally, wordplay draws attention to and/or nuances various figures: humankind ('adam) is drawn from the ground ('adamah), woman ('ishah) is taken from man

14. See the words "garments" and "dress" in Exod. 29:5, 8; 40:14; Lev. 8:7, 13; 16:4. Michael Morales, *Who Shall Ascend the Mountain of the Lord? A Biblical Theology of the Book of Leviticus* (Downers Grove, IL: Apollos/InterVarsity, 2015), 53.

('*ish*), and Eve/Life (*hawwa*) is the mother of all living (*hay*). As we will see, wordplay or punning is a tool used throughout Gen. 1–11.

THEOLOGY and PRACTICE

Having discerned intentional design in Gen. 2 and 3, we can ask, What theology or practice might this intentionality convey? In effect, this two-part story provides three considerations. First, Gen. 2:4–25 draws attention to the union of man and woman, but besides highlighting the role that their union would play in the land, the author draws a principle from it and applies it to future generations with his mention of "father and mother." Second, Gen. 3 yields theological considerations because of "the seed of woman" who will crush the head of the serpent. Third, it indicates an authority structure that will provide practical balance to the personal equality that we saw in the creation of man and woman in the image of God. Our goal in all these considerations is to follow the intentional design and to look for specific ways that the text conveys meaning.

Genesis 2:4–25: The Union of Man and Woman

The application of Gen. 2:4–25 is restricted because, in a sense, the author had not completed his subunit. More content will emerge that shifts the attention. Still, it is obvious that the author wants to say something about the formation of man and woman, because he turns back to and retells the story of their origins. Their story will surely be a centerpiece of what is to come, and, indeed, Gen. 3 bears this out, but the author also does something more. Because of his statement in 2:24, "For this reason," we must pause and ask "For what reason?" It's as if he says "Timeout! I have something to add." He wants to draw a principle from the narrative.

Not only does "for this reason" alert us to a conclusion the author wishes to draw, but the poetry also hints that the narrative has reached its climax. Within the poetry, the author uses repetition and wordplay to emphasize the woman's identity as "bone from my bone, flesh from my flesh." She has come from man's bone and flesh. The wordplay with her name draws out the same point: "This one will be called *woman*, because *from man, she was taken*." What is more, the logic of the narrative in Gen. 2:15–22 points in this direction: man is placed alone in the garden and given the command, but God says that his isolation is not good, so he introduces the animals. When these fail to provide the needed company, he puts man to sleep, takes something from his side, and from that builds the woman, bringing her to the man. The narrator could have simply stated "Two came from one" and ended the story, but instead the subunit culminates in a poetic proclamation. The narrator then alerts us that a principle is to be drawn from these events: "For this reason a man will leave his father and mother and be joined to his wife, and they will be one flesh." Here the narrator steps outside the story by mentioning "father and mother" before figures with these roles have appeared in the account.

Given the passage's emphasis, what applications for theology and practice can be drawn? The story not only commends marriage—the union of one man and one woman—as a foundational institution of God's plan in the land, but it gives it parameters. Polygamy is prohibited; God does not draw multiple women from man. Because man was alone, God made woman from him, thus making two individuals. Two came from one, and marriage joins the two back into one. This is what the author has in mind when he says "for this reason." The story also disallows adultery. The commendation of "being joined" and becoming "one flesh" in their nakedness no doubt draws on the biological attributes of man and woman. The physical union of man and woman underscores the passage's conclusion: "the two were naked"—not three, ten, or more. The narrative's story and conclusion demand this limitation. Finally, it is from here that all other Scripture draws its prohibition of homosexuality. For all the reasons given above, the story disallows this type of union. God did not draw two men or two women from one another or design them for this union. Scripture's portrayal of "woman taken from man" consigns marriage to the union of one man and one woman.[15]

Genesis 3: Authority Structure in Their Union

The design of Gen. 3 emerges in the narrator's sequence of serpent-woman-man, man-woman-serpent, and serpent-woman-man. The flatness of man's figure, the disallowance of the serpent's rebuttal before the onset of the pronouncement of judgment, and the number of words allotted to the pronouncement against the man and land indicate that something had gone awry. Man alone is given the command in 2:16. The author's emphasis is revealed in the serpent's manipulating the command's wording and in the attention placed on the command after the couple's disobedience (3:11, 12, 17) as well as in the man's disinclination to set the serpent right and guard his wife and the command. Our attention also rests on the poetry where the serpent and the land are cursed. The woman's pain in childbirth gives way to hope in a seed,

---

15. It may seem too preposterous to be worth mentioning, but bestiality is also prohibited by the passage.

and the man's food will now come only through toilsome labor. He will also die and become part of the corrupted soil.

From these considerations, several conclusions emerge. First, as surely as woman is a part of humanity, her vanquishing seed will also be a part of humanity. In our panoramic overview of the Pentateuch, we observed the nature of the lion king from his emergence as a human figure of Judah along with his name and divinity as "Most High," "God," and *Shadday*. Now Gen. 3 indicates that this victor will be the offspring of the woman, a member of humanity, which is an important characteristic of the scepter of Judah and star of Jacob.

We can also deduce something else of a practical nature. To the articulation of *personal equality* between man and woman in their image of God and equal stewardship of creation, Gen. 2–3 adds *positional economy*.[16] Because of the narrative's threefold ordering of serpent-woman-man and its reversal, the episode places prominence on the man's reception of the command but also his reluctance to contend for and obey it. When pronouncing judgment, God approaches the man first to take responsibility and issues the longest pronouncement against him. Woman is also held accountable, but the responsibility for correct articulation and adherence to the command was the man's. This structure does not mean that one is less valuable than the other or inferior to the other or that one should be relegated to second-rate tasks while the other wields power without accountability. Each of these caricatures of God's intended order reflects the corrupt consequences of the couple's shattered innocence. Scripture's reorientation of the creation order commends man's authority in the home and, as we can trace later in the NT, in the church to defend, teach, and obey the command. It does not take much introspection to recognize how we flaunt disobedience to God's commands—sexual immorality, manipulation, slander, pride, lying, coveting—and then run and hide in shame from the very God who has provided redemption and life through his Son and Spirit. The so-called fall affects our own relationships and attitudes in the same way it did the first couple. We fear. We distrust. We hide, blame, oppress, and resist acknowledging that we have failed the command.

---

16. From Vernon Steiner in a class in 1997, I received this way of articulating a balance between man and woman's equality and yet also a given hierarchical authority structure. If there is any error in my expression of this concept, the fault is mine.

7

Noah and the Comfort from the Curse (Gen. 4–9)

Up to this point, Genesis has exhibited two types of literature (Gen. 1:1–2:3 and 2:4–3:24) to promote the LORD as the Creator of the world and demonstrate his provision for humanity, even his provision of the male-female relationship culminating in marriage. It has revealed the reason behind the sticky situation in which humanity finds itself, a world less than ideal, full of challenging relationships. The battle between the LORD's nemesis and the woman's seed has also emerged. As it presents new episodes, Gen. 4–9 further develops these themes but also introduces and integrates another genre, genealogy. Since we are now dealing with larger subunits, we must turn from a verse-by-verse treatment to highlighting the most prominent developments. Genesis 4 shows the effects on their progeny of man and woman's disastrous decision. By the end of this multichapter subunit, whose closing boundary appears to be marked by a genealogy (Gen. 9:28–29), one family line will end in polygamy, murder, and judgment, while the other will be the vehicle through which the curse will someday end. But how does the author develop these themes?

Genesis 4

The well-known story of Cain and Abel exhibits the fateful aftershocks of man and woman's disobedience. The woman conceives and "acquires" Cain—a wordplay on the verb "to acquire" (*qanah*) and Cain's name (*qayin*)—from the LORD and births his brother Abel, but the mistrust and jealousy between brothers leads to the world's first murder. In this terse account, the ground that Cain cultivates receives his brother's blood and now cries out to God. Because of his treacherous act, Cain becomes the first cursed human. Even the ground that he worked would no longer produce its fruit for him, and instead, he would be a vagabond and a wanderer in the land. Cain laments that he is banished from the face of the ground, hidden from God himself, a sentence similar to Adam and Eve's banishment from the garden. Cain fears that because he is wandering the earth with no familial protection, strangers will kill him. In response, the LORD threatens sevenfold retribution against anyone killing Cain and places a protective sign on him. This part of the story ends with Cain east of Eden dwelling in Nod (*nod*), a pun on the Hebrew word "wanderer" (*nad*) encountered in Gen. 4:12. Already the author betrays his conviction that connection to the land and community is necessary to enjoy its fruitfulness and security. What will become of Cain's descendants dwelling in Nod?

Cain's descendants live out his sentence by multiplying cities and industries that ultimately lead to wickedness, against which the LORD will bring the flood. By contrast, Abel's replacement, Seth, begins a new era when people "call on the name of the LORD." In Gen. 4:17 Cain is intimate with his unnamed wife, who births a son to him. Without a connection to the land, Cain builds a city and names it after his son Enoch. This birth and naming introduces the genre of genealogy, which the author uses to move the story along and give prominence to figures he will develop. When Cain's genealogical pattern is broken at the seventh generation from Adam, attention falls on Lamech. Unlike Adam, to whom God "brought" Eve and whose union with her brought them into "one flesh," Lamech violates the intended pattern of the institution and "takes for himself two wives." His descendants may seem like an industrious family, but because they have moved away from "working the land," they urbanize and industrialize, apparently fulfilling Cain's fears that they would be in danger.[1] Referring to Cain's sevenfold protection, Lamech demands "seventy-sevenfold" vengeance after committing the same atrocity as his forefather Cain (Gen. 4:23). He poetically menaces that he "slayed" a man and apparently a child! As quickly as Cain's descendants emerge on the scene, they drop out of sight for now.

---

1. T. Desmond Alexander, *From Paradise to the Promised Land*, 3rd ed. (Grand Rapids: Baker Academic, 2012), 130, 149–52, 161–66.

The story returns to Adam and Eve, who births another child. Eve names him "Seth" (*Sheth*), "because God *gave* [*shath*] to me another seed in place of Abel, because Cain killed him" (4:25). In other words, the pun on the name means that Seth was a *gift* from God as a "seed" to replace Abel, whom Cain had slain. What would become of this "seed"? The previous mention of "seed" was in 3:15, the promise that the "seed of woman" would crush the head of the serpent. Although no final answers will come soon, the author strings us along with the name of Seth's son Enosh, whose name is spelled precisely as the word for "humankind." At this time humans "began to call on the name of the LORD" (4:26). The writer does not miss a chance to draw a play on words with these figures whose meaning goes beyond a mere name. While Cain's descendants end up in urbanization and menacing murder, Seth's descendants mark the turning of people to the name of the LORD. When the different progenies are placed next to one another, it becomes clear that Cain's progeny yields destruction, while Seth's is marked by dependence upon God. The account of Cain's line ends with the seventh generation and Lamech the Terrible; we must read on to learn who Seth's seventh generation will be, a striking contrast to Lamech.

Genesis 5:1–9:17

Genesis 5 restarts the story of Adam and Eve from the perspective of a genealogy. Although it is a long and winding story, the genealogy does not end until 9:28–29, after the flood story! Along the way one reads the cryptic anecdote of humankind's proliferation and wickedness (6:1–8), the flood story (6:9–9:17), and Noah's drunkenness (9:18–27)—all spliced into this genealogy! Like the piece of textual tape in 2:4, Gen. 5:1–2 fastens the "stories" that follow onto the *'adam* (man) story from Gen. 1. Apart from the opening ("This is the book of the generations of") and the word "name," the remaining eighteen words in verses 1–2 stem from Gen. 1. The verb and object "to call the name," appear together in Gen. 3:20 and 4:17, 25, 26, each name exhibiting a wordplay with its accompanying explanation.[2] This extraneous clause not only connects the upcoming section (it occurs again in Gen. 5:3) with these naming episodes from Gen. 3 and 4 but also prepares the reader to notice another prominent occurrence of it within the genealogy at Gen. 5:29 and a later vignette in Gen. 11:9. Just as Gen. 2 reprised the sixth day from Gen. 1 in order to articulate for the reader the fruit of man and woman's union, so this story will highlight someone special, Noah. His naming foreshadows God's means of combating

---

2. Consider also 2:23 (without "name") and 2:19 and 20 without a pun.

the ruin that Adam and Eve's progeny have brought upon the land, appearing at the important break in the genealogical pattern in Gen. 5:28–29.

The genealogy begins in Gen. 5:3 when Adam produces a child in "his likeness according to his image." The obvious inclusion of "likeness" and "image" makes the connection to Gen. 1 unmistakable, but what does this connection mean? More will come to light when we examine 6:1–2 below, but just as God "created 'adam [man] in his likeness" (5:1), Adam now begets Seth "in his likeness according to his image." The likeness and image-bearing from 1:26–28 continues despite disobedience, at least through this line of progeny. The clause "he called his name Seth" in 5:3 echoes the same phrase in 5:2, "And he called their name humankind ['adam]," thereby connecting the uses of Adam's "likeness" and "image" in 5:3 with humanity's creation in the "likeness" of God in 5:1 and following Gen. 1:26, when God made humanity "in our image according to our likeness."[3] This lineage from Adam to Seth proliferates in the genealogy until 5:29, where the next "he called his name" occurs with Noah, signifying that this lineage continues the purposes of blessing from Gen. 1. The genealogy's pattern emerges in 5:3 and remains the same except for the variance of years and the child's name until the seventh generation, the same number generation at which the pattern broke in Cain's genealogy. The pattern is as follows:

And [Name A] lived [X number of] years

And bore [Name B]

And [Name A] lived after he bore [Name B] [X number of years][4]

And he bore sons and daughters

And all the days of [Name A] were [X number of years]

And he died

This pattern breaks at Enoch's generation (5:22), where the author gives additional details. What do these details say about Enoch (*Chanokh*)?

The break in the genealogical sequence alerts us that information is forthcoming that will provide a basis for ongoing hope and anticipation. While we expect "And he lived," we instead see that Enoch "walked with God"! Enoch is somehow different. No one has walked with God since God walked in the midst of the garden. Later prominent figures such as Noah, Abraham, and Isaac are also described as "walking with God." A second occurrence

---

3. The order is reversed in 5:3, a case of Seidel's Law.

4. "All the days" and "lived" are reversed from Adam (vv. 4–5) to Seth (vv. 7–8), showing the intentional coordination of Adam with Seth.

of "Enoch walked with God" transpires in the pattern break in Gen. 5:24. And Enoch is simply taken by God. Death has punctuated each patriarch's account—including Adam, Seth, and the others—but somehow it skips Enoch! Although death is the threat and judgment announced due to disobedience in the garden, there must remain hope of escaping it if Enoch somehow managed to do so. How can one walk with God and escape death? Instead of an answer, the genealogy resumes the original pattern.

The reader barely has time to get used to the pattern before it diverges again at the tenth generation with Noah. The variations at Enoch's generation pale in comparison to those for Noah. Just by noticing the divergences in the pattern at the end of the chapter (5:32), we see that the genealogy segments for the first time into the lines of three sons, and to a degree, the remainder of the Pentateuch is about these three sons and their offspring. What do Noah and his three sons have to do with Judah and Jacob's grandson, the lion king? And what do they have to do with the curse of the garden and the seed of woman?

The genealogy's details only hint at what will transpire through Noah and his seed. The pattern initially breaks in Gen. 5:28 when Lamech bears "a son." The genealogy normally divulges the name without indicating that it is a son. This notice of a son leads into 5:29 and the repeated clause, "And he called his name," by which we are conditioned to expect a wordplay with Noah's name. The writer does not disappoint, although its full effect will not be understood until the end of the flood story. For now, however, he is called Noah [*Noach*] because "this one will comfort [*nicham*] us from our work and from the toil of our hands from the ground, which the LORD cursed." With the words "work," "toil," "from the ground," and reference to the curse, the author presents Noah as the one who will bring *comfort* from its effects spelled out in Gen. 3. The first two consonants of the Hebrew verb for "comfort" spell Noah's name, and the words "calling his name" along with the wordplay and its explanation keep our focus on Noah. Additionally, Noah's name (*Noach*) is spelled by reversing the first two consonants of Enoch's name (*Chanokh*), just one more reason to view Enoch as special and to connect the two. So far, the pun involves the following:

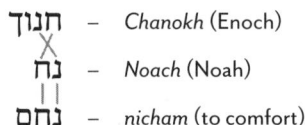

חֲנוֹךְ – *Chanokh* (Enoch)

נֹחַ – *Noach* (Noah)

נחם – *nicham* (to comfort)

FIGURE 7.1. **Enoch, Noah, and Comfort**

Will Noah somehow provide relief from the ground's curse? If so, how and when? The genealogy doesn't close until Gen. 9:29, so we must wait for more information in Noah's story, but a summary of the unique details relating to Noah indicates that the author's attention rests on him.

Details Unique to Noah

No named patriarch, but instead a "son"
The repeated clause "and he called his name" (cf. Gen. 5:3)
Wordplay between "Noah," the verb "to comfort," and "Enoch"
Noah is tenth in the genealogy
The explicit reason for Noah's name, "He will bring us comfort"
Terminology from the curse in Gen. 3
Noah bears three sons, shifting to a segmented genealogy

Genesis 6 interjects several challenging interpretive questions into the primeval history. When read as another episode that the author splices into the larger story, however, the matter fits well enough with its context. The phrases "sons of God" and "Nephilim" are the culprits that cause confusion, but the author frames the short account in 6:1 before he introduces these terms. Genesis 6:1–2 says, "And so it was when men began to multiply upon the face of the land and daughters had been born to them, that the sons of God saw the daughters of men, . . . and they took wives for themselves from whomever they chose." Unfortunately, the chapter break disguises the connection between the "birthing" of sons and daughters in Gen. 5's genealogy and the purpose of this account. The mandated multiplying had taken off and, as the genealogy indicates, sons and daughters had been born. Even though "sons of God" is problematic due to its connection with Job 1:6 and 2:1, Gen. 6:3 constrains its referent by mentioning the limitation on humankind's "days," which here refers to one's lifespan.[5] These men had incredibly long lifespans, and the LORD determined to manage their lifespan, though his "Spirit strove in man." After all, "they are flesh," but what about "sons of God"?

As Gen. 5:1 reiterates, God created Adam in his likeness, and Adam birthed Seth in his image and likeness. While "sons of God" is not used in Gen. 5's genealogy, the root word of "generations" stems from the verb "to birth." Verse 1 reiterates in "the book of the generations [*toledot*, birthings]" that God created Adam. Four clauses repeat that God made humankind, a fifth that he blessed them, with a sixth adding that "he called their name *'adam*

5. Gen. 5:4, 5, 8, 11, 14, 17, 20, 23, 27, 31.

[humankind]." Genesis 5:3 then commences with the pattern of men "birthing" sons and daughters. Though not explicit, through the term "generations" and the repeated references to his creation of humanity, the author implies that Adam is a son of God. And just as important, "he called their name" connects to Gen. 4:17, 25, and 26, all of which involve the naming of a son. Thus, the sons of God refer to Adam's line through Seth and beyond into the genealogy. Despite the long lifespans of those figures, the LORD limits humanity's *days* in 6:3. Genesis 6:4 then harmonizes that ancient time with a period nearer to the author, who is familiar with the Nephilim, the sons of Anak, of which we hear so much in Num. 13 and Deuteronomy. Those "mighty men of the name from ancient time" are forerunners of the Nephilim. Finally, just like the author frames the beginning of this challenging episode with a connection to multiplying (*rov*) in the genealogy, so he betrays his purpose for its inclusion in verse 5: "The wickedness of humankind was great [*ravah*] in the land." The LORD sees it and knows "every formation of the thoughts of their heart was only evil *all the day*."[6] The point of it all? As people multiplied on the earth, their wickedness multiplied to the full length of their days. Consequently, God is cutting their days short and will soon wipe humankind from the earth.

The remaining verses develop the extent of humanity's wickedness before returning to Noah and the wordplay on his name, culminating in Gen. 6:8. Man's wickedness has reached a tipping point, given their proliferation, and the LORD has to "*comfort himself* that he had made man in the land." The same Hebrew word underlying the purpose for Noah's name in Gen. 5:29 [*nicham*] now describes the LORD's own response to his creation, who is now so wicked that he must comfort himself! The conclusion in Gen. 6:6 goes further, saying, "It gave pain to his heart." Similar to the description of Noah in Gen. 5:29, the author associates the LORD's grief with the "pain" introduced in the judgment against the man and the woman in Gen. 3:16–17. In response, the LORD will wipe out all the living things that he created in Gen. 1: "I will wipe out humans, which I have created, from upon the face of the land, from humankind, cattle, creeping thing, and birds of the sky, because I am grieved [*nicham*] that I made them." The creation that he had at one point declared "very good" now becomes so perverted that he must comfort (*nicham*) himself and wipe it out, repeating a second time the verb that describes Noah's role in relieving the curse. Genesis 6:8, the final verse before the next section begins, delivers the punchline: "But Noah found favor in the eyes of the LORD." The verse is grammatically set apart from the narrative

---

6. This wooden translation reveals the connection to the long days of the genealogy's men, the LORD's limiting their days, and the growing wickedness "all the day."

that surrounds it, but also of interest is how the Hebrew word "favor" (*chen*) is spelled. It is an exact reversal of the consonants of Noah's name and contains the same two consonants that Noah's name shares with the Hebrew verb "comfort" and Enoch's name.

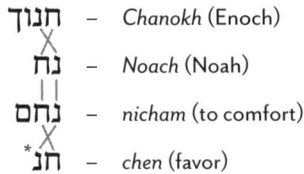

חֲנוֹךְ   –   *Chanokh* (Enoch)

נֹחַ   –   *Noach* (Noah)

נַחֵם   –   *nicham* (to comfort)

*חֵן   –   *chen* (favor)

* I have used the non-final form of this letter (*nun*)
to show the similar spellings of these words.

FIGURE 7.2. **Enoch, Noah, Comfort, and Favor**

In comparison to the flood of wickedness around him, Noah's favor with God is unique. Like Enoch, Noah "walked with God," and the following flood story will disclose his special relationship to the LORD and how he will bring comfort from the curse.

Even though the genealogy that began in Gen. 5 does not end until the close of Gen. 9, Gen. 6:9 opens the next section, "These are the generations of Noah."[7] The introduction of Noah and his sons in 6:9–10 is in stark contrast to what verse 5 reports about the rest of humankind. Instead of wickedness, Noah is "righteous, blameless within his generation." Hebrew syntax does not allow taking this comment to underscore Noah's works so much as a circumstance of the story that the author posts, heightening the narrative's drama.[8] Like his grandfather Enoch, Noah "walked with God." The comment deepens the association between the two figures and poses the question whether Noah might not taste death, a question that is answered at the conclusion of this subunit: "And he died" (9:29). Genesis 6:10 repeats what the genealogy already reported: Noah bore three sons, Shem, Ham, and Japheth. At the other end of the Noah story (9:18–27), the author provides

---

7. The Hebrew word for "generations" (*toledot*; Gen. 2:4; 5:1; 6:9; 10:1; 11:1, 27; 25:12, 19; 36:1, 9; 37:2) initiates Adam's genealogy through Seth in Gen. 5:1–2, so that the author could associate their offspring with the sixth day of creation in Gen. 1 and integrate the punning of names through the phrase "to call a name." The phrase "These are the generations of" appears in 10:1 immediately after the genealogy closes in 9:29, confirming that the boundary of the unit comes with the closing of the genealogy.

8. The syntax and effect are the same in 6:8. See Alviero Nicacci, "An Integrated Verb System for Biblical Hebrew Prose and Poetry," in *Congress Volume: Ljubljana 2007*, ed. André Lemaire, Supplements to Vetus Testamentum 133 (Leiden: Brill, 2010), 99–127, esp. 105.

an inner frame to the genealogy's outer frame by returning to the sons after the flood story. The chiastic structure looks like this:

> Noah's genealogy
>> Noah's sons, Shem, Ham, and Japheth
>>> Flood
>> Noah's sons, Shem, Ham, and Japheth
> Noah's genealogy ends

The author's decision to integrate the flood story within the genealogy gives us a clue as to his point. After the reintroduction, Gen. 6:11 reiterates, "The earth was *corrupted*" and full of violence, "because all flesh had *corrupted* its way upon the earth" (6:12). In response to the *corruption*, the LORD determines to "*corrupt* all flesh" with "floodwaters upon the earth" (6:13, 17). At the end of the flood story, in parallel fashion, God will covenant not to "*corrupt* all flesh" (9:15) and not to "*corrupt* all the earth" (9:11) with "the floodwaters." This mirroring between the onset of the flood story and its conclusion reveals the outer frames of the unit's structure, and we can look within for what has caused the LORD's changed outlook.

> Noah's genealogy
>> Noah's sons, Shem, Ham, and Japheth
>>> *Corruption* of the earth
>>>> Flood
>>> Never again *corrupt* the earth
>> Noah's sons, Shem, Ham, and Japheth
> Noah's genealogy ends

In addition to mirroring the "corruption" mentioned at the conclusion of the flood story, the description in Gen. 6:11–12 of the earth's corruption clarifies why God brings the flood and commands Noah to build an ark. The earth is corrupt; Adam and Eve's disobedience and Cain and Lamech's murders only foreshadowed the impending violence. Evoking Gen. 1's repeated statement, Gen. 6:12 begins "And God saw," but this time he sees not the goodness of creation but the corruption of all flesh. In response, God reveals his plan to Noah: "Behold, I am corrupting them with the earth" (6:13). The focus on the earth's corruption reverberates as "earth" is repeated six times in three verses. Because of this corruption, God commands Noah to make an ark, explaining its proper construction and its purpose in verses 14–17. God expresses his plan to "covenant with Noah" and his family, who are with him in the ark, keeping alive two of everything, male and female. All the creatures and birds after their kinds (as in Gen. 1) are to come into the ark with Noah. The covenant theme, appearing for the first time here, returns at the flood's end in Gen. 9.

> Noah's genealogy
>> Noah's sons, Shem, Ham, and Japheth
>>> Corruption of the earth
>>>> Covenant
>>>>> Flood
>>>> Covenant
>>> Never again corrupt the earth
>> Noah's sons, Shem, Ham, and Japheth
> Noah's genealogy ends

Genesis 7 reports the first half of the flood story to the water's crest. Reflecting later food laws (Lev. 20:25), Gen. 7:1–16 reiterates Noah's unique righteousness and sets forth the LORD's command to bring seven pairs of clean animals and birds, male and female, into the ark. This will keep alive their offspring, because in seven days, the LORD will bring rain upon the ground for forty days and nights in order to wipe out everything that he has made. Noah promptly acts as do the animals, birds, and creeping creatures, and indeed after waiting the seven days, the waters come. For forty days and nights it rains, from the very day that Noah, his family, and the animals enter the ark and the LORD shuts the door. Genesis 7:17–24 chronicles the increase of waters, quite emphatically describing the mountains' inundation, leading to the extinction of everything outside the ark. All flesh creeping upon the earth dies, whether bird, beast, swarming thing, or human. The flood blots out everything except for Noah and those with him in the ark for the "one hundred and fifty days" that the waters prevail.

Genesis 8 mirrors Gen. 7 by reporting the flood's reversal upon the earth, the numbers of days showing the pattern most clearly.[9] The reversal begins in 8:3: "The waters returned from upon the earth . . . after one hundred and fifty days," which corresponds to 7:24, "The waters prevailed upon the earth for one hundred and fifty days." Mirroring the "forty days" of rain in 7:17, Gen. 8:6 reports that after "forty days" Noah opens a window and releases first a raven and then a dove to learn of the flood's decline. When the second

---

9. Gordon Wenham lays out a pattern and slightly different reversal in "The Coherence of the Flood Story," *Vetus Testamentum* 28 (1978): 336–48. I lay out my own in fig. 7.3. As we saw in the genealogy, we must pay particular attention when the pattern is broken.

Entry
  Seven days
    Seven days
      Forty days
        One Hundred Fifty days
        ?
        One Hundred Fifty days
      Forty days
    Seven days
  Seven days
Exit

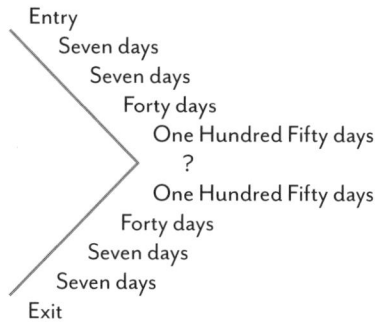

FIGURE 7.3. **Day Structure in the Flood Account**

bird returns, Noah waits "seven days," reflecting the "seven days" that Noah waited for the flood in 7:10, and sends the bird out again in 8:10. This time the dove returns with an olive leaf, and Noah knows that the "waters have decreased upon the earth" (8:11). So Noah waits yet another "seven days" in 8:12, mirroring the "seven days" mentioned in 7:4, before sending the dove out again, and it does not return. God then tells Noah to go out of the ark along with his family and animals in 8:16–17, which they do in verses 18–19, mirroring their entry into the ark in Gen. 7:1–3. The pattern is presented visually in figure 7.3.

The flood story's context and structure emerge in somewhat clear relief. The backdrop is the genealogy, providing the outer frame, with the subsequent multiplication of humankind and their wickedness. Noah's sons provide an inner frame, and "covenant" furnishes yet another frame, before Gen. 7–8 provides an extensive pattern, whose centerpiece and variations in the pattern indicate its prominence: God remembers Noah (8:1).

The story alludes generally to a refashioning of the land like that of Gen. 1, but this time God makes a covenant with Noah, his family, and everything that comes out of the ark never again to corrupt the earth with water.[10] Like we saw with the breaking of the genealogy's pattern, the author's attention rests on the pattern's interruption, especially when other indications of prominence are present. Although minor variations exist within the parallel halves of the flood story, four larger additions coincide with poetry or a wordplay

10. The flood story's content suggests a parallel to Gen. 1: God sends a wind over the waters through which dry land appears. He refashions the land, saving animals, birds, and creeping things after the destruction of life. The narrative ends with the promise that God will not trifle with the ground or wipe out all life as long as the times do not "rest" (Gen. 2:2–3; 8:22). But what, if anything, has changed? See Alexander, *Paradise*, 165.

on Noah's name. What do these interruptions in the pattern indicate about Noah and how he will bring comfort from the curse?

The Noah-Like Aroma (Gen. 8:20–22)

The first variation involves a wordplay on Noah's name and his first action upon exiting the ark: he builds an altar to the LORD, takes clean animals and birds, and offers up a burnt offering. Building an altar to the LORD puts Noah in the rare company of Abraham, Isaac, and Jacob—the only other figures to do so in Genesis. The next sentence repeats the earlier wordplay on Noah's name and shows the LORD's change of heart over humanity's wickedness. Genesis 8:21 says, "And the LORD smelled the *Noah-like* [*nichoach*] aroma and said to himself, 'I will not again treat the ground with contempt because of humankind for the formation of their heart is evil from their youth, and I will not again slay every living thing that I have made.'" The Noah-like sacrifice prompts the LORD never again to treat the ground with contempt or wipe out every living thing. Humans are still sinful, but the LORD's stance has softened.

Protection of Life Because Humans Bear God's Image

The second addition appears in the poetry of Gen. 9:5–6. God's provision for food expands beyond vegetation to include anything "creeping that is alive," but Noah is not to eat flesh with its blood. Blood was associated with life, and that was to be protected. Genesis 9:6 says, "The one pouring out the blood of man, by man his blood will be poured out, because in the image of God, he made him." Now that the land has been cleared of Cain's descendants, the pronouncement intends to prohibit Cain's bloodletting.[11] As if to say that the effect of Adam and Eve's disobedience might yet be minimized, God responds to man's murder with a law announcing judgment on anyone who sheds blood because "he made man in the image of God." With the establishment of the covenant between the LORD and Noah and every living thing, God provides a command to guard against future acts of murder like Cain's and Lamech's.

Extended Explanation of the Covenant

Genesis 9:7 picks up the imperatival blessings from 9:1 (cf. 1:28) that Noah and his sons be fruitful and multiply. That the covenant in Gen. 9:9 is connected

11. Although "poured out" was not the precise description of Cain's fratricide, the verse alludes to Cain's murder in Gen. 9:5's mention of "brother" and since Abel's "blood cried out from the ground."

to verses 1–7 can be seen in the plural pronoun that commences verse 7 ("As for you,"), which refers to Noah and his sons from verse 1, and the singular pronoun in verse 9 ("As for me"), which refers to God. The covenant that God makes is with Noah and his "seed" and every living animal that emerged from the ark—birds, beasts, and every living thing—promising that he will not cut off all flesh or corrupt the earth with water. The sign of this covenant for all generations will be the bow in the clouds: when he brings it about, he will see it and remember his promise not to corrupt the earth with water. "To remember the covenant" is mentioned twice along with the bow that he will see, the sign of his covenant with all flesh and the earth. Noah, a uniquely righteous man, makes an offering that has a Noah-like aroma, which the LORD smells and covenants with every living thing that was with Noah in the ark and indeed with the earth itself, that he will not destroy the earth again with floodwaters.

Noah's Garden

The covenant's description has barely ended (9:17) when in the next verse the author integrates the strange story of Noah's vineyard (9:18–27). By this point, we know that the story's placement is intentional, but what is the author's purpose? As we will see, this story not only completes the *toledot* (generations) of Adam and the genealogy that began in Gen. 5 but also sets the stage for the next phase in God's plan with Abraham.

The first clause relates to the flood story, mentioning Noah's three sons "coming out of the ark," who were last named in 7:13 when they entered the ark as the rain began. The second clause connects this story to later chapters in Genesis, noting that "Ham was the father of Canaan." Canaan is cursed in this narrative, playing into the remainder of the Pentateuch's plot. Genesis 9:19 also connects to the following chapters through the statement that from Noah's three sons "all the land was dispersed."[12] The list of Ham and Canaan's descendants in 10:18 concludes "the families of Canaanites dispersed." The story of Babel that follows in Gen. 11 tells us that its inhabitants do not want to be "dispersed over the face of the earth" (v. 4); yet disperse these inhabitants is precisely what God does. These connections in 9:18–19 form the transition from the flood story into the material in Gen. 10–11. What does righteous Noah have to do with Canaan's curse?

The narrative of Noah's drunkenness begins in Gen. 9:20: "Noah became a man of the ground and planted a vineyard." Because "ground" occurs so

12. The Hebrew word underlying "dispersed" is spelled the same way as a second term for "dispersed," which the author develops in Gen. 10–11. This link between episodes then draws the reader's attention to the word "dispersed," so significant in those chapters.

prominently in Gen. 2–4 and God "planted a garden" in 2:8, Noah's "planting a vineyard" appears similar to Adam's story. Now that the flood has wiped out Cain's descendants, will this story have a happy ending? Noah drinks from the vine, becomes drunk, and is uncovered in his tent, at which point his son Ham "saw the nakedness of his father." Although details are sparse, several emphases emerge. First, the writer establishes Ham's relationship to Canaan in Gen. 9:22: "Ham, the father of Canaan, saw the nakedness of his father." The author repeats Canaan's name an additional three times before the short narrative ends. Second, that Ham saw his father's "nakedness" occurs three times in verses 22–23, indicating the justification for the curse. Yet another connection to the story of Adam and Eve, this "nakedness" is related to the root word that became the theme of the first couple's union and newfound wisdom.

Noah's son Ham and his relationship to Canaan take center stage in this enigmatic narrative. Although details are wanting in the story, passages from Leviticus (18:6–19; 20:11, 17–22) indicate that "uncovering the nakedness" of someone implies sexually depraved acts. That block of legislation commences with the LORD's warning to Moses that they should not practice the depraved deeds of the Canaanites (Lev. 18:3). It makes sense, then, in the ebb and flow of the Pentateuch's story that Ham, who commits this act, would be their progenitor. Despite sparse details, the author leaves no question about what he wants the reader to know. Ham suffers a broken relationship with Noah, becomes a representative of Canaan, and fathers the Canaanites—Israel's greatest nemesis prior to the monarchy. Perhaps most significantly, Ham is cursed because of his actions in this narrative. The author explicitly and repeatedly states these emphases:

> Genesis 9:18: "And the sons of Noah who came out of the ark were Shem and Ham and Japheth; and Ham was the father of Canaan."

> Genesis 9:22: "And Ham, the father of Canaan, saw the nakedness of his father, and told his two brothers outside."

> Genesis 9:25: "And he said, 'Cursed be Canaan! A servant of servants he shall be to his brothers.'"

> Genesis 9:26: "And he said, 'Blessed be the LORD, the God of Shem; and let Canaan be his servant.'"

> Genesis 9:27: "And let Canaan be his servant."

A thorough description of what happened is not offered, but we know that Canaan is cursed. Shem and Japheth, on the other hand, are blessed because of their actions. God later promises to Abram,[13] a son of Shem, that he will inherit the land of Canaan. Genesis 9:28–29 concludes the story of Noah following the typical genealogical pattern with which it began: "All the days of Noah were nine hundred and fifty years, and he died."

--------------------------- **THEOLOGY and PRACTICE** ---------------------------

On the one hand, it seems obvious that the author splices in the narrative of Noah's drunkenness in order to link the story to what comes next in Gen. 10–11 and to how the Canaanites are portrayed in the remainder of the Pentateuch. But how does its insertion into the genealogy provide a context for the promise of the covenant? Let's review the emphases from each of the episodes.

Seth's genealogy ends with "calling on the name of the Lord," a quite different practice than that of Cain's lineage. Through Enoch's prominence, the genealogy highlights the possibility that those who walk with God might not face death. The genealogy concludes with Noah, who will "comfort us from our work and toil of our hands from the ground that the Lord cursed" (5:29). That genealogy provides the wordplay on Noah's name, noting that he found favor in God's eyes. The flood story confirms Noah's uniqueness as the one with whom God establishes his covenant, telling Noah of his plans to corrupt the earth, remembering Noah in the middle of the flood's pattern, and sending his Spirit to dry up the waters. Noah demonstrates his special status with God by making an offering. When God smells the Noah-like aroma, he promises that as long as earth remains, he will not again treat the earth with contempt.

Meanwhile, Gen. 9 links Noah and his family's exit from the ark with Gen. 1 and the command to be fruitful and multiply. Like Gen. 1, God arranges for other food but prohibits eating flesh with its blood because blood involves life. Consequently, murder is prohibited because humans are made in the image of God. Along with this new command comes the confirmation of a covenant and a sign that God will remember all flesh, indeed anything alive, and will not corrupt the earth again.

But the story of Noah's vineyard reminds us that the curse of Gen. 3 ("cursed is the ground") and the curse of Gen. 4 ("cursed are you from the

---

13. God changes Abram's name to Abraham in Gen. 17. To avoid confusion, I use Abraham throughout this book.

ground") still vexes Noah and his sons, whose sins are a constant reminder for us today. Not only does the fruit of the ground cause Noah's drunkenness, but apparently something of Cain's curse passes through Noah's seed, coming to rest on cursed Ham. Nothing has changed with the ground. It still causes painful toil, still brings forth sin, broken relationships, and ultimately leads to death. What has become of Noah's *comfort* from the curse? Apparently we must wait to see if Noah's other seed will establish a new covenant.

Abraham

God's Solution to a Worldwide Problem (Gen. 10:1–12:3)

The previous chapters have demonstrated that the author links episodes to one another to weave together smaller text units into a longer story. This practice shows the author's selection of particular episodes and provides coherence to the larger story, demonstrating the author's intentionality in their arrangement. Along with the links, we also saw how Noah's story and the flood interrupts the *toledot* (generations) of Adam in Gen. 5. While Gen. 5 begins as a genealogical retelling of Gen. 2–4, it quickly moves beyond Adam and Seth to the highlighted characters, Enoch and Noah. That genealogy, as well as the now-incorporated story of Noah, continues until Gen. 9 and concludes by recounting Noah's own experience as "a man of the ground" and his death. Was Noah's "comfort from the curse" merely the promise that God will never destroy the earth with water?

The Nations and Noah's Grandson, Abraham

Table of Nations

Genesis 10 chronicles the *toledot* of Noah's sons, summarizing the proliferation of all humanity after the flood. The chapter begins, "Now these are the generations of the sons of Noah: Shem, Ham, and Japheth. And

sons were born to them after the flood." Genesis 10's segmented genealogy
records each of Noah's sons as they bear children and disperse in the land.
Given the attention on Shem's blessing at the end of Gen. 9, we should notice
that he is the first of the sons listed in Gen. 10:1 and the last son mentioned
in 10:31. His name will receive more attention as the subunit moves forward
even though Japheth and Ham's descendants unfold next.

Verses 2–4 list Japheth's sons before summarizing in Gen. 10:5: "From these
the islands of the nations were divided into their *lands*, each according to his
language, according to their *families*, in their *nations*." Ham's annals begin in
10:6, enumerating several prominent Canaanite families before concluding in
similar fashion to Japheth's in 10:20 (see statement compared below). Finally,
Shem's descendants are enumerated with yet another closing statement in
10:31. The final verse of the chapter summarizes all that has been said about
Noah's sons, concluding with a statement similar to the closing statements
for Japheth, Ham, and Shem.

> Genesis 10:5: "From these the islands of the nations were divided into their lands,
> each according to his language, according to their families, by their nations."
>
> Genesis 10:20: "These are the sons of Ham, according to their families, accord-
> ing to their languages, by their lands, by their nations."
>
> Genesis 10:31: "These are the sons of Shem, according to their families, accord-
> ing to their languages, by their lands, according to their nations."
>
> Genesis 10:32: "These are the families of the sons of Noah, according to their
> genealogies, in their nations, and from these the nations were separated in the
> land after the flood."[1]

Repetition conveys the structure: the same population groupings appearing
for each son's descendants, separating according to their families, according
to their languages, in their lands, and according to their nations.

To discern the author's message, let's summarize what we've seen thus far.
The strange story of Noah's drunkenness emphasizes that Ham is the father
and representative of Canaan, resulting in Canaan's curse because of Ham's
actions. Shem and Japheth, on the other hand, receive the LORD's blessings.

---

1. This narrative is also connected with the flood narrative through the word "family" that
emerges in 8:19 from which every living thing came out of the ark: "Every beast, every creeping thing, and every bird, everything that moves on the earth, went out by their families from
the ark."

Genesis 10's Table of Nations records Noah's sons settling into their respective populations that make up the then-known world. Genesis 11 turns our attention to the occupants of a plain with their own plan, as well as another genealogy related to Noah's son Shem.

Tower of Babel

Genesis 11:1–9 tells the story of the inhabitants of Shinar and their attempt to build a great tower. They explain their intention in Gen. 11:4: "Come, let us build for ourselves a city and a tower whose top is in the heavens, and let us make for ourselves a name, lest we be *dispersed* over the face of all the land." What does God do in response? He disperses them: "And the LORD *dispersed* them from there over the face of all the land, and they stopped building the city" (11:8). The short account concludes "Therefore, its name was called Babel,[2] because there the LORD confused the speech of all the land; and from there the LORD *dispersed* them over the face of all the land" (11:9). How is this little narrative interconnected with the surrounding material?

At first glance, the connection between the story of Babel and Gen. 10's Table of Nations seems negligible, even contradictory. Genesis 11:1 opens "And the entire land had one language and words."[3] By contrast, Gen. 10 reiterates that each son's descendants divided into their respective "tongues." The purpose for the juxtaposition of the chapters comes into focus when we notice a wordplay on Shem's name. The focus on Shem—which begins with Shem's blessing in Gen. 9 and continues through the fronting of his name in the genealogy—develops in the tower of Babel, continues into the *toledot* of Shem in 11:10–26 and the subsequent *toledot* of Abraham's father Terah in 11:27–32, and concludes in the blessing of Abraham in Gen. 12:1–3! Not only does this wordplay fasten together these seemingly unconnected textual units, but it also reveals how and why the author places prominence on these characters and concepts.

The wordplay is a pun connecting three Hebrew homographs (words spelled with the same consonants): the name Shem, who is the last of the sons' families that dispersed in Gen. 10:31; the adverb "there" (*sham*) in Gen. 11:2; and the noun "name" (*shem*) in 11:4. Genesis 11:2 reports, "And so it was when they journeyed from the east that they found a plain in the land of Shinar and dwelt *there*." The plain's inhabitants determine to use bricks and mortar to build a city and tower whose head reached into the heavens.

---

2. Literally, "He called its name . . ."

3. A more literal translation is "And the entire land had one language and *one* words," seemingly emphasizing the oneness of language.

They want to make a *name* for themselves, which they think will keep them from being "dispersed over the face of all the land." But the LORD has his own plan for a *name* and a means to gather his people. What's his plan, and how does it involve Shem?

Genesis 11:5 states that the LORD "came down" to see the city and tower that the "sons of Adam" had built. The inhabitants of the valley think that the tower they are building is quite high, reaching even to heaven, but the LORD must still descend to see it. Even so, he reasons that their unity will give them the fortitude to do anything, so he decides to thwart their intentions. In language that mirrors what the inhabitants said in verses 3 and 4, "*Come, let us* make bricks" and "*Come, let us* build the city," the LORD declares, "*Come, let us* go down and confuse *there* their language" (Gen. 11:7). Having repeated the pun "there" (*sham*) in verse 7, the author does it again in verse 8: "The LORD dispersed them from there [*sham*] over the face of all the land," the exact opposite of their intention stated in Gen. 11:4. Genesis 11:9 draws together the conclusion of the story with three final occurrences of this homograph: "Therefore, its *name* was called Babel because *there* the LORD confused the language of all the land and from *there* the LORD dispersed them from over the face of all the land." To keep our eyes on Shem, the author distributes occurrences of "name" and the adverb "there" throughout Gen. 11:7–9.

Generations of Shem

Without so much as a conjunction, Gen. 11:10 transitions to the *toledot* of Shem. As if to leave no doubt that Shem's genealogy will lead to another important development, Shem's name is repeated twice at the beginning of Gen. 11:10 before the genealogy continues through the rest of Gen. 11. Shem is the first son blessed after the debacle with Noah's drunkenness, the first of Noah's sons mentioned in the settlement in 10:1, and his descendants are the last listed in the Table of Nations in 10:31. His name is punned with two other terms in the story of Babel, including one that will play a central role in 12:1–3. Who does the genealogy of Shem lead to? Just as the genealogical pattern in Gen. 5 highlights the tenth son, Noah, Shem's genealogy segments at the tenth generation and leads to Abraham!

This genealogy unfolds according to the usual pattern until it arrives at Abraham's father Terah in Gen. 11:26. After Terah's generation, the genealogy divides into three sons: Abraham, Nahor, and Haran. Terah's genealogy expands in 11:27, but the genre quickly transitions to narrative before the genealogy resumes at the close of the chapter with the death of Terah (11:32). In this shift to narrative, we see several plot developments that are important for understanding Abraham's story. It's hardly an exaggeration to say that the remainder of the Bible has to do with Abraham's descendants, but the author draws our attention to a problem. The genealogy reports that generation after generation men fathered sons and daughters, but now we read that Abraham's wife was barren. How will Shem's line continue if Sarai is barren? This question and God's promise to Abraham in Gen. 12:1–3 will reverberate throughout the remainder of the Bible and beyond.

Other plot developments are also noteworthy. Terah, Abraham's father, is taking his family to the land of Canaan, but as we learned in the story of Noah's vineyard debauchery, Canaan is cursed. Will God then curse Terah and Abraham because they are living in Canaan? As the chapter closes, the author draws attention one more time to the letters of Shem's name. Repeating the word "there" from the Babel account, Gen. 11:31 reads, "And they came unto Haran, and they dwelt *there*." Will God continue to thwart man's plan of making a name for himself? How will the curse of Ham, the curse of Canaan, the curse of Cain, and the curse of the garden be dealt with? Will Adam and Eve's descendants be dispersed forever?

The Blessing of Abraham

Genesis 12:1–3 answers these questions and resolves the tension raised in Gen. 2–11. The promise of Noah's name through the destruction of the flood will find its ultimate fulfillment in the seed of Abraham. The promise to Abraham will overcome the curse of the ground, of Cain, of Ham and the dispersion of the nations, will remedy Babel's pagan plans, and will solve the problem posed by Sarai's barrenness, which threatens to end Shem's genealogy. The solution will flow through Abraham to all nations:

> And the LORD said to Abram, "Go from your land, and from your birthplace, and from your father's house to the land that I will show you. I intend to make you a great nation, and I will bless you, and I will make your name great; and it will be a blessing and I will bless those who bless you, and the one who curses you I will curse. And in you all the families of the land will be blessed." (Gen. 12:1–3)

With the tensions of the previous narratives as the backdrop, we learn that the LORD has a plan to bless Abraham. Five times in three verses, the word "bless" appears. The writer juxtaposes the first use of "bless" with two parallel clauses. "I intend to make you a great nation" precedes the first promise of blessing, and "I will make your name great" follows it. A fourth clause, "and it will be a blessing," concludes verse 2.

The author composes Gen. 12:1–3 from the same language and ideas that flow out of Gen. 1–11. To put it another way, the textual fabric that makes up 12:1–3 materializes from the narratives that precede it. Anyone who fails to grasp this point will misunderstand the purpose of 12:1–3. God's promise to bless Abraham and the transition into the patriarchal narratives are connected to the universal context of God's creative act in Gen. 1, the universal context of the garden and the curse that results from Adam and Eve's disobedience in Gen. 2–3, the universal context of the *toledot* of Adam with its integrated destruction of the flood in 5:1–9:17, the universal context of the curse of Ham in 9:18–29 and the Table of Nations in Gen. 10, and Abraham's emergence through the *toledot*s of Shem and Terah along with Sarai's barrenness in Gen. 11. We simply cannot ignore the first eleven chapters of the Bible at this important juncture.

Although we acknowledge the importance of Abraham and his blessing, we often tend to map his story onto the history of ancient Israel and Abraham's physical offspring rather than connecting it to the universal story of Adam and Eve. Observing this misunderstanding, Gerhard von Rad, a leading OT scholar, states:

> The story of the Tower of Babel ends without grace, and therefore, as we have already said, the main question which the primeval history [Gen. 1–11] raises for the reader is that of the further relationship of God to the nations. Is it now completely broken, and is God's grace finally exhausted? The primeval history gives no answer to this question. . . . The answer to this most universal of all theological questions is given with the beginning of the saving history, the call of Abraham and Yahweh's plan for history indicated therein, to bless "all the families of the earth through Abraham." . . . The whole of Israel's saving history is properly to be understood with reference to the unsolved problem of Yahweh's relationship to the nations. . . . Genesis 12:1–3 thus teaches that the primeval history is to be taken as one of the most essential elements in a theological aetiology of Israel.[4]

Do you want to understand the origin and purpose of Abraham, Isaac's supernatural conception, and Israel's story? Then you must recognize it as God's solution to the universal human condition encountered in Gen. 1–11, ultimately coming to pass through Abraham's promised "seed." The book of Genesis is about not only Israel but all humankind.

Textual Production: Following the Author's Breadcrumbs to Genesis 12:1–3

Genesis 12:1 resumes Abraham's story from 11:31. The author splices in Terah's death notice from the genealogy to "close the book" on him before

---

4. Gerhard von Rad, *Old Testament Theology* (Peabody, MA: Prince, 2005), 1:163–64.

developing the story of Abraham. God instructs Abraham to leave his *land* and father's house and go "to the *land* that I will show you." Verse 2 continues, "And I will make you into a great *nation*." Here, the author draws upon three prominent cues. Abraham is the tenth generation highlighted in Shem's genealogy, and the play on Shem's name encourages the reader not to miss Abraham's role in the story. Noah's descendants after the flood each settle into his own *nation*. Now Abraham is to go to a *land* that God will show him. Once we read of a "great nation," we know that the author is drawing on the account from the Table of Nations. In doing this, he shows how Abraham will result in something more than the dispersion into the different families, languages, and lands. The Table of Nations passage closes with Noah's sons settled "according to their *families*, according to their *languages*, by their *lands*, by their *nations*" and concludes "The nations spread in the land after the flood" (10:31–32). God intends to make a great *nation* from Abraham, something beyond what we see in Gen. 10–11.

The LORD's blessing will bring about this greatness. The next clause states somewhat simply, "And I will bless you." "Bless" occurs six times in Gen. 1–11, including God's imperatival blessing to humanity on the sixth day to "be fruitful and multiply," his blessing of the seventh day, and his blessing to Noah to "be fruitful and multiply." Just as Adam and Eve have multiplied, and as Noah and his sons have multiplied, Abraham will also be fruitful and multiply (Gen. 17:6). However, this blessing concerns a "great nation," which must mean something more than large numbers of people and separation into tongues, families, nations, and lands. This has already happened with Noah's sons. What will this great nation look like?

Genesis 12:1–3 in the Context of the Whole Plotline

To grasp the importance of Gen. 12:1–3, perhaps we should consider the whole story. Later in Abraham's story, God promises, "I will surely bless you and multiply your seed like the stars of the heavens, and like sand that is on the seashore. And your seed will possess the gates of his enemies, and in your seed all the nations of the earth will be blessed, because you have obeyed my voice" (22:17–18). In that blessing we find many of the same words and ideas that appear in Gen. 12:2–3, including Abraham's many descendants and the blessing of all nations. But an additional idea emerges: in the later restatement, it is "in Abraham's seed" that "all the nations of the earth will be blessed." Who does this refer to?

Through the stories of Abraham's children that follow Gen. 12, the author slowly builds toward his big reveal, which comes to fruition in Abraham's distant son, the lion king of Gen. 49:8–12. Genesis 12 does not yet hint about

Abraham's offspring Isaac and Jacob, but the reader soon learns that the blessing will come through Sarah's seed, a "son," even though she is barren! The episode in 15:1–5 recounts the story of Abraham's childlessness and raises the question of who will be his future heir. God has promised him that someone from his own "loins" will inherit his house and pass it on. Abraham and Sarah miraculously produce Isaac, who produces Jacob, who fathers the twelve sons of tribal Israel, one of whom is Judah. Judah's descendants eventually bring forth David, and the rest of the OT looks to the promise given to David that he will have a divine-human son who will sit on God's throne forever. We already saw the three poems that foretold a lion king, 'El Shadday, the Most High, who would come in the last days as a descendant of Jacob and Judah, grandsons of Abraham. In addition, we now know to trace Abraham's lineage backward from Shem to Noah to Seth to Adam, which links the promise of this seed to the seed promised to Eve in Gen. 3:15, the offspring who would crush the head of the serpent, their nemesis. This promise in Gen. 12:2–3 therefore arises from the failure of Adam and Eve. Moreover, because the author has highlighted Abraham as the tenth generation in the line of Shem, we know that he intends something special for him. Abraham is special not because he is unique among humans but because he is the instrument through whom God's blessing will flow. As Gen. 12:2 launches into the next section, we learn that God will make Abraham a great nation and bless him through one of his sons.

The Great Name (Shem)

The next clause in Gen. 12:2, "And I will make your name great," draws on another important connection to Gen. 11. As we saw earlier in Gen. 11:1–9, the author uses wordplay involving the personal name Shem and the Hebrew words for "name" (*shem*), and "there" (*sham*)—all three words spelled with the same sequence of Hebrew consonants, making them homographs. This builds on earlier occurrences of the word, such as in the story of Noah's vineyard and the Table of Nations, where the author highlights Shem. Not only is Shem the one whom the LORD blesses, but he is also the first and last son mentioned in the genealogies. Then Gen. 11 begins with the sons of 'adam (humankind), who find a plain and decide to build a city "there." These inhabitants also build a "tower," which is spelled with the same Hebrew letters as the adjective "great." Through this second use of wordplay, the author establishes yet another link between the episodes, just as he did with *shem* when the inhabitants wanted to make a "name" for themselves so they wouldn't be dispersed. Although God thwarts the people's plan to make a name for themselves, we do not see the extent of God's purpose until now: God intends to make a name through Abraham! The word "great" makes a second appearance in God's promise. It will be a great name and a great nation.

The theme of blessing appears in the final clause of Gen. 12:2 and the first clause of Gen. 12:3 with God's declaration "It will be a blessing, and I will bless those who bless you." For reasons that we will see in a moment, this blessing has some elements in common with Isaac's blessing of Jacob in Gen. 27:27–29. At this important juncture, we should note *where* the author draws his material from and *how* he arranges it. Genesis 27 tells how Jacob obtained Isaac's blessing through deception, but God's decision to bless the younger son is final. In chapter 4 we discussed Balaam's prophecy, where this same blessing appears (Num. 24:9), which indicates the writer's intention to associate Jacob's blessing in Gen. 27:29 with Balaam's vision of the lion king.

The Blessing's Corresponding Curse

Let me illustrate the significance of the writer's selection and arrangement of small clauses from these passages. The English translations of Gen. 12:3, 27:29, and Num. 24:9 sound similar, invoking blessing on those who bless and cursing on those who curse. The stories contained in Gen. 27 and Num. 24 involve themes of blessing and cursing throughout, but until Gen. 12:3, the immediate context of 12:1–3 has nothing to do with cursing. While the word for "blessing" is the same throughout Genesis and Num. 23–24, different Hebrew words for "cursing" are used in the three passages. The differing words allow us to see how the author takes the language from one context and uses it in another. The story of Balak and Balaam has seven occurrences of the verb "curse," including the phrase "the ones cursing you are cursed" (Num. 24:9).[5] The Hebrew verb in these seven occurrences is *'arar*. The Hebrew word for curse in Gen. 27, on the other hand, is from the root *qalal* (27:12–13). The word *'arar* from Num. 22–24 does not appear in Gen. 27 until we reach Isaac's blessing, at which point the author appears to have inserted the blessing and curse from Balaam's vision into the blessing of Jacob. The same words are used in each sentence, but the order of blessing and cursing is reversed, suggesting that something has been excerpted from another context.[6]

When we look at Gen. 12:3, things get even more interesting. Although English versions often translate the two words for curse in the same way as in Gen. 27:29 and Num. 24:9, the author draws on different words for curse

---

5. A different, unrelated word for curse appears in Balak's speeches. It is not used in the blessing formulations.

6. I mentioned this as a case of Seidel's Law.

in Gen. 12:3.[7] Attempting to capture this difference in English, the ESV translates, "Him who dishonors you, I will curse." The first word (*qalal*), which
the ESV translates "dishonor," occurs in Gen. 8:21, where God promises after
the flood never again to "curse" the ground because of man's sinfulness. The
second part of Gen. 12:3, "I will curse," uses the word *'arar* found in Num.
24:9 and Gen. 27:29 as well as in the garden curses (3:14–17), the cursing of
Cain (4:11), and the cursing of Canaan (9:25). What has the author done
in 12:3? Unlike Gen. 27:29 and Num. 24:9, which contain the single lexeme
for "curse," 12:3 combines two distinct words for cursing. The author has
adapted the curses from the later passages to include *both* of the words for
curse found in Gen. 1–11. Furthermore, unlike the plural references to "those
who curse you" in Gen. 27:29 and Num. 24:9, the threat in Gen. 12:3 refers
to a singular figure, suggesting that the author intentionally changed it from
plural to singular.[8] Through these adaptations, the author shows that it is
through the blessing of Abraham that God will remedy the universal problems
that have unfolded in Gen. 1–11.

A Blessing for All Families

The blessing of Abraham, then, is a blessing for all families! The final clause
in Gen. 12:3b says, "In you all the *families* of the ground will be blessed."[9]
As the author has already repeated the words "land," "nation," and "name"
from Gen. 10–11, here he repeats the word "family." How will Abraham bless
all the *families* of the ground? And who do these families represent? In Gen.
11, where Abraham is introduced, the author told us at the end of Shem's
genealogy that Abraham's wife was barren. How will this blessing take place
if Abraham cannot have children? And who are the "families of the ground"?
Besides Gen. 10, the phrase "families of the ground" is taken from other passages in Genesis where the LORD blesses Abraham, Isaac, and Jacob.[10] As we
saw earlier, it is through Abraham's seed that the blessing will come! With
Isaac's miraculous birth, the LORD ensures that the promise in 28:14 will now
continue to Jacob until the "scepter from the tribe of Judah" comes.

Who do the "families of the ground" represent? As we have seen, this
word "family" is one of the four categories repeated throughout the Table of

---

7. See, e.g., the NASB: "And the one who *curses* you I will *curse*."

8. It is possible that the singular points to the serpent in Gen. 3, but apart from the switch
to singular, there is little evidence to support this connection.

9. I translate it "ground" here so that the reader recognizes that the word is different from
"land" in Gen. 10.

10. Genesis 28:14 reflects the Hebrew wording in Gen. 12:3, while Gen. 22:18 and 26:4
promise blessing for the "nations of the earth."

Nations. Noah's descendants spread out into their *families* after the flood.[11] The "families of the ground" whom God promises to bless in Gen. 12:3b can be none other than all the families and nations that descended from Noah, even cursed Ham and all humankind! The LORD's promise to bless the families of the land points us to Gen. 9–10 when Ham was cursed. Even so, Ham's descendants spread into "families" just as Shem and Japheth did. The seed of Abraham will bless all families and remedy the curse of Ham—indeed, even the curse of the garden. Abraham and his seed will be the answer to every problem encountered in Gen. 1–11.

─────────── **THEOLOGY and PRACTICE** ───────────

At the time the author began writing this section, he already had in mind the perspective of the entire work, including its end. As we saw earlier in chapters 3–4, the author has given us a unified work, and already in this first part (Gen. 1–11) he has integrated ideas and phrases from later in the book. His concern with the people of Israel/Judah is no surprise. However, the first eleven chapters of the Bible show us that the Pentateuch is concerned with every land, nation, tongue, and family. The author envisions Abraham's seed affecting *all* humanity.

The phrase "families of the ground" in Gen. 12:3 refers to the descendants of Noah in the Table of Nations as they dispersed into their families, languages, lands, and nations. This should not surprise us, because the lion king provided the *re'shit*—that is, time and the cosmos—for himself. The earth and all it contains are his portion, including the families of the earth. The Pentateuch has not yet revealed how the nations will hear of this king or submit to him, but the author has not finished "speaking" yet. We will have to wait until the end of his book to learn of the LORD's plan to make people from all families of the ground *his* people. From the perspective of the entire canon, "families of the ground" culminates in Rev. 5:9, where John declares, "And they sang a new song saying, 'You are worthy to take the scroll and open its seals because you were slain and you ransomed with your blood *people* for God from every *family, language, people,* and *nation.*'"[12] Already in the Pentateuch this international reach is evident. God's mission for the seed of Abraham was always intended to benefit all nations.

11. "Family," "language," "land," and "nation" occur in Gen. 10:5, 20, 31, and we read in verse 32 that the "families" of Noah spread out in the "land."
12. Or consider its association with the Great Commission in Matt. 28:19–20.

We also saw in an earlier chapter how God will vanquish the serpent through the "seed of woman," a promise that would ultimately result from the marriage between the man and woman. In the promise to Abraham, the author makes the point that the seed the reader is to await is indeed a human descendant, born from the "bowels" of Abraham. Just as the son of Judah and star of Jacob is a human figure, this promise concerns a human being, albeit one who is himself the very "image of God," whom the author also awaits. The dual nature of Christ is consistent with these early chapters of Genesis that project hope in God's promise to Abraham and his seed.

Moses

*God's Mediator and the Deliverance
from Egypt (Exod. 1–15)*

As I indicated in the last chapter, Abraham's story and blessing continues in Gen. 12–50 through Sarah's offspring. The theme of a promised seed is developed through the stories of Abraham (Gen. 12–24), Isaac (Gen. 25–26), Jacob (Gen. 27–34), and Joseph (Gen. 37–50). I have tried to treat the significance of these stories by means of the promised seed of blessing and victory over the enemy. The theme of a promised "land" remains significant throughout the Pentateuch as Israel treks toward it. I also drew connections to the lion king's ultimate inheritance of the "land"—that is, time and the cosmos. Additionally, Gen. 49's poem draws upon themes from the Joseph story in order to highlight a future sovereign of Judah. Exodus 1 now picks up the end of that story and connects it to a new story involving Moses.

Moses and the Sons of Jacob

Exodus 1–15 tells the story of the LORD's resolve to show his power in all the earth and to dwell among his people. Much of the story focuses on Moses, God's mediator for the people of Israel. But what about Abraham, Isaac, and Jacob? What happened to Joseph and his brothers in Egypt? We must consider how the entire account of the exodus—as well as the next section of legal codes framed by narratives—has been juxtaposed to the narratives of Abraham, Isaac, Jacob, and Joseph. When the story opens, Exod. 1:1 virtually copies Gen. 46:8, "These are the names of the sons of Israel coming to Egypt," before stating the names of Jacob's offspring. But apart from this superficial restatement, the end of Genesis and the beginning of Exodus are not made from the same "literary" material, even though both are mostly narratives.

Their content is not the same; nor do they naturally follow one another chronologically. Rather, they are coordinated with one another by means of literary links in Exod. 1. Besides the literary link between Exod. 1:1 and Gen. 46:8, Exod. 1:6 restates Joseph's death (Gen. 50:26) along with all his brothers and the whole generation. Alluding to Gen. 1, Exod. 1:7 anticipates why the most powerful man in all Egypt would fear the Israelites: because they "were fruitful, swarmed, multiplied, and grew very, very numerous." A new king has arisen who does not know Joseph, verse 8 reports, indicating that a later period is in view. In fact, the author passes over the decades/centuries after Joseph's death with hardly a word, arriving at his purpose in Exod. 1–11: Moses's deliverance of Israel from Egypt. The closing chapters of Genesis show the families of Joseph and his brothers thriving. Why would they need deliverance?

Moses's Birth and Miraculous Salvation

Moses's introduction into the story is epic. After connecting the book to Jacob's sons, Exod. 1 portrays an insecure, concerned Pharaoh, who oppresses the Israelites because he fears their vast numbers, just as Balak did in Num. 22. Not content with oppressing them only through slavery, Pharaoh tells the Hebrew midwives to kill all the newborn Israelite boys and allow only the girls to live, a decree that puts Moses's life in jeopardy. In contrast to anxious Pharaoh, the midwives appear confident, strong, and victorious. Because they revere God and are cunning, they overcome one of the most powerful men on the planet, who by comparison, appears anxious, insecure, and wavering. Despite Pharaoh's efforts to oppress the Israelites and limit their numbers, they "multiply" (Exod. 1:7, 12, 20). Outwitted and outmaneuvered by the midwives, he commands his people to throw any son into the river, setting the stage for Exod. 2 and the miraculous circumstances of Moses's birth.

Every detail in these stories sets the stage for Moses's epic role as Israel's savior. Exodus 2 covers Moses's birth and development up to his marriage to the daughter of a Midianite priest, whom Moses works for as a shepherd.[1]

1. Just as non-Israelite prophet Balaam plays a role in helping Israel to overcome Balak, so a non-Israelite priest plays a role in helping Moses overcome Pharaoh. I first learned about

Given Pharaoh's plot to drown all Israelite sons in the river, Moses's emergence and survival portends the outsized role he will play in the upcoming story. He is destined for greatness. When a Levite couple bears a son, the mother must hide the child as long as possible. When this is no longer feasible, she puts him into an ark in the river. Who should come along and find the child? None other than Pharaoh's own daughter, establishing an important background to Moses's upbringing in Egypt. Moses's sister, who has been watching in hiding, volunteers to fetch a Hebrew woman to nurse the child, and who better to ask than Moses's own mother? Pharaoh's daughter then proceeds to pay Moses's mother to nurse and care for the child, a stunning reversal of fortune! When the child has grown up, his mother returns him to Pharaoh's daughter, who "called his name Moses," a play on the verb for "draw from water" (Exod. 2:10). Moses's showdown with Pharaoh awaits.

Moses in Midian

After Moses has grown up—notice the absence of any details regarding Moses's childhood—Exod. 2:11 reports that he visited his kinsmen in their labor and sees an Egyptian taskmaster abusing a Hebrew slave. Thinking that no one is watching, Moses kills the taskmaster, but the murder becomes known to the Pharaoh, forcing Moses to flee to Midian. While sitting by a well in Midian, Moses meets a priest's daughters, whom he "saves" (2:17), eventually marrying one of the daughters and becoming a herdsman in the region where he ultimately meets God at the burning bush. All of this sets the stage for the Midianite priest to play an important role in Exod. 18 before the central event in Exod. 19, where God plans to meet with the Israelites on Mount Sinai.

Before turning to the miraculous story of the burning bush and Moses's role in the upcoming drama, Exod. 2:23 returns to the Hebrews' plight under Pharaoh, who has now died and been succeeded by another ruler. The Israelites continue to groan and howl because of their labor, and their complaints rise to God. God "heard" their groaning, "saw" them, and "knew." And just like he remembered Noah (Gen. 8:1), he "remembered his covenant" with Abraham, Isaac, and Jacob (Exod. 2:24–25). Exodus 3:1, meanwhile, provides the background for the burning bush. Moses is shepherding his father-in-law's flock when he comes upon the "mountain of God, Horeb."[2]

---

the many correspondences between Pharaoh and Balak in a conversation with Seth Postell, November 2024.

2. The mountain plays an important role in Exodus and serves as a reference point in Deuteronomy, where Moses exhorts the Israelites to look back to Sinai.

Moses and the Burning Bush

The mountain Moses encounters is not only "holy" (Exod. 3:5) but will become part of the "sign" that the LORD has indeed sent Moses when the Israelites "serve God on this mountain" (3:12). When a "messenger of the LORD" appears to Moses "in a flame of fire in the midst of a bush," Moses turns aside to see "the great appearance," at which point "God called to him from the midst of the bush" (3:3–4). After warning Moses that the place is holy, God tells him, "I am the God of your father, the God of Abraham, Isaac, and Jacob" (3:6). Using the same three verbs that appear in 2:24–25, God continues, "I have surely *seen* the affliction of my people in Egypt. I have *heard* their howling from their oppressors, for I *know* their pain" (3:7). God announces his plan to bring the Israelites out of their bondage to the land of the Canaanites, as God had foretold to Abraham in Gen. 15:19–21. But the catch comes in Exod. 3:10: he plans to send Moses to do it!

Moses, however, is not comfortable with this idea. When he questions his role in the plan, God assures him that he will "be" (*'ehyeh*) with him, using the Hebrew verb "to be" that occurs in the revelation of his personal name *YHWH* (Exod. 3:12).[3] Moses counters God's proposal by maintaining that the Israelites will not know God and will ask what his name is. In response, the LORD delivers the well-known formulation, "*I am* who *I am*. Thus you will say to the sons of Israel, '*I am* has sent me to you'" (3:14, using *'ehyeh* three times). Based on the Hebrew verb "to be" and itself a pun on *YHWH*'s name, he again repeats, "Thus you will say to the sons of Israel, '*YHWH*, the God of your fathers, the God of Abraham, the God of Isaac, and the God of Jacob has sent me to you.' This is my name forever, and this is my memorial from generation to generation" (3:15). The word "memorial" is from the root "to remember," alluding to God remembering his covenant with Abraham, Isaac, and Jacob in 2:24. The LORD's very name reflects his commitment to the covenant with Abraham and is a reminder that he *was* and *is* with his people, *seeing*, *hearing*, and *knowing* their pain (2:24–25). Besides revealing that he, *YHWH*, is the God of Abraham, Isaac, and Jacob, he reveals his plan to use Moses to bring Israel out of Egypt to the land promised to Abraham. The task will not be easy, though, and will take a "strong hand [*yad*]" (3:19). The LORD will "send his hand and smite the Egyptians" (3:20), but who will be his hand?

---

3. Here and in other places where the revelation of the "name" is significant, I use the Hebrew name *YHWH* [*Yahweh*] so that the pun with the verb "to be" (*yihyeh*) is obvious. Otherwise, I follow the modern practice of using "LORD" to represent *YHWH*.

Moses, the LORD's Hand

Exodus 4 reinforces Moses's role in the LORD's plan for the upcoming plagues. Moses himself will mediate between the LORD and Pharaoh. Even after hearing the plan, Moses is not satisfied and continues to argue, but in the end, his arguments reveal to an even greater extent his paradigmatic role in the upcoming deliverance from Egypt. Moses's first retort expresses his concern that the Israelites will be unwilling to "listen to his voice" and that "they will not believe in me" (4:1). It is therefore significant that the conclusion to the exodus narratives reads as follows: "Israel saw the great *hand* that the LORD had done in Egypt and the people feared the LORD and they *believed* in the LORD and in Moses, his servant" (14:31). The people believed in the LORD and Moses. Why? Because they had seen "the great hand [*yad*] that the LORD had done [*'asah*] in Egypt." What hand did they see?

Exodus 4 explains the role that Moses's hand will have in the LORD's deeds. Upon hearing Moses's retort in Exod. 4:1, the LORD asks, "What is this in your hand [*yad*]?" Moses replies, "A staff." The word "hand" occurs twelve times in Exod. 4, and all uses are intimately connected with God's power through which Moses will "do" (*'asah*) God's deeds. The LORD even explains to Moses in 4:21, "Look! All the wonders that I have put in your hand [*yad*], you will do [*'asah*] them before Pharaoh." Likewise, 4:17 connects the wonders with Moses's hand, "And this staff you will take in your hand [*yad*], with which you will do [*'asah*] the signs." Exodus 4:20 calls it "God's staff," saying, "Moses took the staff of God in his hand." Back in Exod. 3:19, the LORD had warned Moses that Pharaoh would not free the people unless compelled by "a mighty *hand*," and verse 20 continued, "I will send my *hand*, and I will smite the Egyptians with all my miracles." Moses's hand and staff are the LORD's means to accomplish his purposes.

The connection between God and Moses is so close that even in Moses's objections, God promises to be with him in special ways. After Moses quarrels over his ability to speak, the LORD assures him, "Now go, I will be with your mouth, and I will teach you what to say" (4:12). When the LORD grudgingly sends Aaron along in 4:15, he reassures Moses that he will be with his "mouth" and goes so far as to say that Moses would be "like God" to Aaron. The chapter closes with Moses and Aaron meeting on the "mountain of God," Aaron speaking for Moses to the people, and Moses "doing" [*'asah*] the signs before the people.[4] And similar to how the exodus narrative closes in 14:31, Exod. 4 concludes with the people believing: "And the people believed, and

---

4. They meet on the "mountain of God" in Exod. 4:27. Aaron "speaks words" and Moses "performs signs" in 4:30. The enigmatic episode concerning Zipporah and circumcision in

they heard that the LORD had visited the sons of Israel and that he had seen their affliction, and they bowed and worshiped" (4:31). Will Pharaoh and the Egyptians be as easy to convince?

Let My People Go

Exodus 5:1 reveals the central expression that unites the entire deliverance story: "Let my people go so that they may hold a feast to me in the wilderness!" When Moses and Aaron tell Pharaoh that the LORD has instructed him to let the people go, Pharaoh incites the taskmasters to increase their workload by forcing the Israelites to gather straw instead of the Egyptians providing it. "Let my people go" occurs an amazing forty times, from its emergence in Exod. 3 through to the Israelites' deliverance in Exod. 14. Accompanying "let my people go" is the clause's purpose statement, "so that they may hold a feast to me in the wilderness." The LORD's objective to be with his people first emerges in the revelation of the LORD's name in 3:12, that they will "serve God on this mountain." This purpose is repeated many times in three similar clauses in Exod. 3–14: "to serve the LORD God" (fifteen times), "to sacrifice to the LORD God" (twelve times), and "to hold a feast to the LORD" (twice). These repeated clauses unite the plague narratives with Moses's introduction to the LORD in Exod. 3–4. What is more, nouns from these three verbal roots—feast, sacrifice, service—occur in the celebrations of the Passover and Unleavened Bread in Exod. 12–13, integrating these cultic sections into the plague narratives. These feasts reveal a central motif in Exodus through Num. 10: the LORD's intent that his people serve and celebrate him in his presence.[5] But first, he must deliver them from servitude to Pharaoh.

The face-off between the LORD and Pharaoh shows the same concerns that Moses had about the Israelites' response to his mission. In Exod. 5:2, Pharaoh says, "Who is the LORD that I should listen to his voice to let Israel go? I do not know the LORD, so therefore, I will not let Israel go!" This was Moses's precise concern in 4:1, 8–9, and the reason God has given him the signs in his hand. Pharaoh's response sets up his conflict with the LORD. Will Israel serve the LORD or Pharaoh? No sooner have Moses and Aaron made their request than Pharaoh increases the workload, requiring the same quota of bricks and blaming the increased workload on Moses and Aaron. Israel's foremen also accuse Moses and Aaron, and in response, Moses turns to the

---

4:24–26 is to show that Moses submits to the rite of circumcision just like Abraham, whose story returns in Exod. 6.

5. "Feast" occurs in Exod. 10:9; 12:14; 13:6; "service" occurs in Exod. 12:25–26; 13:3, 5, 14; and "sacrifice" occurs in Exod. 10:25; 12:27; 13:15.

LORD and asks why he has done evil to the people. The LORD's answer in Exod. 6:1 emphasizes what we have seen in the story: with a strong hand (*yad*), the LORD will act (*'asah*) and Pharaoh will let them go. But the rest of the chapter raises several questions.

The Splicing of Abraham's and Moses's Stories

Exodus 6 is well-known for its apparent dissonance with what has already transpired in Exodus.[6] Notwithstanding the obvious peculiarities in the chapter, the problem lies not so much with the text but with modernity's expectation that it be "cut from the same cloth" as its surroundings. When we recognize that the author has selected various stories or texts and arranged them next to one another, the problem leads us to ask *why* this episode is integrated into this context. The author splices Exod. 6:2–30 into this context for several reasons.

First, Exod. 6 reiterates that the God who made a covenant with the patriarchs is this *YHWH* now commissioning Moses and Aaron. Likewise, Moses and Aaron's story stems from God's promise to Jacob. Verse 2 asserts that he is *YHWH*, before explaining in verse 3 that he has not made himself known to the patriarchs by this name. Verse 4 continues that he has, however, made a covenant with them over the land that they sojourned in, the covenant that compelled him to act when he heard the Israelites' groaning. Because of this covenant, God is taking the Israelites to be his people, and he their God, bringing them to the land of promise. This subsection concludes as it began: "I am *YHWH*" (Exod. 6:2, 8). The LORD's revelation of his name to Moses and the Israelites' deliverance to the land are in accord with his promise to Abraham. How else does the author connect this story with Jacob?

The remainder of Exod. 6 deals with Moses's "uncircumcised lips," a description that provides a frame around its genealogy (6:12, 30). Verse 9 reports that Moses spoke to the people about the LORD's plan to take them as his people, but they would not listen because of their harsh servitude. When the LORD tells him to tell Pharaoh "Let the people go," Moses understandably questions how Pharaoh will listen when the people do not listen. After all, he is "uncircumcised of lips." The description "uncircumcised" undoubtedly characterizes Moses's perceived lack of eloquence, a problem he mentions in 4:10. Regardless, 6:14–29 alleviates any questions about the lineage of Moses and Aaron by integrating the segmented genealogy that centers on Levi's

6. Brevard Childs, *The Book of Exodus*, Old Testament Library (Philadelphia: Westminster, 1975), 111–20.

descendants, concluding with the Levite brothers, Moses and Aaron.[7] In spite of Moses's "uncircumcised lips," Moses and Aaron are part of Jacob's story and God's promise to Abraham. Finally, Moses's reticence in Exod. 6 sets up an incredible assertion from God in 7:1.

The Ten Plagues

Despite Exod. 6's peculiar language and genealogy, Exod. 7 picks up on its plot and develops the purpose of the plague narratives. Will Israel serve the LORD or Pharaoh? Will Israel, Pharaoh, and Egypt know the LORD and his power? Despite the hype, it will not be much of a fight. In response to Moses expressing concern about his "uncircumcised lips" in 6:12, the LORD's response in 7:1 shows Moses's incredible role in the story: he will be "God" to Pharaoh, while Aaron will be Moses's prophet! The author goes to great lengths to characterize Moses's mediatorial function between Pharaoh and the LORD.

Exodus 7:2 returns to the mantra that Pharaoh must "let the sons of Israel go" from his land, and the LORD reveals his strategy in 7:3. He will harden Pharaoh's heart and do many signs and wonders in the land. This will not only accomplish the purpose of freeing the Israelites, but "the Egyptians will know that I am the LORD" (7:5). To some extent these ideas explain the remainder of the plague narratives. Pharaoh refuses to let the people go but instead harshly increases their workload. The LORD hardens Pharaoh's heart so that he can multiply his signs and wonders (10:1). In response, Israel and Egypt—indeed, "all the earth"—will hear of the LORD's power (9:16). While many have sought a theological explanation for how the LORD hardens Pharaoh's heart, the question misses the point of the story. Egypt's pharaohs had enslaved Israel and refused to let them go free to serve the LORD. To show that there is no comparison between Pharaoh and him, the LORD demonstrates his power over not just nature but even Pharaoh's own heart.[8]

---

7. Exodus 6:26–27 contains a chiasm that displays "Moses and Aaron" on either end with "their host" at its middle:

    Aaron and Moses
        bring out sons of Israel
            Egypt
                their host
            Egypt
        bring out sons of Israel
    Aaron and Moses

Verses 28–29 offer their own repetition with "I am YHWH" at the center.

8. The English translation "to harden the heart" stems from the translation of three Hebrew verbs: *chazaq*, *qashah*, and *kavad*. *Chazaq* ("strengthen") occurs in 4:21; 7:13, 22; 8:19 (8:15

The one sign and ten plagues from Exod. 7–13 demonstrate to Pharaoh, the Egyptians, the Israelites, and the whole earth who the LORD is.⁹ At the introduction to the eighth (locusts) and ninth (darkness) plagues, Exod. 10:1–2 explicitly indicates that the LORD was doing these things in the midst of the Egyptians so that future Israelites will hear of how he dealt with Egypt. Through these signs, they will know that he is *YHWH*, connecting the plague narratives with the revelation of his name in Exod. 3 as well as the association with the patriarchs in Exod. 6:2–8, which begins and ends with "I am *YHWH*."¹⁰ What is more, 9:13 blends the original command to "let my people go [*shalach*] that they may serve me" from 4:23 with the purpose of his name's revelation in 3:12. Exodus 9:14 adds, "This time, I am sending [*shalach*] the plagues" so that Pharaoh will know there is no one like *YHWH* in the earth, while verse 15 notes that he will "send [*shalach*] his hand" to smite Pharaoh and his people. Pharaoh exists to demonstrate the LORD's power and make known his name in all the earth (Exod. 9:16).¹¹ The entire account from *YHWH*'s appearing to Moses through the plague narratives has to do with the revelation of *YHWH*'s name. Despite the signs and wonders, Pharaoh hardens his heart so that there remains one more wonder before dividing the sea.

Before the LORD brings his last plague upon Pharaoh in Exod. 12–13, Exod. 11 summarizes the result of the plagues and foretells the death of all the firstborn in Egypt. Exodus 11:1–2 expresses the LORD's plan for Israel to plunder the Egyptians, while 11:3 reports that Moses has become great in the land of Egypt, to Pharaoh's servants, and to the people. Exodus 11:4–7 then recounts how Moses tells Pharaoh the LORD's plan, concluding with the statement in verse 8, "And all your servants will come down to me and bow down to me!" Finally, verses 9–10 summarize the point of the plagues: "'Pharaoh will not listen to you so that my wonders may be multiplied in the

---

MT); 9:2, 12, 35; 10:20, 27; 11:10; 14:4, 8, 17. *Kavad* ("heavy") occurs in Exod. 7:14; 8:15, 32 (8:11, 28 MT); 9:7, 34; 10:1. *Qashah* (stubborn) occurs in 7:3; 13:15. The use of *kavad* connects the "heaviness" of the plagues with the "heaviness" of Pharaoh's heart, both from the same root. *Chazaq* may connect the LORD's "*strong* hand" (3:19; 6:1; 13:3, 9, 14, 16) with his "hardening" of Pharaoh's heart, both from the same root. Likewise, *qashah* may connect the "*harsh* service" of 1:14 and 6:9 with the "hardness" of Pharaoh's heart in 7:3 and 13:15, both from the same root.

9. The list is as follows: serpents (Exod. 7:8–10); water becomes blood (7:15–21); frogs (8:1–15 [7:26–8:11 MT]); gnats (8:16–19 [8:12–15 MT]); flies in Egypt, not in Goshen (8:20–32 [8:16–28 MT]); livestock dies (9:1–7); sores on skin (9:8–12); hail (9:17–35); locusts (10:3–20); darkness (10:21–29); death of the firstborn (11:1–13:16).

10. "I am the LORD [*YHWH*]" occurs in Exod. 6:2, 6, 7, 8, 29; 7:5, 17; 8:22; 10:2; 12:12; 14:4, 18; 15:26.

11. The story in Josh. 2:8–11 demonstrates that the inhabitants of the land do indeed hear of the LORD and fear him.

land of Egypt.' Now Moses and Aaron had done all these wonders before Pharaoh, and the LORD had hardened the heart of Pharaoh, and he had not let the people go from his land." Now that the LORD has accomplished his purpose in the plagues through Moses and Aaron, what more will come of *YHWH*'s name?

The Passover and the Feast of Unleavened Bread

Exodus 12–13 establishes the Passover and the Feast of Unleavened Bread and relates these to the last plague, the death of the firstborn. Exodus 12:1–11 gives the instructions for the Passover before verse 12 explains that the LORD will pass through Egypt and smite all the firstborn of Egypt, concluding with "I am *YHWH*." This associates the feast with the revelation of his name in the upcoming plague. Verse 13 clarifies that the LORD will see the lamb's blood on the doorpost and will "pass over" them. Verse 14 establishes that the day will be a memorial and that they will "*feast* a *feast* to the LORD. . . . As an eternal statute, you will hold the *feast*," linking this celebration with the original expression in 5:1 that Pharaoh should let the people go so that they can hold a *feast* to the LORD.

Before relaying the Passover instructions to the Israelites, Moses gives instructions for the Feast of Unleavened Bread as a reminder of when they left Egypt. Then Moses calls the elders to go and select Passover lambs, to spread blood above the doorposts, and not to go outside. The destroyer will pass by, see the blood, and not enter. Exodus 12:25 indicates that when they enter the land, they are to keep "this service [*'avodah*]." That way, when their sons ask them about "this service," they can say that it is a "sacrifice of the Passover to the LORD when the LORD passed over the houses of Israel in Egypt when he struck the Egyptians and delivered our houses." Like "feast" in Exod. 12:14 links to 5:1, "service" links the celebration to the LORD's original sign in 3:12—namely, that Israel will "serve [*'avad*] God on this mountain." Their "service" to Pharaoh was the reason they had groaned, and their cry for help because of their "service" (*'avodah*) had risen to the LORD (2:23). In the end, would they *serve* the LORD or Pharaoh? Just as they bowed and worshiped at the end of Exod. 4, so they bow and worship in 12:27. The people do what the LORD commanded Moses and Aaron, and so the LORD strikes Egypt. The Israelites plunder the Egyptians as they leave, baking dough without leaven as the LORD established earlier in the chapter (12:39).

After the last plague, Exod. 13:1–16 associates the Passover and the Feast of Unleavened Bread with what has just taken place and the revelation of his name. When the LORD brings them into the land, the "service" (13:5) and the "feast" (13:6) are to be a sign of all that the LORD has done, bringing them out of Egypt with a "strong hand" (13:3). "Strong hand" occurs four times in Exod. 13, which is yet another connection to the revelation of God's name in 3:19, where the LORD warns Moses what it will take to go free.[12] The adjective "strong" originates from the verb *chazaq*, used to describe the "hardening" of Pharaoh's heart, showing that the demonstration of the LORD's victory over Pharaoh encompasses his "strong hand" in "hardening" Pharaoh's heart. Exodus 13:14–15 explicitly associates these two actions with the memorials: "And it will be when your son asks you in the future saying, 'What is this statute?' you will say to him, 'With a *strong* hand the LORD brought us out from Egypt, the house of slavery. When Pharaoh *hardened* to let us go, the LORD slew all the firstborn in the land of Egypt. . . . Therefore, I am sacrificing to the LORD any firstborn males opening the womb, and all my firstborn sons, I redeem." The Passover and Feast of Unleavened Bread become a law and a statute to remind Israel how the LORD brought them into the land (13:9–10). Although chapters 12–13 concern statutes about festivals, they are integrated into the exodus narratives with reminders of the LORD's resolve that the Israelites serve him and not Pharaoh. In the following chapter, these cultic regulations will help us understand why the author includes so many legal sections in the Pentateuch. What is the LORD's goal with these regulations?

The LORD's Glory in the Crossing of the Sea

Exodus 13:17 initiates the final phase in Israel's deliverance before Moses's poetic song in Exod. 15. The narrative turns again to the situation of the Israelites after they have departed Egypt, explaining why they go into the wilderness. These verses connect this deliverance through the Red Sea to the LORD's miraculous guidance in Exod. 13–14 as well as Num. 14 by means of the pillar of cloud and fire. Also, Moses takes Joseph's bones as promised, while the pillar of cloud and fire goes before them. The LORD's miraculous parting of the sea shows the same emphases as the revelation of his name and the plague narratives. The LORD *hardens* Pharaoh's heart so that he pursues the Israelites, and the LORD is glorified. The Egyptians know that he is *YHWH*, in keeping with the revelation of his name throughout the plague narratives. *Kavad*, one of the three verbal roots used to convey the LORD's "hardening" of Pharaoh's heart, is also used as a recurring theme in Exod. 14: the LORD will be "glorified" (*kavad*) occurs in 14:4, 17, and 18.[13] In other words, it is through

---

12. Exod. 3:19; 6:1; 13:3, 9, 14, 16.
13. *Kavad* is the same root translated as "harden" and "glorified." *Kavad* also occurs in Exod. 14:25, but there it refers to the wheels of Pharaoh's chariots moving "with difficulty."

Pharaoh's *hardening* (*kavad*) that the LORD accomplishes his purposes: to be *glorified* (*kavad*) and make his name known to all the earth.

Just as the LORD planned, Pharaoh's heart changes about letting the Israelites go, so he gathers his army, pursues Israel, and overtakes them by the sea. Portending the trouble that the Israelites' lack of faith will later cause in the wilderness, Exod. 14:10–12 reports their fear, how they cry out to the LORD and castigate Moses for bringing them to die in the wilderness. Moses encourages the people to stand still and see the LORD's salvation, but the LORD censures Moses, instructing him to tell the people to move forward. Not only that, but in 14:16, two words from Exod. 4, "staff" and "hand," again take center stage. Moses is to lift his *staff*, stretch out his *hand* over the sea, and split it! Verses 17–18 repeat the same trio of words that Exod. 14:4 put forward: harden, glorify, and know. The LORD will "harden the heart"—this time of all the Egyptians—and the LORD will be "glorified" [*kavad*] so the Egyptians will "know" that he is the LORD. Like 14:4, Exod. 14:17–18 twice reiterates that the "hardening" is for the LORD's glory, demonstrating again the connection between the act of hardening and the LORD receiving glory.

As the showdown draws to a close, Moses stretches out his hand over the sea and the LORD drives the sea back with a strong east wind until it becomes dry, splitting the waters (14:21). Israel walks through with a wall of water on either side, but when Egypt pursues, the same pillar of cloud and fire confuses the Egyptians, causing their chariots to careen. Before Pharaoh's forces can flee, Moses stretches out his hand at the LORD's command and brings the waters upon the Egyptians. The water returns, the LORD sweeps the Egyptians into the midst of the water, and not one of them survives. The account ends in 14:30–31 with its own twist: the LORD saved Israel from the "*hand* of the Egyptians . . . and Israel saw the great *hand* that the LORD did in Egypt and the people feared the LORD and they believed in the LORD and in Moses, his servant." Moses is the LORD's *hand* through which he saved Israel, causing Israel to believe in the LORD and in Moses, his servant. Although the story itself ends there, the author is not finished. He integrates one final piece into his composition.

The Song of Moses

The author finishes the account with a poem that blends the LORD's fight against Egypt with the later victory over the promised land. The poem begins in Exod. 15:1 with Moses "singing" a song: "I will sing to the LORD because he has certainly exalted himself! Horse and rider, he has tossed into the sea." In like manner, the poem concludes with Miriam (a prophetess and Aaron's sister) singing the same words (Exod. 15:1, 21). In verse 3, the poem takes up the theme of the LORD as a warrior who "fights" for Israel. This theme appears in the plague narratives in Exod. 14:14, 25 and can be traced to later narratives in Exod. 17, Num. 21 and 31–32 (where Moses defeats several kings in battle), and Josh. 4–11 (where Joshua leads Israel to its victories). The poem describes the LORD's watery victory over Pharaoh and his army. It was the LORD's "breath" (*ruach*) that first divided the waters and then brought them back on the Egyptians (Exod. 15:8, 10). Exodus 15:11 asks, "Who is like you among the gods, LORD? Who is like you, glorious in holiness, awesome in deeds, working a miracle?" The Hebrew word for "miracle" comes from the same root as "wonders" in Exod. 3:20. "Glorious in holiness" draws attention to the LORD's character but also to the "place of his holiness" appearing in 15:13. No doubt alluding to the holy mountain of God where Moses first met the LORD, 15:17 betrays a later perspective with the term "sanctuary" (coming from the same root as "holiness"), which indicates already a concern for the future sanctuary where the LORD will dwell among his people. Why is the author writing about the sanctuary before it exists?

This future perspective is evident also in Exod. 15:14 with the mention of the Philistines. Were they involved in the exodus? Of course not, but we see the author's retrospect as verse 15 draws upon the exodus to note Edom's terror, Moab's trembling, and Canaan's "melting." Suddenly, the poem expresses not merely information about the defeat of Egypt but the conquest of the promised land. Indeed, just as the LORD had declared, his name is being told in all the earth! The nations of the promised land have heard and have been put on notice that the LORD will bring about his covenant promises to Abraham. Exodus 15:15b says "All the inhabitants of Canaan have melted," a description that comes to pass in Joshua.[14] The LORD uses his mighty deeds, accomplished in the exodus, to make his name known and facilitate Israel's conquest of the peoples living in Canaan. Exodus 15:17 indicates that the LORD will bring Israel to his mountain, his inheritance, where he dwells, his sanctuary. Will the LORD now dwell in the midst of his people as they serve him? Not so fast.

The poem reflects a perspective from the end of the Pentateuch. The LORD will dwell among his people and prepare them to go into battle against the people of the land. Exodus 25:8–9 explains that the sanctuary is the tabernacle in which the LORD will dwell among his people. Exodus 15:18 even claims that the LORD will be king over his people forever, noting his victory over

---

14. A similar clause occurs in Josh. 2:9, 24, introducing a key motif in the conquest narratives of Joshua: the "inhabitants in the land" heard of it and "melted." See also 2:11; 5:1; 7:5.

Pharaoh and portending future trouble between the LORD and Israel when they choose another king in 1 Samuel. And just as it began, Miriam's song concludes the poem. One might think that the Israelites and the LORD will live happily ever after. After seeing these miracles, shouldn't the Israelites trust the LORD? Exodus 15:22 begins as if indeed it might be so.

Just like the LORD instructed Moses at the beginning of the story in Exod. 3:18, the Israelites are now set to travel three days into the wilderness to sacrifice to the LORD! In Exod. 3:18, Moses was to tell Pharaoh, "Let us walk a three-day journey into the wilderness and let us sacrifice to the LORD our God."[15] Now Exod. 15:22 suggests that they will do just that! They set out from there and journey "three days in the wilderness," but they do not sacrifice to the LORD. Instead, they are struggling to find water! How will they respond? Will they trust in the LORD and Moses his servant and in their ability to provide? Will they sing another song to the LORD celebrating his accomplishments? The remainder of Exod. 15 transitions to the contentious next chapter in the LORD's relationship with Israel.

THEOLOGY and PRACTICE

Exodus 1–15 is not an independent textual unit. Although only superficially juxtaposed to the book of Genesis, it is extensively integrated with what follows in Exodus through Numbers. Since this unit is dependent on material that unfolds in subsequent chapters, our ability to draw theological and practical conclusions from it is limited; the author is not done talking. However, we can say a few things.

First, Moses is undoubtedly God's chosen mediator. He is an Israelite, but he was also raised as an Egyptian, and this dual connection makes him an ideal mediator between the two peoples. More importantly, he relates directly to God and performs his signs, mediating between the LORD and his people. Although the theme is only minimally set forth in Deut. 33, through his giving of the law, Moses is portrayed as a type of the coming law-giving lion king, who will inherit the cosmos. Moreover, Moses is the paradigm whom the writer of Deut. 34 types as the future prophet that the people of God are awaiting. These narratives in Exodus and the legal codes in Exodus through Numbers will increasingly set forth his office, but in the meantime, we should ponder that it is Moses, the babe drawn from water, whom the LORD sends to save his people. As he did with Noah, and Abraham, God chooses a man

15. The same clause occurs in Exod. 5:1, 3; 7:16; 8:27–28 (8:23–24 MT).

through whom to work to save his people. Should we expect something different with the Messiah?

Second, the LORD's deliverance of Israel from slavery in Egypt is the prime pattern for salvation in the OT. The Ten Commandments ground Israel's identity and activity in the LORD's deliverance; Leviticus ubiquitously comments on it; Num. 23 and 24 establish the exodus as a type for future deliverance; and Deut. 4, 26, and 28 use it positively and negatively as a ground for the LORD's future activity. Even Joseph's story in Gen. 37–48 anticipates deliverance from Egypt. Furthermore, the crossing of the Jordan in Josh. 3–4 is portrayed as another crossing of the Red Sea. These texts are only the beginning as indeed the remainder of Scripture uses the miracle of the exodus as God's paradigmatic salvation event: we are enslaved to sin and death, and release from these is our own exodus out of Egypt through the waters of baptism.[16] And as God brought Israel out of Egypt, so he also brought the lion king, the son of Judah, through it. As this lion king overcame death, so will we.

Third, these narratives set forth the LORD's intent to dwell in the midst of his people. This connection was the consistent purpose set forth by Moses to Pharaoh, "Let my people go that they may serve me."[17] The LORD's determination to be with his people shows from the outset in his instruction to Moses in Exod. 3:12: "When you bring the people out of Egypt, you will worship God on this mountain." On the one hand, the Pentateuch resolves this issue by means of the tabernacle, which will turn out to be less than ideal and temporary. On the other hand, at the end of the Pentateuch, Moses will introduce another, permanent solution. The permanent solution will be God's greatest act of condescension and is the Pentateuch's announcement of the gospel.[18]

Fourth, the LORD's desire that his glory be known to Egypt and Israel and to all nations is merely the preamble to future acts of judgment and salvation. Exodus 9:16 indicates most clearly his desire: "But for this purpose I have raised you up, to cause you to see my glory, and in order to proclaim my name in all the earth." No fewer than twelve times we read that the LORD is doing this so that Israel, Egypt, and future generations will know that he is *YHWH*.[19] God has a desire that his glory be known to all people through both judgment and salvation.

Fifth, the great salvation that the Israelites witness also sets the stage for Israel's greater need for deliverance from stubbornness and rebellion. One would think that after experiencing such miracles, the Israelites would have

16. For themes of the exodus and baptism, see Ezek. 20:33–34; 36:24–27.
17. Exod. 5:1; 7:16; 8:1, 20, 21; 9:1, 13; 10:3, 4.
18. See chap. 11 for this solution.
19. Exod. 6:7; 7:5, 17; 8:10, 22 (8:6, 18 MT); 9:14, 29; 10:2; 11:7; 12:26–27; 14:4, 18.

believed God's goodness and his ability to provide, and would obey him. Does it not remind you of Adam and Eve's disobedience and lack of trust in the garden? For Israel, the next episodes in Exodus portray their grumbling and rebellion, indicating that humanity has a desperate need if they are ever to dwell in the Lord's midst. The people of Israel demonstrate unholiness and the need for a way—albeit temporary—for the Lord to dwell among his people. What will that way be, and how does it relate to the permanent solution mentioned above? Before we come to either, we must better understand the nature of Israel's stubbornness and rebellion.

The Law

An Unsuccessful Journey to God's Presence
(Exod. 15:22–Num. 36:13)

Exodus 15:22 through Num. 36:13 forms the next major subunit in the Pentateuch. It tells the story of Israel's journey toward the promised land, but it also contains extensive catalogues of legal codes. The LORD took action against Egypt in part because he had promised Abraham and his descendants a place for them to dwell. He demonstrated his glory through Pharaoh's defeat, culminating in the song Israel sang after the LORD's deliverance. But as we will see, all is not well in the wilderness.

This next section reveals the LORD's purposes and patterns through their wilderness journey, Moses's leadership, and the giving of the law: God is determined to dwell among his people and for them to serve him rather than Pharaoh. Not unlike the legal sections in Exod. 12–13 regulating the feasts, the catalogues of legal codes in this section do not stand alone as independent documents. Rather, the larger narrative of the journey and its purpose provides the context. Treating them as isolated documents leads to seeing them merely as a list of dos and don'ts. Instead, this material must be understood within the boundaries and purposes the author provides. How does the narrative frame shape our interpretation of this material?

As part of the larger story spanning Genesis to Deuteronomy, Israel's journey begins when the LORD tells Abraham that his offspring will return to the land after servitude (Gen. 15:12–16). God also speaks to Moses about this journey, saying that he will bring Abraham's offspring to their land after delivering them from their oppressors (Exod. 3). As a sign that this promise has been fulfilled, they will "serve God on this mountain." While the LORD's purpose in the exodus is that his "name be proclaimed in all the earth," he also desires Israel to draw near and know who he is (Exod. 16:9–12). Repeatedly, the LORD said, "Let my people go that they might serve me." In light of the power he displayed in the plague narratives, wouldn't it make sense for the people to celebrate the LORD in their midst? But this is not what happens. Just as Abraham's story culminated in a poem about a lion king who will come in the end of the days, so this story culminates in Balaam's poem about a lion king. Israel's journey is not only about the past.

The Pattern of Narratives (Exod. 15:22–18:27; Num. 10:10–21:35)

In Exod. 15:22–Num. 36:13 we read about Israel's journey through the wilderness and the LORD's giving of his law. But these Scriptures do not merely report what transpired and give the content of the commandments; they do something more. The author wants to say something about the future. We have already seen how the author uses the deliverance from Egypt in the Balaam poem to say something about the star of Jacob, the lion king who will come in the end of the days. How do these narratives and legal codes fit into that promise? The author establishes a pattern within the narratives that tells us something about humanity, our attempts to draw near to God, and a mediator who accomplishes God's purposes.

Exodus 16 commences the next leg of Israel's journey, a journey that continues until the end of Numbers, when they arrive at the border of the promised land. The narratives in Exod. 16–18 cover events immediately following the exodus, while Exod. 19–Num. 10 describe the people's yearlong stay at Sinai. Numbers 10–21 also flow out of their exodus experiences, even though these narratives are separated by many chapters of legal codes. Tellingly, the pattern of events in Exod. 15:22–18:27 transpires again after the wandering in the wilderness in Num. 10–21, as the following series of figures illustrates (see figs. 10.1–4).[1]

---

1. The pattern I'm presenting is based on John Sailhamer, *The Meaning of the Pentateuch: Revelation, Composition, and Interpretation* (Downers Grove, IL: IVP Academic, 2009), 366, but I have expanded it significantly.

FIGURE 10.1.

Wilderness Pattern with Intervening Legal Material

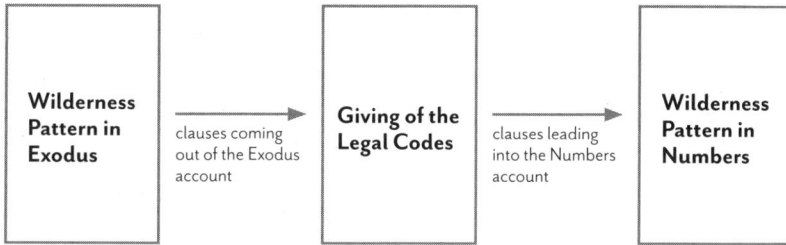

FIGURE 10.2.

Clauses Coming out of the Exodus Account Mirror Clauses
Leading into the Numbers Account

[Jethro, Moses's father-in-law, brought an offering and sacrifices to God (Exod. 18:12)]
    Jethro, priest of Midian, father-in-law of Moses (Exod. 18:1)
        Jethro rejoiced over the good that the LORD did for Israel (Exod. 18:9)
        and he walked to his land (Exod. 18:27)
        and they journeyed (Exod. 19:2)
burnt offerings and sacrifices of peace offerings (Num. 10:10)
    Moses said to Hobab . . . the Midianite, father-in-law of Moses (Num. 10:29)
        "We will do good to you because the LORD spoke good concerning Israel."
        (Num. 10:29; see also 10:32)
        "I will not walk with you; rather, to my land . . . I will walk." (Num. 10:30)
        and they journeyed (Num. 10:33)

FIGURE 10.3.

Word, Clause, and Episode Patterns in the Wilderness Wanderings:
Exodus and Numbers Accounts Compared

Exodus	Numbers
wilderness of Shur (15:22)	wilderness of Sinai (10:12)
Moses made Israel journey (15:22)	sons of Israel journeyed . . . by Moses (10:13)
three days (15:22)	three days (10:33)
he called its name (15:23)	he called its name (11:3)
grumble (15:24)	complain (11:1)
"What shall we drink?" (15:24)	"Who will give us meat to eat?" (11:4)

Exodus	Numbers
he cried out to the LORD (15:25)	the people cried out to Moses (11:2)
in Egypt (15:26)	in Egypt (11:5)
murmuring (16:1–4)	complaining (11:1–4)
pots of meat (16:4)	meat (11:4)
bread from heaven (16:4)	manna (11:6)
the people go out and gather (16:4)	the people went out and gathered (11:8)
dew went up (16:13–14)	dew came down (11:9)
quail (16:13)	quail (11:31)
manna, like the seed of coriander (16:15, 31)	manna, like the seed of coriander (11:7)
gathered the bread (16:22)	gathered the quail (11:32)
ate the manna (16:35)	eat meat (11:18, 21)
forty years (16:35)	forty years (14:33–34)
water from rock (17:1–7)	water from rock (20:1–12)
all the congregation of the sons of Israel (17:1)	all the congregation of the sons of Israel (13:26)
wilderness of Sin (17:1)	wilderness of Zin (20:1; cf. wilderness of Paran, 13:26)
there was no water (17:1)	it did not have water (20:2)
the people contended with Moses (17:2)	the people contended with Moses (20:3)
the people complained against Moses (17:3)	they complained against Moses (14:2)
"Why did you bring us from Egypt to cause us to die?" (17:3)	"If only we had died in the land of Egypt!" (14:3)
"Cross before the people . . . take your staff." (17:5)	"Take your staff and assemble the congregation." (20:8)
"Strike the rock and water will come out, and the people will drink." (17:6)	"Speak to the rock . . . and you will cause water to come out and give drink to the congregation." (20:8)
Moses did thus (17:7)	Moses smote the rock "times" with the staff (20:11)
Meribah over the contending of the sons of Israel (17:7)	*Meribah*, where the sons of Israel contended with the LORD (20:13)

Exodus	Numbers
they tested the LORD (17:7)	they tested me (14:22)
Amalek (17:8)	Amalekites (14:28)
Israel fights Amalek while Moses holds up the "staff of God in his hand" (17:8)	Edom would not let Israel pass through land and meets them with strength (20:14)
Moses's hands were faithful; Joshua leads (17:8–13)	Aaron dies and Eleazar succeeds him; Eleazar leads (20:23)
Amalek fought Israel (17:8)	the Canaanite . . . fought against Israel (21:1)
battle (17:14–16)	battle (21:1–16)

FIGURE 10.4.

Departures from the Exodus Pattern in Numbers

Chapter	Event
11	Spirit of the LORD on men
12	Miriam and Aaron speak against Moses
13	Moses sends spies to the land
14	the people want to pick a new leader and return to Egypt
	"How long will this people not believe in me in spite of all the signs I have done in their midst?" (14:11)
	spies die, except for Caleb and Joshua
15	offerings in the land
16	the earth swallows rebellious Korah
17	censers made holy, and Aaron's rod buds
18	Aaron and his sons bear the iniquity of the priesthood; tribe of Levi in the sanctuary
19	law of the red heifer, touching the dead, and clean/unclean
20	instructions change from "strike the rock" (Exod. 17) to "speak to the rock" (Num. 20) even though he "smote" is portrayed in both places
	"Because you did not *believe* me to cause me to be regarded as holy before the eyes of the sons of Israel, therefore you will not bring this assembly into this land that I have given them." (20:12)

Chapter	Event
21	the people spoke against the LORD and against Moses (21:5)
	bronze serpent
	"Gather the people, and I will give to them water. . . . 'Go up, well, and sing to it,' the well that the princes dug, the nobles of the people dug it, with the one making rules, with their staffs." (21:16–17a)

Several points emerge from the patterns presented in figures 10.1–4. First, Israel's actions before and after the law is given are the same. In a way, Exod. 16:4 sets up the entire wilderness wanderings as a test to see whether Israel will walk in the LORD's laws. They fail the test. The legal codes do not change the people, do not stop their grumbling, and do not increase their faith. If anything, the people appear more rebellious after the legal codes are given, as evidenced by the constant contention against Moses in Num. 14–17, narrative episodes that do not have a counterpart in Exod. 15:22–18:27 (see fig. 10.4).

Second, the pattern shows that, as in the exodus narratives, Moses fills the role as mediator between God and the people. His function will take on special prominence when we consider Exod. 19, and even more so in later narratives, culminating in his sentence to die outside the promised land because of his failure in Num. 20.

Third, the pattern and the legal codes show the LORD's determination to dwell among his people, but they must be made holy. This purpose emerges immediately in Exod. 16:9, when they are to draw near to the LORD, and in Exod. 19, when he tells the people to assemble on the mountain. When assembling on the mountain in his presence fails to materialize, Moses becomes the mediator until the tabernacle and the cult are established, although these too fail to establish the holiness of the priests and the people.

In the remainder of this chapter, I will assume these conclusions from the pattern's outer frame of Israel's rebellion as seen in figs. 10.1–4. I will next treat the remaining narratives that provide the context for the blocks of legal codes, while reflecting on these three purposes from Exod. 15:22 to Num. 36:13.

The Scene on Mount Sinai (Exod. 19:1–20:21)

Exodus 19 contains a pivotal moment in Israel's relationship with the LORD. Israel encamps at the base of the mountain, confirming the promised sign (see 3:12) that he is with them on their journey toward the promised land. A chronological note in Exod. 19:1 locates the story in the third month after they had left Egypt. This begins an almost one-year stay in the Sinai region, which ends in Num. 10:11. While it may seem simply to tell a story about Israel's interaction with God on the mountain, when looked at closely, the chapter exhibits several discrepancies that show that the author is up to something in its composition.[2] With Israel encamped at Mount Sinai, Moses goes up the mountain, and the LORD speaks to Moses and reminds him of all that happened to the Egyptians and how the LORD has brought Israel to him. Verse 5 begins with two important details. First, the LORD says, "If you certainly obey my voice and keep my *covenant.*" Practically nothing about a covenant has been said before this in Exodus apart from a passing reference to the covenant with Abraham in 2:24 and the "covenant to give [the patriarchs] the land of Canaan" in 6:4–5. Second, what should we think about the "if"? God's covenant with Abraham was a promise of blessing that contained no "if," no conditions that must be met.

The LORD's words to Moses contain other mysterious details, such as, "You will be to me a kingdom of priests" (Exod. 19:6). Priests mediate between God and others, and a kingdom implies royalty. Both would make sense given the LORD's deliverance of Israel from Egypt and special selection of Abraham's descendants. The problem emerges later in the chapter when we find Moses, Aaron, *priests*, and *people* having differing levels of access to the LORD (19:24). The notion of a kingdom is not seen again until the end of Numbers! A kingdom of priests might also make sense since the LORD had said in Exod. 3:12 that they would serve him on the mountain. Once the necessary preparations were made for sanctification and the trumpet blew, they were to go up *on the mountain.*[3] But verse 17 says that they stood at the foot of the mountain. And later in the chapter, the people are no longer permitted to go up the mountain at all (19:24). The LORD also indicates that they are to be a "holy [*qadosh*] nation" (19:6). This makes sense given the instructions in Exod. 19:10–12 that Moses was to make the people "holy" and put a "border" around them so that they could meet with the holy LORD (Exod. 15:11; Lev. 11:44–45). But again, later in the

2. For those unable to see the challenges in the Hebrew text, a side-by-side comparison of English translations reveals the difficulty in translating the Hebrew.

3. Unfortunately, English versions translate the verse differently, some construing the Hebrew to mean that when the trumpet blew they were to come up *to* the mountain (e.g., ESV), others, to come up *on* it (e.g., NRSV). Besides the Hebrew verb "go up" (*'alah*) and the preposition "in" (both in 19:13), based on the LORD's original stated purpose in Exod. 3:12, I understand 19:13 to mean that they were to be *on* the mountain in God's presence. In spite of the preparations to meet God, the people "stationed themselves *at the bottom of the mountain*" (19:17). Moreover, in 19:21 the LORD tells Moses, "Go down and warn the people." Since the people had not moved since verse 17, they were not yet on the mountain.

chapter, it is the mountain that is "bordered" and made "holy" (19:23) and no longer the people. Why the change in who can approach God and what is holy?

The chapter also reveals Moses's special role between the people and the LORD. Although the locations of the conversations between the LORD and Moses and between Moses and the people are not always explicit, no fewer than eight exchanges between the parties take place. Moses is often told to "go up" or "come down" when it is not clear where he is located. He is certainly the go-between between the LORD and the people. Consider also what the LORD says to Moses in Exod. 19:9: "I am coming to you in a thick cloud so that the people will hear when I speak with you and *believe in you* forever." The people's perception of the communication between the LORD and Moses was to promote faith in Moses forever. Besides this occasion, in the Pentateuch "faith in" someone is directed only toward the LORD. This unique description for Moses suggests his outsized role in the story.

The heart of the chapter is Exod. 19:16–19. The people have prepared for this moment on the third day. They tremble in the camp when thunder, lightning, and a thick cloud descend upon the mountain and a loud horn sounds. According to verse 13, this is the moment when the people should have gone up the mountain, but Moses has to bring them out of the camp, and they stand at the bottom of the mountain (19:17). Verse 18 reiterates that the entire mountain was smoking with fire and shaking because the LORD had come down on the mountain. Verse 19 begins with the horn sounding louder and louder. In a mysterious interaction, Moses suddenly initiates conversation with God, and God answers him in a voice. However, the verse does not say how God answers him. Exodus 19:20 apparently shifts settings, because it switches to using "the LORD" rather than "God" (v. 19). It also describes the LORD's descent to the head of the mountain and his calling Moses, who ascends to the head of the mountain. What was God's answer in Exod. 19:19? What are we to make of these issues?

Three other passages also describe this incident: Exod. 20:18–21, Deut. 4:10–14, and Deut. 5. Exodus 20:18–21 follows the giving of the Ten Commandments and describes the same scene on the mountain as 19:19. The scene in 20:18–21 uses the name "God" from Exod. 19:19 and indicates that the mountain smoked and thundered and that the horn still blared. Twice it mentions that the people "stood at a distance" because they were afraid (20:18, 21). It reports the frightening scene as if the events of 19:16–19 were still happening, but we know from 19:21–25 that the scene had moved on, with Moses going up and down to warn the people. Why the second report of their fear and distance?

Deuteronomy 4:10–14 reports the same incident albeit with a different purpose. Still, it indicates that the people "stood at the bottom of the mountain" and heard the Ten Commandments from the midst of the fire. Reporting the incident a third time, Deut. 5:4–22 declares that the LORD spoke the Ten Commandments "face to face" on the mountain from the midst of the fire, with Moses standing between the LORD and the people who were too afraid to come up the mountain. It is clear from these three passages that God spoke the Ten Commandments from the midst of the fire, presumably during the exchange recorded at 19:19.

But why do the Ten Commandments not appear in the narrative until Exod. 20:1? And who is speaking the Ten Commandments in 20:1? Is it God or Moses? Exodus 19:25 reports, "Moses went down the mountain to the people and said to them . . ." The final verb "said" (*'amar*) usually introduces direct discourse in such a setting. Instead, Exod. 20:1 begins with the same type of narrative verb form but with a different word for "speaking." It reports, "And God spoke [*dabar*] all these words," followed by a recitation of the Ten Commandments. But where is God? The narrative situation in 19:19–24 has completely changed, with only Moses and Aaron allowed to approach God in 19:24 and with Moses back at the bottom in 19:25. So who spoke the Ten Commandments, and when were they spoken?

Adding to the complexity of the narrative is the unfortunate chapter transition that interrupts the narrative flow. The author waits until Exod. 20:1–17 to list the Ten Commandments, even though it appears that this actually transpired in 19:19. Why did he do this? *Because he wanted to elevate Moses's role as the giver of the law.* Moses is the mediator of the covenant. Even though God speaks the Ten Commandments, it is Moses's role to bring them to the people and to stand between the LORD and the people. Therefore, the author elevates Moses to the one who speaks with God for the people and reveals God's will and word to the people. The people are to believe in Moses forever and fear God. According to Exod. 19–20, then, the people *stood at a distance* (Exod. 20:18, 21a), and as their mediator, Moses alone *drew near* to the thick darkness where God was (20:21b).

Law Codes and Narratives (Exod. 20–40)

The Covenant Code and Exodus 24

By this point, it is clear that Moses alone can approach God. This will receive increased emphasis until hints of trouble appear at the end of Exodus. In the meantime, Exod. 20:22 declares that the LORD has indeed spoken to them from heaven (from the mountaintop). Consequently, more legal codes follow, beginning with the command not to make gods of silver or gold. Commonly known as the Covenant Code, Exod. 20:22–23:33 contains various legal codes providing Israel with a code of conduct. This block of legal codes is grammatically connected to Exod. 24:1 and the narrative contained in that chapter, indicating that the two passages are presenting simultaneous events.[4] The two sections should therefore be taken together, Exod. 24 containing another narrative providing the framework that constrains the interpretation of the Covenant Code.

Exodus 24 begins with the same emphases as Exod. 19. Moses is to come up by himself, while even Aaron, his sons, and the elders are not allowed to approach. The people also cannot come up. Moses returns to them and reports the words and the "judgments" (24:3), presumably those enumerated in the Covenant Code (21:1). As mediator of the covenant, Moses performs a covenant ceremony. This includes a covenant ritual in which he takes blood from a sacrificed bull, tosses half upon the altar, and reads the "book of the covenant" to the people, with which they unanimously agree to comply. Moses then tosses the other half of the blood upon the people and says, "Behold, the blood of the covenant that the LORD cut with you according to all these words" (24:8). The Covenant Code provides instruction for the people and the agreed-upon stipulations for the covenant. The covenant ritual seems to indicate a joining of altar and people by means of the agreed upon adherence to the words of the covenant. Will this covenant enable the LORD to dwell among the people?

The situation seems hopeful as Moses ascends with his crew: they see God, and they eat and drink (24:9–12). Moses plans to go up and receive the tablets of law and commandments for their instruction while the others stay behind. Taking Joshua with him, Moses goes up the mountain, and the cloud covers it. The glory of the LORD appears like a consuming fire at the top of the mountain, and Israel can see it. As if to elevate Moses in yet another way, the narrative reports that Moses enters the cloud and goes up the mountain, staying there forty days and forty nights (24:13–18). While agreement to the Covenant Code appears to offer some hope that the people may yet dwell in

---

4. This coordinating clause begins in Exod. 20:22, "And the LORD said to Moses," while Exod. 24:1 responds with the opposite Hebrew verbal order, "And to Moses he said." There are no intervening narrative verbs or verbs of speaking with the LORD as the subject. See Bruce K. Waltke and M. O'Conner, *An Introduction to Biblical Hebrew Syntax* (Winona Lake, IN: Eisenbrauns, 1990), 650–51. A better description of this phenomenon is found in John Sailhamer's unpublished "Notes on Biblical Hebrew Syntax," 110–15. This construction occurs when the same verb is repeated in an opposite verbal tense (see, e.g., Gen. 1:5).

the Lord's presence, Aaron, his sons, and the elders must still worship "at a distance" while Moses alone enters the cloud. And what about all that the people agree to? Will they be able to obey all the judgments and commandments? Will they be able to perform even the first one?

The Tabernacle and the Golden Calf (Exod. 25–40)

Exodus 24 leaves the reader watching Moses as he disappears into the cloud, but Exod. 25 lets us in on the scene on top of the mountain as God speaks to him. Israel is to take an offering and make a *holy* place (*miqdash*, a sanctuary, 25:8) so the Lord will dwell in their midst! This is exactly what Israel needs to be holy and how they can dwell with God. Exodus 25:21–22 explains that once the holy place is made according to the pattern and once the mercy seat and testimony are in their proper place, God will meet with Moses and speak with him about all that he commanded for Israel. "Holiness" is included in all of its plans! Exodus 26–27 explains that this will be a dwelling place with curtains, a tent (often called a tabernacle) with furniture and vessels made of pure gold, bronze, and other fine materials. This is to be done according to the pattern that Moses sees on the mountain, to separate parts of the tabernacle, including the holy place, from the holy of holies (26:33). Will a holy place make Israel holy?

Exodus 28 explains the role that Aaron and his sons will play as priests. The craftsmen must make holy garments so that Aaron and his sons will be made holy for the priesthood (twice in 28:3–4).[5] Aaron's clothing and jewelry will symbolize the twelve tribes, the sons of Israel, so that he will bear them before the Lord in the holy place and bear their judgment on his heart before the Lord continually (28:29–30). Aaron's turban and its jewelry will bear the guilt of the "holy things" (all their "holy gifts") that the sons of Israel "make holy," so that they will be accepted before the Lord (28:38). Their outer garments are also intended to "make them holy" to serve as priests, while their undergarments cover their naked flesh when they go into the holy place so as not to bear their iniquity and die (28:41, 43).

Exodus 29:1 begins in the same way, emphasizing the need for Aaron and his sons to be made holy to serve as priests. The entire chapter resounds with different types of offerings to atone for Aaron and his sons and make them holy. Exodus 29:43–44 reiterates that the Lord will meet with them there and that the tent of meeting, the altar, Aaron, and Aaron's sons will be made holy. Verse 45 goes on to say that in this way the Lord will "dwell in their midst"

---

5. The root for "holy" (*qadosh*) is used throughout these chapters, indicating the attempt to make Israel holy, fit for the Lord's presence.

and be their God. Exodus 29:46 concludes the chapter by echoing the plague narratives, stating that the people will know that he is the LORD God who brought them out of Egypt *so that* he can dwell in their midst. But will more priests usher Israel into God's presence?

Exodus 30–31 contains instructions for the altar, the census offering, the bronze basin, anointing oil, and incense—always to make things holy or for atonement. Sabbaths also were holy and intended to make Israel holy (31:13–14). The root word "holy" occurs an overwhelming fifty-eight times in these two chapters as an obvious clue that the tabernacle was to make Israel holy so that the LORD could dwell among them. With all these instructions and provisions, could Israel be made holy so God would dwell in their midst? Exodus 31:18 concludes the tabernacle instruction, saying God gave Moses the two tablets of testimony, written by the finger of God. What would Moses do with the tablets? And will these additional measures make the people holy so that they may dwell with God? Unfortunately, the next chapter reports a devastating turn of events.

Exodus 32–34 reports the story of the golden calf and Moses's intercession for the people. While Moses tarries at the top of the mountain, the people grow impatient and convince Aaron to build a golden calf. Upon engraving it with a tool, they proclaim, "These are your gods, O Israel, who brought you up from the land of Egypt" (32:4, 8). Moses has just received the tablets with the Ten Commandments—the first two of which prohibited the worship of another god and the making of an idol—and Aaron and the people have already disobeyed. The LORD threatens to consume them in his anger and to make a great nation from Moses, but Moses intercedes, urging the LORD in two commands to turn and relent over his plan. Reminding the LORD of his covenant with Abraham, Moses convinces the LORD not to destroy the people. Descending the mountain with the two tablets of the LORD's commandments, Moses sees the calf and the dancing and throws the two tablets from his hand, shattering them. The broken commandments represent the broken covenant. The people have failed to live up to the conditions of the covenant, rebelling against the first two commandments (Exod. 20:2–4, 23). After destroying the calf and rebuking Aaron, Moses leads those who side with the LORD into battle. The sons of Levi fight against their fellow Israelites, killing three thousand men. Moses goes up the mountain to the LORD to atone for Israel's great sin, even offering for his own name to be blotted out, but the LORD retains the right to punish them as he sees fit.

The sin of the golden calf threatens to undo the LORD's plan to dwell in the midst of Israel and reveals that they are a "stiff-necked" people (Exod. 33:2–5). The LORD therefore elects to send an angel before the people in his stead.

With such a development threatening a central purpose for Israel's deliverance from Egypt—that the LORD would dwell in the midst of his people—Exod. 33–34 elevates Moses's role to new heights. Not only does he speak to the LORD face to face as one speaks with a friend, with all Israel watching, but he also convinces the LORD to go with his people and is allowed to see the back of the LORD's glory. This scene culminates in the famous proclamation of the LORD's character in 34:6–7: "The LORD, the LORD, a compassionate and gracious God, slow to anger, great in lovingkindness and truth, keeping lovingkindness to thousands, forgiving iniquity, transgression, and sin; but he will by no means leave the guilty unpunished, visiting the iniquity of the fathers upon the sons and grandsons to the third and fourth generations."

Having remained on the mountain with the LORD for forty days and forty nights, Moses receives more stipulations to ratify the covenant. With new tablets in hand, Moses comes down from the LORD's presence with "horns of light" radiating from his face (34:29). Just as Israel was afraid of God's presence on top of the mountain, now they are afraid to draw near to Moses! (34:30) So Moses put a veil over his face whenever he would speak to them. The sin of the golden calf elevates Moses's position before the LORD. He remains the only one who can be in the LORD's presence!

The sin of the golden calf threatened to stall God's plan to dwell in the midst of his people, but the plan resumes with Moses's intercession. Exodus 35–40 describes the implementation of the tabernacle's plans. The entire tabernacle is produced according to the command of Moses in the way that the LORD commands him (38:21–22). After its first occurrence in 38:22, the clause "as the LORD commanded Moses" occurs an overwhelming eighteen times in Exod. 39–40, and its sentiment is ubiquitous through Leviticus and Numbers. When Moses completes the work, the cloud covers the tent, and the glory of the LORD fills the tabernacle (40:34). But a problem ensues: Moses cannot enter the tent of meeting! Even though he has spoken to the LORD "face to face," now that the tabernacle is complete and the glory of the LORD fills it, Moses is unable to go in (40:35). The cloud of the LORD is upon it by day and a fire is in it by night before the eyes of all Israel in their journeys (40:36–38). If Moses cannot go into the tent of meeting, who will intercede for Israel? Will the LORD not dwell in their midst? Will he not go with them and before them to the promised land?

Entrance into the LORD's Presence (Leviticus)

Leviticus 1:1 opens with the same problem. The LORD calls to Moses *from* the tent of meeting. Is there a way for the Israelites to approach God? The

LORD's instruction would provide a way. The first block of legal codes in Lev. 1–7 deals precisely with this problem. Moses must explain to the Israelites what transpires when someone brings an offering. Although the process is perplexing at first, the underlying Hebrew words illuminate the ritual.[6] The word for "offering" (*qorban*) originates from the verb "come near" (*qarav*). Translated woodenly, Lev. 1:2 says, "If anyone wants to *bring near* a thing that *brings near*, from the cattle, from the livestock, from the sheep you will *bring near* your thing that *brings near*." These *bring near* things have different purposes—whether to atone for sin, establish peace, or deal with sin—but ultimately they make provision for the person to *come near* to the LORD. This liturgy is the plan for Israel to be made holy! The LORD will then dwell in their midst during their journeys.

Leviticus 8 makes provision for the priests themselves to approach, to come near, the LORD. The entire chapter deals with the process to sanctify the tabernacle, its utensils, and Aaron and his sons and to atone for the priests' sin so that they can come near. Will these preparations be enough to enter the LORD's presence? What were once a few ambiguous preparations for the covenant in Exod. 19, the Covenant Code with offerings and blood ritual for the covenant in Exod. 24, the tabernacle instructions in Exod. 25–31 and 35–40, and the new Ten Commandments for the covenant in Exod. 34 now take up eight chapters of preparation in order for the priests to *come near* to the LORD. To put the matter another way, ever-increasing ritual acts and personnel layers progressively put Israel at a distance from the LORD. And it does nothing to make them *be* holy!

All the instructions in Lev. 1–8 lead to this moment. Will Aaron or Moses be able to enter the LORD's presence? Will the provisions to *come near* work? Will Aaron make it out alive? Leviticus 9:4 indicates that after all the necessary preparations, this is the day that the LORD will appear to them. The anticipation and anxiety have not been this high since the scene in Exod. 19! The entire congregation *comes near* to the tent of meeting and stands before the LORD while they await the appearance of the glory of the LORD (Lev. 9:5–6). Aaron, of course, must *bring near* an offering and make atonement for himself and the people (9:7). With grave fanfare, Aaron does according to all that the LORD commanded Moses, tossing blood on the altar, reminiscent of the covenant ritual in Exod. 24:6, 8 (Lev. 9:12, 18). Then Moses and Aaron enter the tent of meeting, come out, and bless the people, and the glory of the LORD appears to the people! As if to confirm the acceptance of the ritual, the

---

6. Michael Morales, *Who Shall Ascend the Mountain of the Lord? A Biblical Theology of the Book of Leviticus* (Downers Grove, IL: Apollos/InterVarsity, 2015), 124.

fire of the LORD consumes the offering and fat. When the people see it, they shout and fall on their faces. Will this ritual be enough? Will the people obey the LORD, and will he accompany them on their way to the promised land?

Unfortunately, the trouble is just beginning. Without interruption, Aaron's sons put strange fire in their censers to try to *come near* to the LORD in a way that "he did not command them" (Lev. 10:1). Just as the fire had come out from the LORD and consumed the offering of Moses and Aaron, so now fire comes out from the LORD and consumes Aaron's sons, killing them before the LORD (10:2). Spoken by Moses, the LORD's response may seem harsh but reveals the purpose of the entire episode: "When someone comes near to me, I will be treated as holy; before all people, I will be glorified" (10:3). The word "come near" is the key word in Leviticus. Everything is oriented around this idea of *coming near* to the LORD. The ritual is intended to make holy the priests, the vessels, the clothing, and the tabernacle so that Moses, Aaron, and his sons can come near. But all must be done in the way that the LORD has commanded. It remains the LORD's purpose to dwell among his people, but it will be on his terms—as communicated by Moses—not on theirs. Although the tabernacle meets with initial success, the rituals are a laborious process that must be carried out in detail. The remainder of the chapter reiterates that coming near to the LORD requires careful obedience.

Leviticus 11–15 continues the mass of ritual and legal code that Israel must perform to come near to the LORD and to make something holy to the LORD. Leviticus 11 concerns the clean and unclean, which 10:10 initiates. The LORD's own holiness demands that the Israelites distinguish between clean and unclean (11:44–45). Leviticus 12–15 concerns other issues of cleanness and uncleanness before Lev. 16 returns to the death of Aaron's sons, indicating that not even Aaron can enter the holy place within the veil, or he too will die! In the cloud over the mercy seat, the LORD will appear. The remainder of the chapter details a new laborious process for making everything holy, so that once a year Aaron can enter into the sanctuary of the holy place to make atonement (16:33–34).

One might think that after such a process, people will be free to serve the LORD. But instead, Lev. 17–25, 27 present other law codes addressing a long list of items: proper slaughter, sexual sins, codes of conduct, child sacrifice, mediums, necromancers, blemishes, holy things, feasts, oils, breads, blasphemy, lex talionis, sabbaths, property, and slaves.[7] After these chapters,

---

7. The references are as follows: proper slaughter (Lev. 17), sexual deviancy (Lev. 18), and "Be holy for I am holy" (Lev. 19:2). For different codes of conduct, see offering children to Molech, mediums, adultery, sexual sin, clean/unclean, holy to the LORD (Lev. 20); blemishes (Lev. 21); holy things (Lev. 22; note that *holy* occurs 3× and *profane* 1× in Lev. 22:2 and 22:32); feasts (Lev. 23); oils, breads, blasphemy, death penalty/lex talionis (Lev. 24); sabbaths, property, slaves (Lev. 25).

Lev. 26:3 begins with an "if" reminiscent of the encounter in Exod. 19, but Lev. 26 adds a frightening proposition: "If you walk in my statutes, keep my commandments, and do them," then the LORD will bless them (26:3–13), but if not, 26:14–39 details the many curses that the LORD will bring on them. He will remember Abraham's covenant only if they confess their contrary ways (26:40–45). Leviticus 27 closes out the book by returning to its opening theme: in order to *come near* (*qarav*) with things that *bring near* (*qorban*), particular codes concerning vows and valuations must be enacted. Will this increasing mass of regulation be enough for the LORD to dwell in the midst of Israel on their journey to the promised land?

Who May Enter? (Num. 1–10)

Without explanation, the book of Numbers opens with Moses in the tent of meeting (Num. 1:1)! Were the huge mass of regulations, the laborious process on the Day of Atonement, and the threat of curses for disobedience enough to grant Moses entrance into the tent of meeting? Will Aaron and his sons be able to enter? Will the remainder of the Israelites be able to serve the LORD in his presence?

Numbers 1 reports the census taken for all the tribes, but the tribe of Levi is not listed among the Israelites. Instead, they are to keep and care for the tabernacle (1:47, 50–54). No one from the other tribes is allowed to "come near" to the tent![8] If they do so, they are to be put to death. The other Israelite tribes are to camp around the tent of meeting, while the Levites are in its midst as they journey (2:17). The Levites will report to Aaron to serve him; an entire tribe will mediate between Israel and the high priest! No one else can get close to the LORD's presence. Numbers 3:6–13 reiterates that the Levites belong to the LORD to come near and keep charge of the tabernacle because the LORD redeemed every firstborn of Israel when he smote the firstborn of Egypt, but any outsider attempting to come near will be put to death (3:10, 38)! This frightening threat doesn't sound like dwelling in the presence of the LORD. One of the Levite families, the Kohathites, will care for the holy of holies and all the holy things, but if they even touch them, they will die (4:15, 17–20).

Numbers 5–6 gives regulations concerning impurity, jealousy, and Nazarite vows for people to come to a priest who will "bring near" the thing that "brings near." In this way, the priest atones for their sin or makes them holy. Numbers 7 details the completion of the tabernacle, its anointing, and the "making holy" of all its furnishings. The chiefs of the people "come near" with a great many

---

8. Num. 1:51; 3:10, 38; 16:10; 18:4, 7. The Hebrew word *zar* has to do with an unauthorized person or stranger in a relationship. See the use of *zar* in Lev. 10:1; 22:10, 12, 13.

animals to bring their "brought-near" thing. But now they bring them to the Levites; they themselves are unable to come near to the tent of meeting. And in the end, only Moses enters the tent of meeting to hear the voice of the LORD.

Numbers 8 concerns the cleansing of the Levites so that they can render service for the tabernacle and atone for the people. They are needed to do service in the tabernacle and make atonement so that no plague will come among the Israelites who approach the holy place (Num. 8:19). Israel is certainly on a journey, but will they ever arrive in God's presence? Will the promised land provide that place?

Not only do they walk toward the promised land, but they increasingly receive more ritual and code to make them holy, and more cultic personnel stand between the Israelites and the presence of the LORD. The movement of the cloud and fire prompts the Israelites to journey or to stay, while special trumpets are made to give warnings or commemorate special events. Finally, in Num. 10:11–12, the cloud lifts, but the people of Israel wander in the same pattern of rebellion that occurred before the one year stay on Mount Sinai. The legal codes have had no effect on their holiness! What is more, the invitation for the entire nation to meet with the LORD seems a dream at this point. While Numbers presents the Levites as ministering to Aaron and taking care of the tabernacle, any wrong move means death, and they cannot enjoy God's presence. Only Moses can meet with God. Although a great deal of ritual and priestly functions have been enacted to make the people holy, it has not worked.

Unfortunately, the last chapters of Numbers offer little hope. Because of Phinehas's actions, Num. 25 establishes the Levites as those who stand between the LORD and the people after the people played the harlot at Baal Peor. Corresponding to the census that opened the book of Numbers, Num. 26 records a second census. With little mention of the tabernacle or the tent of meeting, attention turns toward dividing the promised land (Num. 26–27). Even so, Israel must still bring near their offerings to the Levites so that they can offer their "bring-near" things (Num. 28–30). Along the way, the Israelites must do battle with past enemies and prepare for the battles of the promised land. They remain on a journey until they arrive at their ultimate destination, and the rest of Numbers offers instructions for their boundaries, cities, and inheritances there.

THEOLOGY and PRACTICE

This chapter covers the large textual unit of Exodus–Numbers. What have we discovered? The LORD chose Moses to deliver, mediate, and give his word to the Israelites. Whether Moses's portrayal in this subunit rises to the level of typology, he certainly uniquely represents God to the people and the people to God. In the end, Moses rebels and requests that the LORD appoint a man to shepherd the congregation (Num. 27:14–17). Moses dies outside the promised land, and Joshua becomes that man according to Numbers and Joshua. But in Deuteronomy, Moses does become the type of one the people of God still await.

The journey also demonstrates the people's failure to grow in holiness. They continually contend against Moses and the LORD, even though the rituals and legislation continue to accumulate. The commands do not improve their holiness and do not bring them into the LORD's presence. If such commands did not work for Israel, they also have no agency for us in their current form. The legal code was not intended as an absolute or eternal codification of stipulations to enter into covenant with the LORD. Instead, they show us that the Sinai covenant was temporary and poorly suited to compel Israel to obedience. The end of Numbers leaves the reader wondering what it will take for God's people to reflect his holiness and to dwell in his presence. The tabernacle, while certainly attempting to make provision for the LORD to dwell among his people, remains laborious, life-threatening, and ill-suited as a permanent measure to accomplish its purpose. The reader awaits a more permanent solution, one that returns us to the invitation in Exod. 19 or even Gen. 2.

11

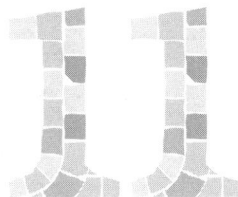

Two Covenants or One?
(Deut. 1–31)

Deuteronomy contains Moses's first-person reflection on many of the events that transpire from Exodus through Numbers as he and the Israelites stand at the border to the promised land. He also recasts the legal code as they prepare to enter the land of promise. In a way, he presents lessons for the Israelites to learn based on the past, but he also discusses at least two different covenants, the second of which has important implications for the future people of God due to its theological foundation and innovative formulation.

Israel's Relationship to the Sinai/Horeb Covenant (Deut. 1–5)

Deuteronomy 1:1–5 provides the outer frame to Moses's words in which "he begins to explain this law" (1:5). But he doesn't take up legal codes just yet. Rather, the remainder of Deut. 1–3 focuses on the rebellion of the first generation from Egypt and Israel's defeat of the kings after they journeyed from Sinai, reminiscent of Numbers. Moses makes clear that all the men of the first generation died except for Caleb (Deut. 1:34–35; 2:14–16). He also references the covenant the LORD cut with them at Sinai (Horeb) when he gave them the Ten Commandments (4:13, 23). The LORD made this covenant with them at that time, Moses says, but also with those now standing with Moses

some thirty-eight years after the incident of the burning mountain when the
LORD spoke from the midst of the fire (2:14). According to Deut. 5:1–26,
this incident was the occasion in Exod. 20:18–21 when they were afraid and
asked Moses to speak with God so that they would not die. They told Moses
at that time, "Go near and hear all that the LORD our God says and speak
to us all that the LORD our God says to you, and *we will hear it and we will
do it*" (Deut. 5:27). What the people promised in Exodus, they failed to do.
Will this generation finally listen to Moses's words and do them? Moses will
return to this statement about *hearing and doing* at the end of Deuteronomy
with a solution quite unlike any other.

Israel's Uncircumcision and Rebellion (Deut. 6–28)

Deuteronomy 6–28 contains Moses's exhortation to the Israelites to adhere
to the LORD's commands when they go into the land. He begins with "the
commandment" in Deut. 6:1—that is, the "statutes and judgments" that the
LORD commanded him to teach them, beginning with the so-called greatest
commandment to love the LORD with all their heart, their soul, and their
might. With great encouragement—and reminiscent of stories from Egypt,
Sinai, and the wilderness—Moses reminds his hearers of the LORD's commitment to them and their need to obey. But he also repeatedly reminds them
of their own rebellion, how they were "stiff-necked" and close to destruction
except for his intercession and the LORD's mercy (Deut. 9:6, 7, 13, 23–24).
Moses exhorts his hearers again in Deut. 10:12 to fear, love, and serve the LORD
with all their heart and soul. But one gets the impression that Moses knows
a deeper problem besets the Israelites: the uncircumcision of their hearts! In
10:16 he commands: "Circumcise the foreskin of your heart and do not be
stiff-necked any longer!" Is this even within their power to accomplish? Is the
Sinai covenant with its many laws not enough then?

Unfortunately, Moses has seen their rebellion and stiff-necked ways for as
long as he has known them; nothing has reformed them to that current day
(Deut. 31:27). He reminds them again of all the LORD did in Egypt and the wilderness before adding blessings and curses to compel them to obey (Deut. 11).
In chapters 12–26 Moses then turns to yet another law code reminding them of
how to act when they enter the land. This code itself concludes in Deut. 27–28
with more rituals upon entrance into the land as well as blessings if they obey,
but a number of horrific curses are invoked if they fail to obey (28:15–68). It
feels like we already covered this territory in Exodus and Numbers. Will it be
any different this time? Will Israel *hear* the words of the LORD and *do* them?

A New Covenant (Deut. 29–30)

The Covenant in Addition to the Covenant at Sinai

Deuteronomy 29:1 begins, "These are the words of the covenant that the LORD commanded Moses to make with the sons of Israel in the land of Moab, *besides* the covenant that he had made with them at Horeb."[1] Although some have argued that this verse indicates a covenant renewal, the word "besides" declares that this covenant is in addition to the covenant made at Sinai. As we will see, it is not merely a renewal of the covenant of legal codes made in Exod. 19–Num. 10. Obviously, he already "made" (past tense) the covenant at Sinai decades earlier, so what covenant is this? Does it refer to all the coaxing and additional stipulations from Deut. 4–28, or does it refer to the upcoming proclamation in Deut. 29–30?

The verse numbered Deut. 29:1 in our English Bibles is actually the last verse of Deut. 28 in the Hebrew, which suggests that it concludes the discussion from chapters 4–28. By placing it at the start of Deut. 29, English versions suggest that the verse refers to the upcoming chapters. The fact that it begins in the same way as Deut. 1:1, "These are the words . . ." may also lead us to conclude that the English versions are correct in having it open a new section in Deuteronomy. More convincing, however, are the many references to "covenant" in Deut. 29:1–15 and 30:1–14 that refer to a future covenant he enjoins them to enter, which has not yet been realized. Moses says in Deut. 29:1, 11–12 that he is making this covenant right then! The Sinai covenant was clearly in the past. The language in Deut. 6–7 demonstrates that the Sinai covenant was made and has ongoing implications for those with whom the LORD made that covenant—namely, Israel. Those implications and stipulations are put forward to Moses's audience in Deut. 4–28 and they return in 29:16–29 and 30:15–33:29. In contrast, the covenant references in 29:1–15 and 30:1–14 pertain to those standing there before Moses *and* to a future people who are not there.[2] What do we know about the covenant references in Deut. 6–7?

The Sinai Covenant's Ongoing Requirements for the Israelites (Deut. 6–7)

The LORD expects the Israelites to keep his testimonies, statutes, judgments, and commandments stemming from the Sinai covenant that he has *already cut* with them (Deut. 4:23; 5:2–3). Deuteronomy 6:25 concludes, "And it will be righteousness for us if we are careful to do all these commandments

---

1. Horeb is a specific place on Mount Sinai.
2. I will say more about this below, but Deut. 29:14–15 explicitly mentions those who stand among them then and people who are not there with them.

before the LORD our God as he commanded us." The conditional "if" requires "careful" obedience to all the commandments. We already know, however, from Deut. 9:4–6 that they will not be able to say, "Because of our righteousness the LORD has done these things." Moses goes on to explain that when they enter the land, they must not make a covenant with the surrounding nations and serve their gods, because God has chosen them to be a holy (*qadosh*) people and a "special possession" (7:6). These descriptions are the exact words of Exod. 19:5–6, indicating the ongoing expectations of the covenant the LORD made with this generation (Deut. 4:13, 23, 5:1–3). Moreover, Deut. 7:9–12 indicates that it is "because you *hear* these judgments, keeping them to *do* them, that the LORD will keep with you the covenant and lovingkindness that he swore to your fathers." The commandments pertaining to the ongoing demands of the Sinai covenant from Exod. 19, reaffirmed in Exod. 24 and 34, are contained in Deut. 4–28. What about the "covenant besides the covenant" in Deut. 29–30?

This New Covenant's Impact on the Heart

Besides the contrasting time orientations of the Sinai covenant and the "covenant besides the covenant," Deut. 29:1–15 and 30:1–14 show that the two are conceptually different. Despite all that the LORD has done for Israel, something is still missing. The "heart" is an important topic in Deuteronomy, with Moses and the LORD often urging Israel to engage the heart. Deuteronomy 10:16 expresses the issue clearly: "Circumcise the foreskin of your heart and do not be stiff-necked any longer!" Clearly something at the core of their being is wrong. The same sentiment emerges in Deut. 29:4 when Moses says that despite the LORD's past actions, to that day he has "not given them a heart to know, eyes to see, and ears to hear." The LORD's future action toward his people will remedy this precise problem. But how?

The covenant in Deut. 30 is conceptually set in contrast to the one at Mount Sinai and functions differently from the Sinai covenant. This point will become clearer in Deut. 30:6, but the author consistently points out the negative side of the Sinai covenant. As we saw in the narrative frame around the legal codes in Exodus–Numbers, the Sinai covenant did not produce the faith and obedience needed to dwell in the LORD's presence. The LORD knew that they would break the Sinai covenant, saying in Deut. 31:20, "For when I have brought them into the land flowing with milk and honey, which I swore to give to their fathers, and they have eaten and are full and grown fat, they will turn to other gods and serve them, and despise me and break my covenant." Moses himself reiterates in 31:27, "For I know how rebellious and stubborn you are. Behold, even today while I am yet alive with you, you have been rebellious against the LORD. How much more after my death!" These threats and many more throughout the book show that the LORD and Moses have no expectation that the Sinai covenant will last. The people will break it because the Sinai covenant does not treat their "heart" problem. So what was the purpose of the Sinai covenant?

The Sinai covenant was made with external stipulations. It is significant that they came on tablets of stone; they were external to the people. The LORD gave these stipulations because the people needed to be taught how to approach him safely on their journey to the land and how to behave in a way that would keep them safe and healthy. But clearly these codes did not provide the enablement to empower them to love the LORD and dwell in his presence. The people needed something that treated their whole being, something internal to them. What sort of covenant would do this, and when would it emerge? Would only leaders such as Moses or the high priest participate in the glory of this covenant, or would women and foreigners get to participate?

A Covenant for Anyone

Just as one might expect, Moses begins in Deut. 29:10 with the elders, the leaders, and officers, indeed, the men of Israel, but verse 11 quickly adds that women and children will also participate in the benefits of this covenant. Even the foreigner in their midst is able to enter this covenant! Surprisingly, Moses says in verses 14–15 that the covenant is not just for those who are there with him that day but also for those who are not there! Can anyone participate in this covenant? Even though the covenant is also for those who are *not* there, Moses clearly wants his immediate audience to enter into this covenant. Even though those standing there had participated in the Sinai covenant, this was something new, a covenant they had not yet entered. Deuteronomy 29:12 makes this clear: "*so that you may enter* into the covenant of the LORD your God and his oath." Not only this, but verse 13 suggests that this covenant will distinctly establish them as children of Abraham: "*in order to* establish you today to be his people and he to be your God as he spoke to you and swore to your fathers, to Abraham, Isaac, and Jacob." In other words, just as those who perished in the wilderness would not enter the land, the people in Deut. 29 have not yet entered into this covenant. Moses seeks to compel them that day to enter it, along with those not there that day. What about those who fail to heed this covenant offer? What will happen to them?

Judgment Under the Sinai Covenant

Deuteronomy 29:16–29 addresses the man, woman, or tribe who fails to take these words seriously. If their heart turns away that very day, the LORD will not forgive them and will put on them all the curses written in that book, casting them into another land! Before they are even in the land, Moses warns them that they will be cast out of it.

Deuteronomy 30 begins with this same perspective: "And it will be when all these things come upon you, the blessing and the curse, which I have set before you, and you will call them to mind in all the nations where the LORD your God has driven you . . ." Several important factors emerge in this verse. The first is that it clearly begins with a future tense, "And it will be," and proceeds to discuss a distant possibility. When is this future period? The time "when [the blessings and the curses] come upon you." What blessings and curses? The blessings and curses listed in Deut. 11 and 28. Historically and biblically speaking, the worst of these came in the early sixth century BC when Babylon exiled the elites from Jerusalem and a decade later destroyed the city, apparently negating Israel's central promises of land, temple, and king. From Moses's vantage point, this destruction was 750 years in the future! From the viewpoint of Deut. 30, the covenant will not be enacted anytime soon.

The last half of Deut. 30:1 is even more dramatic than the first. Moses says that they will "call them to mind in all the nations where the LORD your God has driven you." After a long journey through the wilderness and the first generation already dead, while still awaiting the fulfillment of God's promise to Abraham, Moses warns the nation that they will be driven from their land, and not just by anyone. God himself will drive them from the promised land. Verse 2 contains the same verb as "to call to mind" (*shuv*) in Deut. 30:1, "And you will return [*shuv*] to the LORD your God and hear his voice." The "calling to mind" and "returning to the LORD" is much more than a relocation. This return brings with it a "listening to his voice with all your heart and all your soul." How will such a feat take place? This is the kind of obedience that the LORD requires of them but they fail to produce.

Restoration and the Promise to Abraham

Deuteronomy 30:3 foretells an even greater mystery. After they are exiled among other nations, the LORD will "return them from captivity." Moses uses the verb "to return" [*shuv*] for the third verse in a row, this time indicating a restoration from some future captivity. In this future period, the LORD will have compassion on them, return (*shuv*) them, and gather them from all the peoples where he had dispersed them. Even if they are at the "end of heaven," the LORD will gather them from there (30:4). This "return from captivity" is the same mantra that appears in Jeremiah's prophecy of the restoration to Jerusalem seventy years after Babylon has sacked the city and temple. Later he and others speak of a worldwide restoration![3] Deuteronomy 30:5 associates this return with the Abrahamic covenant, saying, "The LORD your God will bring you to the land that your fathers possessed, and you will possess it." This statement would have been quite bewildering to Moses's audience, since they were not even in the land yet. Moreover, as noted above, the issue here is not primarily their location but their heart's disposition. Because it is portrayed as Moses's speech, the only fathers who had possessed land at that point were Abraham, Isaac, and Jacob. (They had purchased their burial plots.) God will do good to them and multiply them more than their fathers. This "restoration" cannot be immediate, of course, because they have not yet been driven from the land. As they stand on the edge of the Jordan River before crossing into the promised land, Moses already envisions them entering the land, being driven from the land, and returning to the land. Can this pledge be merely another iteration of the land promise to Abraham?

Although Moses seems to be speaking of only a return to the land, Deut. 30:6 demonstrates the innovative and far-reaching content of Moses's speech. The problem since the garden has been obedience. Through narratives, patterns, and content, this theme intensifies in Exodus through Numbers. Deuteronomy highlights the issue through the narrative of the golden calf, attention to idolatry, the spies' unbelief, and the Israelites' contentions with Moses. The author has made clear that something must be done that the Israelites cannot do themselves. The LORD must do something to their innermost being. He must act upon their heart: "The LORD your God will circumcise your heart and the heart of your seed, to love the LORD your God with all your heart and with all your soul in order that you may live." This action is one that the LORD takes upon himself to produce in his people a love for God, and he does so for the sake of their very lives! But how can the LORD circumcise a heart?

Circumcision of the Heart

Circumcision of the heart is a metaphor that combines the sign of the covenant given to Abraham with a "cutting" of an individual's inmost being, leading to love for and submission to the LORD. The LORD is the one who will do this. He will "circumcise" their hearts. Moses's statement in verse 5 that

---

3. English versions: Jer. 29:14; 30:3, 18; 31:23; 32:44; 33:7, 11; 48:47; 49:6, 39; Ezek. 16:53; 29:14; 39:25; Hosea 6:11; Joel 3:1; Amos 9:14; Zeph. 2:7; 3:20; Pss. 14:7; 53:6; 85:1; Job 42:10; Lam. 2:14.

they will possess "the land that your fathers possessed" and that the LORD will "do good to you and multiply you more than your fathers" underscores the blessing the LORD made to Abraham to "multiply your seed like the stars of the heavens and the sand which is on the seashore, and your seed will possess the gate of their enemies" (Gen. 22:17–18). This covenant in which the LORD circumcises the hearts of his people is the author's last word on what constitutes the LORD's covenant with Abraham. Genesis tells the story of God's promise to Abraham and of circumcision as its accompanying sign. Now at the end of the Pentateuch, the author invests circumcision and God's covenant promise to Abraham with its intended content. God will someday take action on an individual's heart—regardless of gender, social class, and nationality—so that they can obey with their full being and live faithfully in the land. From the author's perspective, the sign of circumcision points the reader to this future act of God when he will enliven his people so that they can obey him and remain "in the land." Perhaps most provocatively, the recognition that Israel still needs to be circumcised in order to love God and live indicates to the reader that physical ethnicity is not the primary qualification for a life lived in obedience to God. God himself will act to ensure their devotion. So what about the many stipulations in the Pentateuch? What does Deuteronomy say about the commandments, judgments, and statutes?

The Word That Is Near, Unlike the Commandments

Deuteronomy 30:7–15 returns to the issue of these stipulations. Verses 7–10 associate this new act of God with his application of "oaths" on their enemies. On the surface, this future action appears to refer to the curses written in Deuteronomy, but the word "oath" first emerges in 29:11–20, when Moses urged his audience to enter this covenant. The writer apparently envisions more than those curses, possibly even an unwillingness to enter this covenant.[4] Moses also returns to the many commandments and statutes (30:10) that his audience will now obey. God will make them prosperous because they will obey him with all their heart and all their soul. This new ability to obey comes into focus as the commandments and statutes become a single "commandment" in Deut. 30:11, a formulation also seen in 6:1, where Moses says, "This commandment, the statutes and judgments that the LORD your God commanded to teach you to do in the land . . ." But in Deut. 30 after the circumcision of the heart, "this commandment" soon becomes a "word" set in contrast to statutes and commandments (30:11–14). What is unique about "this word"?

4. See the usage of the Hebrew word translated "curse/oath" in Ezek. 16:59; 17:13, 16, 19.

This word is different from any other expression of "commandments." Deuteronomy 30:11–14 says: "For this commandment that I command you today is not too miraculous for you, and it is not too distant. It is not in heaven, to say, 'Who will go up for us to heaven to receive it for us, that we may hear it and do it?' It is not across the sea, to say, 'Who will cross over the sea for us to receive it for us, that we may hear it and do it?' Rather, the word will be very near you, in your mouth, and in your heart, to do it." The author finally clarifies what will be different in this future experience of a circumcised heart. On the day Moses is speaking to them, written stipulations remain in force to reveal what they must do on the other side of the Jordan, but a future day holds a different experience. Deuteronomy 29:29 describes it as a secret thing, and 30:11 describes what "this commandment" is not: it is not "too miraculous." Most English versions translate the Hebrew word underlying "miraculous" as "difficult" or "hard," but this Hebrew root is used to describe the miracles of the plagues in Exod. 3:20 and 15:11. This future work of God will not be like the exodus miracles that he performed through Moses for the world to see.

The conclusion of Deut. 30:11 adds yet another contrast: "It will not be distant." Four times Exodus describes the people's position as "distant" when the LORD appears.[5] Only Moses is able to approach God (Exod. 20:21). Their disposition and the increasing number of rituals and legal codes put a distance between them and the LORD. This commandment, however, will not be like that. To further explain what he means, the writer continues in Deut. 30:12: "It is not in heaven, to say, 'Who will go up for us to heaven to receive it for us, that we may *hear* it and *do* it?'" This allusion likewise looks back on the incident in Exod. 20:22, where the LORD spoke to them from the top of the mountain, "from the heavens." Deuteronomy 30:12 also indicates that someone had to "go up" for them "to take it" so that they can "*hear* it and *do* it." Moses "went up" to meet the LORD on the mountain no fewer than ten times for different durations, receiving instructions to bring back to the people, and they witnessed his ascent into the cloud.[6] But this commandment will not be like that situation. No one will need to go up to get this word and bring it down for them to *hear* it and *do* it.

Deuteronomy 30:13 provides yet another contrast. This contrast alludes to God's miraculous deliverance of the Israelites from Egypt. "It is not across the sea, to say, 'Who will cross over the sea for us to receive it for us,

5. Exod. 20:18, 21; 24:1; 33:7.
6. Exod. 19:3, 24; 24:1, 9, 12, 13, 15, 18; 32:30; 34:4.

that we may *hear* it and *do* it?'" This commandment will not be like the awe-inspiring deliverance that Israel experienced when God delivered them from the pursuing Egyptian army, after which Moses received instruction for them to do. The identical three clauses concluding verse 12 and verse 13 emphasize the point of the contrasts. Moses had to go up the mountain and cross the sea to obtain the laws and statutes. Moreover, each incident involved making them *hear* the commandments so that they would *do* them. Whatever act this commandment is compared with, it will not be like those awe-inspiring events.

What exactly is this commandment? Unlike each of those incidents, this commandment is unique. Deuteronomy 30:14 simply says, "Rather, the word will be very near you, in your mouth, and in your heart, to *do* it." Unlike the "commandment" in Deut. 6:1, this commandment is merely a word, and the word's nearness is the opposite of a "distance." It is so near to you and so much a part of you because it is in your mouth and in your heart! And because it comes from your heart, you will "*do* it," the exact verb that concludes verses 12 and 13. Unlike these other great acts of God, this future circumcision of the heart will result in a change in the inner person.

Blessing or Curse?

The remainder of Deut. 30 returns to Moses's immediate audience and the choice he is setting before them "this day." Will they choose life and blessing or curse and death? Deuteronomy 31 provides the answer. Even though Moses appoints Joshua to lead them into the land, eventually they will abandon the Sinai covenant, breaking it and committing idolatry (31:16). Moses writes a song as a witness against them (31:19), puts the book of the law in the ark as a witness against them (31:26), and even calls the heavens and the earth as a witness against them (31:28). Moses's own words testify that they have been rebellious and stiff-necked "today" while he is alive, so why wouldn't they be so after his death (31:27)? Verse 29 then returns to the future, "Because I know after my death, you will indeed act corruptly and turn aside from the way that I commanded you, and evil will meet you in the end of the days because you did evil in the eyes of the LORD to provoke him with the work of your hands." The "evil" that will meet them refers not only to the idolatry in 29:18 and 31:18 but also to the "blessing and the curse" of 30:1. From Moses's perspective, the idolatrous breaking of the Sinai covenant will usher in a period of great evil. It will be in this "end of the days" that the LORD will circumcise the hearts of his people that they may obey and dwell again in the land.

THEOLOGY and PRACTICE

Deuteronomy 29–30 contains Moses's exhortation to the second generation of Israelites to walk in the updated stipulations of the Sinai Covenant and at the same time to look to a time in the end of the days when the LORD will transform their inner disposition so that they love and obey him. The implications of this action in this future time are breathtaking.

First, the circumcision of the heart means that mere ethnicity is not enough to love and obey the LORD and remain in the land. The author certainly intends the Israelites' future offspring to partake in the circumcision of the heart, but the fact remains that the LORD is the only one who executes it, while some may not experience it (Deut. 29:18). Significantly, according to Deut. 29:10–11, 14–15, men, women, children, foreigners, and even those "not here with us today" are adjured to enter into this covenant. Can the LORD not choose those on whom he will have compassion? Also, not to obtain "the circumcision of the heart" means that one remains "rebellious and stiff-necked," leading to disobedience, idolatry, being dispossessed of the land, and being sent away from the LORD's presence and blessing. From Deut. 30, one cannot fully explain all that the metaphor of the circumcised heart means, but it does lead to a love for the LORD and obedience to his word. From Moses's perspective, this enablement is the good news that the Israelites need. Although God has given them his stipulations out of care for them, they have been unwilling and, in a sense, unable to obey (Deut. 29:4). But this future act of God will enliven them to love the LORD and live in his presence.

Although Deuteronomy does not contain a full description of how the metaphor will take place or what all it entails, it does describe a particular time, the end of the days. The Pentateuch has already described this time frame as the time during which the law-giving lion king from the tribe of Judah will come, and the obedience of the nations will be his (Gen. 49:1, 10; Num. 24:7–9, 16–19; Deut. 33:21). The Greek translation of the OT translates "the end of the days" as the *eschaton tōn hēmerōn*, the eschaton. For those of us who believe that Jesus fulfills the prophecy of the lion king, it follows that the end, the eschaton, has begun with the emergence of Jesus, son of Judah, son of David. His emergence indicates that *the last days* have been inaugurated, and that the LORD will circumcise every "seed" that enters into the covenant. Whether man or woman, Jew or gentile, this circumcision will bring about an entrance into a new relationship with the LORD and a "restoration from captivity" to the land of promise. What does a restoration from captivity look like?

Other texts and communities also look forward to the restoration. Almost every OT book after Kings (in the *TaNaK* order) contains the phrase "restore from captivity" or "restoration" to the land, or can be understood as a function of waiting for this restoration. Jeremiah 30–33 and Ezek. 36–37 clarify more of what the restoration entails, whether it be a "new covenant" written on the heart or God's spirit "given in your midst."[7] Another well-known community not too far from the shores of the Dead Sea still awaited restoration in their time, even though they were already back in the land. They read Deuteronomy and looked forward to a restoration.[8] Their own scrolls remind us of this.[9]

Another community of God's people also looked forward to the restoration. In Acts 1:6 the disciples ask Jesus, "Lord, will you at this time restore the kingdom to Israel?" His answer in 1:7–8 is telling: He does not say yes, as if it would come in a moment. Instead, they are to leave the timing to the Father, but they will receive power from the Holy Spirit and will be his witnesses, starting there and proceeding to the "end of the land." The apostle Paul mentions Deut. 30 in Rom. 10:8 when talking about the righteousness from faith: "But what does it say? 'The word is near you, in your mouth and in your heart'—this is the word of faith that we preach." This word is your confession that you believe in the resurrection of the Lord Jesus, expressed by Paul in Rom. 10:9 as "if you confess with your mouth . . . and believe in your heart." It is an internal change in perspective that produces a love for God and love for his people.[10]

Why then do we not yet experience the fullness of this obedient life to which God has enlivened us? It is because the last days have not yet drawn to an end. Trouble still abounds. We are like refugees in a land yet to be cleansed (Ezek. 38–39). Although we have his Spirit and faith, we are still dealing with the effect of a corrupt creation. Paul reasons in Rom. 8:19–24, saying,

> For the longing of creation awaits the revelation of the sons of God. For the creation was subjected in futility, not itself willingly, but because of him who subjected it in hope that the creation itself will be set free from its bondage of corruption into the freedom and glory of the children of God. We know that the whole creation groans and suffers as in the pains of childbirth up to the present time. And not just that, but we ourselves, who have the firstfruits

7. Jer. 31:31, 33; Ezek. 36:27; 37:14.

8. Jason A. Staples, *The Idea of Israel in Second Temple Judaism* (Cambridge: Cambridge University Press, 2021), 259–87.

9. Lawrence Schiffman, *Reclaiming the Dead Sea Scrolls* (New York: Doubleday, 1995), 203–21.

10. The NT refers to these matters often, but consider Acts 2:1–36; Col. 2:9–14; 2 Pet. 1:3–4.

of the Spirit, groan inwardly, awaiting adoption to sonship, the redemption of our bodies.

God has saved us. We know the Spirit's work in our lives and hope in that day about which the prophet Isaiah writes when we will dwell in the new heavens and the new earth, and all flesh will worship the LORD (Isa. 66:22–23).

12

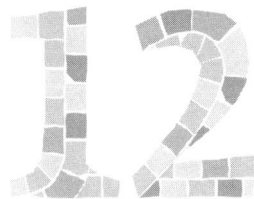

A Witness Against You
(Deut. 32)

Deuteronomy 32's song is a witness against Israel that they will turn to other gods after entering the promised land (31:19–22). Unfortunately, neither Moses nor the LORD expect that Israel will remain devoted to God. Before the song, Moses speaks of the future—a time he calls "the end of the days" (31:29)—when the LORD will carry out his plan in response to Israel's idolatry. Although Moses enjoins the people to keep the commandments of the LORD and partake of his covenant, he has seen their character since Egypt and knows nothing has changed. What will the LORD do, given his expectation that the people will turn away?

Besides Moses's song witnessing against the people, the LORD also calls heaven and earth as witnesses against Israel.[1] Deuteronomy 31:28–29 says, "Gather to me all the elders of your tribes and your officers and let me speak these words in their ears and call heaven and earth to witness against them. Because I know after my death, you will indeed act corruptly and turn aside from the way that I commanded you, and evil will meet you in the end of the days because you did evil in the eyes of the LORD *to provoke him with the work of your hands.*" Besides the chapter's theme of idolatry, this final clause

---

1. Deuteronomy's genre stems from an ancient covenant formula, which often includes a historical preamble, stipulations, blessings and curses, and witnesses.

reveals an important clue about the song. They have disobeyed the LORD and made him jealous with the idols that they have made with their own hands. Besides the "evil" that will meet them, what else does Deut. 32 envision?

The People's Idolatry

Deuteronomy 32 opens with a call to the heavens and earth to listen. God and his ways are perfect, but his sons have "acted corruptly" (32:5). The LORD alone found Israel in the wilderness and provided for their needs, but Israel grew fat and complacent and forsook God (32:15). Even though he had taken them as his own, they somehow lost sight of that and spurned him. Israel's apostasy begins as gluttony but deteriorates into adultery and idolatry. Five verbs occur in quick succession in Deut. 32:15a, each pointing to Israel's finding of satisfaction in food and plenty, before the verse concludes with two verbs expressing Israel's foolish rejection of their Savior God. Moses often warns Israel against such attitudes before they enter the land (Deut. 6; 8; 11). They know that they are entering a bountiful land, and God warns them lest they forget that he is the one who has given it to them and they instead look to other gods.

Deuteronomy 32:16 commences a string of echoes related to false worship in other passages. Each clause alludes to an incident in which Israel is warned against idolatry or commits it. Verbal associations and puns abound throughout and demonstrate the central theme of idolatry in the chapter and beyond. The passage acts as an intersection where many roads meet, having on and off ramps to a larger road system. The many roads are analogous to numerous situations of idolatry that the Pentateuch addresses. To extend the analogy, the LORD's indictment against Israel is the larger road system, while the destination becomes a partial repudiation of his people, including an interesting twist! Deuteronomy 32:16 begins with the central theme, "They made him jealous with strangers. With abominations they provoked him to jealousy."

The LORD's Jealousy

The notion of jealousy, occurring three times in Deut. 32:16–21, is used in every context of the Ten Commandments where false gods are expressly forbidden because of God's jealousy.[2] The Hebrew verb "made him jealous" is

2. Exod. 20:5; 34:14; and again when the Ten Commandments are reiterated in Deut. 4, 5, and 6.

the verbal parallel to the adjective "jealous" found in these and other passages, including Num. 5, where a husband becomes jealous of his wife. Deuteronomy 32:21 uses this same verbal form, denoting Israel's propensity to make God jealous with other gods, concluding the string of allusions with a plan to kindle Israel's affection.

The word in Deut. 32:16 glossed as "strangers" has to do with an outsider, sometimes referring to a stranger in the marriage bed.[3] Here the term refers to foreign gods that are not related to Israel's covenant-making God, the LORD. God consistently warns Israel not to play the harlot with the gods of other nations (Exod. 34:12–16; Deut. 6:12–15). Any relationship with a foreign nation carried the potential threat of being seduced into worshiping the gods of that nation. The obvious connotation is that Israel has made the LORD jealous with gods that are outside the confines of their covenant with the LORD.

Deuteronomy 32:16 continues, "With abominations they provoked him to jealousy." The term "abomination" also occurs in contexts of idolatry, such as Deut. 27:15: "Cursed is the man who makes an idol or a molten image, an abomination to the LORD."[4] The LORD abhors the idol because it is not a true thing and leads his people away from his work on Israel's behalf as their true God. The verb used in the clause "provoke to jealousy" (*hikh'is*) appears so commonly in so-called Deuteronomistic literature that Samantha Joo has devoted an entire monograph to the verb.[5] This word becomes a shorthand way of expressing how Israel has made idols with their hands and provoked God to jealousy with their images. Joo says, "When קנא [*qana'*, jealous] is used of God against Israel, the nouns as well as the verbal forms occur in contexts involving other gods: God is stirred to jealousy because of Israel's idolatry. If one looks at the context of Deut. 32:21 . . . this is also evident. The idolatrous context of קנא/קנאה [*qana'ah/qana'*, jealous] is crucial in understanding the Hiphil attestations of כעס [*hikh'is*, provoke to jealousy] which occurs primarily in indictments of Israel for their idolatry."[6] Four times in Deuteronomy (4:25; 9:18; 31:29; 32:21) this verb expresses the Israelites' predisposition to provoke the LORD to jealousy by pursuing other gods.[7]

One of these instances, Deut. 9:18, occurs in Moses's description of the golden calf incident. The entire chapter is a rehearsal of the people's rebellious nature, intended to remind them that it is not because of their righteousness

---

3. Jer. 5:19; Ezek. 16:32.

4. See also Deut. 7:25–26; 12:30–31; 13:1–19; 17:2–5; 20:18.

5. Samatha Joo, *Provocation and Punishment: The Anger of God in the Book of Jeremiah and Deuteronomistic Theology* (Berlin: De Gruyter, 2006).

6. Joo, *Provocation and Punishment*, 25.

7. The nominal forms occur in Deut. 32:19, 27.

that the LORD will go before them and dispossess other nations of the land. Referring to the golden calf, 9:7 uses a synonym of "provoke to jealousy" (*hikh'is*) to warn Israel not to forget: "Remember and do not forget how you *provoked to wrath* the LORD your God in the wilderness. From the day you left the land of Egypt until you arrived at this place, you have been rebellious with the LORD." Moses also recounts his intercession for the people in which he gives a summary of the people's sin. He fasted over "[their] sin, when [they] sinned to do evil in the eyes of the LORD to *provoke him to jealousy*" (9:18). This statement—absent from Exod. 32's account of the golden calf incident— demonstrates not only Israel's tendency to worship idols but also how their idolatry moved the LORD to jealousy because they betrayed him for another.

"Provoke to jealousy" also occurs in Deut. 31:29 in association with the end of the days. Calamity will meet Israel because they will do evil in the eyes of the LORD, "provoking him to jealousy with the work of their hands." The four uses of this term "to provoke to jealousy" within Deut. 32 demonstrate the prominence of the notion within the chapter. The provocation by the sons of Israel through their acts of idolatry, specifically the idolatry of the golden calf to which Deut. 9 refers, will cause the LORD to respond in like manner and attempt to provoke them to return to him because of their own jealousy (32:21).

The Enemy Idols

The focus on idolatry continues in Deut. 32:17: "They sacrificed to demons, not a god, gods they did not know, new ones who came recently, whom your fathers were not acquainted with." "Demons" translates a rare Hebrew noun found only in this passage and Ps. 106:37, where the verb "sacrifice" refers to the abhorrent practice of child sacrifice. Though the noun is rare, it suggests some image, perhaps an angelic realm or a "non-god" of the surrounding nations, as the next clause indicates: "not a god, gods they did not know." What is more, the prepositional phrase "to demons" may be related to a curious phrase in the golden calf narrative in Exod. 32:25. There Moses sees that the people "lacked restraint because Aaron had let them loose for derision *from the ones rising against them*." But who are "the ones rising against them"?

In his commentary on Exodus, Brevard Childs questions what exactly the phrase might mean.[8] The Hebrew word underlying the English translation of Exod. 32:25 suggests a wordplay with "demons" in Deut. 32:17. This

---

8. Brevard S. Childs, *The Book of Exodus: A Critical, Theological Commentary*, Old Testament Library (Philadelphia: Westminster, 1974), 570.

type of wordplay is called an athbash, in which a letter is replaced with its corresponding opposite in the alphabetic sequence. In the English alphabet, for example, an *a* (the first letter of the alphabet) would replace a *z* (the last letter of the alphabet), a *b* would replace a *y*, a *c* would replace an *x*, and so on.[9] In this case, the Hebrew letters that correspond to the word "enemies" in Exod. 32:25 spell the word for "demons" in Deut. 32:17.[10] The author uses athbash to connect the worship of the golden calf with the notion of sacrificing to "demons"—that is, to "non-god(s)" and "vanities" (Deut. 32:16, 21).

Not only do they not know these non-gods, but Deut. 32:17 also expresses that they are "new ones who came recently, whom your fathers were not acquainted with." The word translated "not acquainted with" relates to Lev. 17. In Lev. 17:1–9, the LORD speaks to Moses concerning the slaughter of animals. He tells Moses to instruct Aaron, his sons, and the sons of Israel regarding the proper place for sacrificing animals. They must bring their sacrifices to the opening of the tent of meeting to present them to the LORD. This is contrasted with sacrifices to "goat idols" (Lev. 17:7). The verb "to be acquainted with" (*saʿar*) is spelled similarly to the "goat idols" (*saʿir*) and provides another link between Deut. 32 and a passage where idolatry plays a central role.

Leviticus 17 shares other common terminology with Deut. 32 and the golden calf incident in Exod. 32:7–20. The people are no longer to "*sacrifice sacrifices* to goat idols" (Lev. 17:7). The verb "sacrifice" and its corresponding noun "sacrifices" occur together in Exod. 32:8 and Deut. 32:17. This verb is also taken up in God's instructions to Moses in Exod. 34:15, where God warns Moses not to covenant with another nation lest the Israelites *play the harlot* with this nation's gods and *sacrifice* to them. Likewise, Lev. 17:7 portrays their sacrificing to goat idols as "*playing the harlot* after them."[11]

9. In the Hebrew alphabet, the letter aleph (first in the alphabet) corresponds to the letter taw (last in the alphabet), a bet corresponds to a shin, a gimel corresponds to a resh, and so on. An example of this type of wordplay occurs in Jer. 25:26 and 51:41, where the Hebrew word *Sheshach* is understood to represent the corresponding word *Babel*, something the church father Jerome mentions in his Jeremiah commentary. Aaron Demsky, writing about inscriptions found in the biblical city of Aphek, observes, "Jerome, in his commentary on the Book of Jeremiah, accepts the Jewish Hebrew *ʾa-t/b-s* system, which in principle, he states, is similar to the elementary practice in learning the Greek alphabet, i.e. *alpha-omega, beta-psi*." See Aaron Demsky, *Aphek-Antipatris, 1974–1977: The Inscriptions* (Tel Aviv: Tel Aviv University, Institute of Archaeology, 1978), 2:53.

10. For those familiar with the Hebrew alphabet, ב in בקמיהם ("the ones rising against them") corresponds to the ש in the plural term שדים ("demons"). The letter ק in בקמיהם corresponds to the ד in שדים, the letter מ corresponds to the י, and the letter י in בקמיהם corresponds to the final ם in שדים.

11. Numbers 25:1–2 portrays another incident of idolatry using similar words: sacrifice, playing the harlot, and worshiping other gods.

The LORD's Response

Deuteronomy 32:18–20 transitions from Israel's neglect and provocation of the LORD to his action against them. They have forgotten the one who metaphorically "birthed" them (v. 18). Having seen their provocation, verse 19 describes the LORD's contempt for them and how he would "hide [his] face from them and see what their end will be." After all, they are perverse and lack faith (v. 20). What does it mean that the LORD will hide his face from them? Deuteronomy 32:21 explains: "They, they made me jealous with not-a-god. They provoked me to jealousy with their vanities. So I, I will make them jealous with not-a-people. I will provoke them to jealousy with a nation lacking sense." As if to emphasize the themes of "jealous" (*qana'*) and "provoke to jealousy" (*hikh'is*), both root words occur twice in verse 21, whereas they occur only once each in verse 16. The phrase "not a god" that occurred in verse 17 also reappears here. Moreover, the grammar and vocabulary of verse 21's first half mirror the grammar and vocabulary of the second half. It is intended to convey a tit-for-tat response, except for the last parallel element in the verse. They have made him jealous and provoked him with idols that are not true deities. Consequently, corresponding to their actions, he will act. They made him *jealous*; he will make them *jealous*. They *provoked* him to jealousy, so he will also *provoke* them to jealousy. They made him jealous with "not-a-god"; he will make them jealous with "not-a-people." They *provoked* him to jealousy with "vanities," so, emphatically, "with a foolish nation" he will *provoke* them to jealousy. But what does "a foolish nation" mean?

The adjective and underlying verbal root occur in the Pentateuch only here in Deut. 32. Deuteronomy 32:6 calls Israel a "foolish people," explaining this in a parallel line as "not wise." They are corrupt (v. 5). God is a rock, perfect in his ways, the song begins. He has found and provided for Israel (32:10), and they should have known him, but they have neglected and forgotten him (32:18). The adjective often refers to one "who has no perception of ethical and religious claims."[12] What nation will the LORD use to provoke Israel to jealousy? He'll use those who lack any religious and ethical sense, people who have no understanding of the true God like Israel did: the gentiles.

Scholars often suggest that God will "provoke" Israel by bringing a foreign army to defeat them,[13] but that does not match the passage's correlation

---

12. Francis Brown, S. R. Driver, Charles A. Briggs, *The Brown-Driver-Briggs Hebrew and English Lexicon* (reprint, Peabody, MA: Hendrickson, 1996), 614.

13. Gerhard von Rad, *Deuteronomy*, Old Testament Library (Philadelphia: Westminster, 1966), 198; J. G. McConville, *Deuteronomy*, Apollos Old Testament Commentary (Leicester: Apollos, 2002), 456–57.

between the Lord's jealousy at Israel's betrayal and his intention to provoke them to jealousy. And while the subsequent verses include the coming of the "sword" (32:25), God's means of judging Israel extends beyond military conflict. The Lord will allow them to endure many calamities (32:23–24). Conquest and exile will not accomplish God's intent to "provoke them to jealousy." Rather, it will come about when the Lord has compassion on non-Israelites and makes his dwelling among all flesh, not only among Israel (e.g., Jonah; Joel 2:28–31).

The last section of the poem affirms the Lord's uniqueness. Israel has been foolish and pursued non-gods. The Lord is the only God. There is no God besides him, says Deut. 32:39; he "puts to death and makes alive," he "wounds and heals," and no one snatches from his hand. He will bring judgment and will return vengeance upon his enemies, accomplishing that by his arrows and his sword, which will be drunk on blood and consume flesh. However, his people are told to rejoice over his judgment (32:43). And who are his people?

The nations are his people! Deuteronomy 32:43 concludes the poem, "Rejoice, O nations, his people!" Why should they rejoice? Because he will avenge his servants and take vengeance upon his enemies, the next clause answers. The Lord will win! Most English versions add "with"—"Rejoice, O nations, *with* his people"—but there is no preposition in the Hebrew. Rather, the gentile nations are identified as being his people. Though some balk at the idea that the nations would be called God's people, 29:11–15 has already affirmed that the foreigner can enter the covenant. Deuteronomy 30:6 affirms that God seeks a circumcised heart, not a particular ethnicity. Finally, Deut. 32:21 alludes to the Lord's provoking Israel to jealousy by showing interest in another nation, just as they had pursued false gods. Indeed, the nations will also be God's people.

THEOLOGY and PRACTICE

The end of Deuteronomy speaks of a time when the Lord will embrace those from all nations as his covenant people. This should not surprise us. The Pentateuch begins with a universal perspective. Adam and Eve are not Israel, nor is Abraham when he is called. And as certainly as the Israelites are included if they have believed in the Lord, so will others if the Lord circumcises their hearts to love him and obey his commands. The book of Hosea seems to pick up on this theme when Hosea names his child "Not My People" because the Lord said that Israel was not his people, and he would no longer be "I am" to them (Hosea 1:9). Hosea 1:10 (2:1 MT) continues, "Because in the place it was said to them 'You are not my people,' it will be said to them 'Sons of the living God!'" Where had "Not my people" been said?

Apparently, "not-a-people" in Deut. 32:21 attracted Hosea's attention. Similar to the punishment that Deut. 32's song envisions for Israel, so Hosea 2 threatens their judgment. But that's not the last word. Rather, Hosea 2:23 (2:25 MT) indicates that the LORD will say to Not My People, "You are my people," and they will respond, "My God." Regardless of Israel's betrayal and their many days without a king, Hosea 3:5 concludes, "Later, the sons of Israel will return and seek the LORD their God and David their king, and they will be in awe of the LORD and his goodness in the end of the days." Indeed, Israel will be front and center in the worldwide return to the LORD in the end of the days. They too will seek "David, their king" and obey the LORD with their whole heart.

The apostle Paul also cites Hosea in Rom. 9:25–26 to explain God's purpose with the gentiles saying, "As indeed he says in Hosea, 'I will call the one "Not My People" "My People," and her who was not beloved, "Beloved." And it will be in the place where it was said about them, "You are not my people," there they will be called "sons of the living God."'" The gentiles are included in God's plan.

Paul becomes even more explicit later in Romans. In making the case that it was God's plan all along to save gentiles, Paul quotes Deut. 32:21: "But I say, did Israel not understand? First, Moses says, 'I will make you jealous by that which is not a nation, by a nation without understanding I will provoke you'" (Rom. 10:19). Again, in Rom. 11:11, Paul argues, "So I ask, did they stumble in order to fall? By no means! Rather, by their trespass salvation has come to the gentiles in order to make them [Israel] jealous." The LORD elected Abraham and his descendants, through whom his seed would come, and gave them his commandments and oracles. It was an act of grace, and the encouragement of the gospel is theirs, but Abraham's time awaited a later day. His was not the time of the end of the days but the promise of a time when his seed would possess the gates of his enemy. When the seed had conquered death, the LORD would pour out his Spirit on his people, raising them from their watery graves to walk in newness of life. No, the King must come first. Then and only then will the time of the end, the eschaton, begin.

Conclusion

A Prophet like Moses (Deut. 34)

Deuteronomy 34 picks up the narrative thread after the conclusion of the song in Deut. 32, almost ignoring Deut. 33. The LORD tells Moses to ascend Mount Nebo, see the land, and die. Moses does just that, at which point another writer traces the Pentateuch's conclusion with an eye to the future. The fact that "no one knows his burial place *to this day*" suggests the distant perspective that the writer has on Moses's time (Deut. 34:6). Joshua's own "spirit of wisdom" comes from Moses's laying on of hands. Despite Israel's disobedience to the LORD while Moses was alive, this writer announces that Israel listened to Joshua and did as the LORD commanded Moses! What a different perspective.

Deuteronomy 34:10 is even more remarkable: "And a prophet has not arisen yet in Israel like Moses, whom the LORD knew face to face." How could a prophet have arisen unless some time had passed? Such a statement requires a lengthy period. Moreover, it suggests that the office of prophecy had become prominent in Israel. Although "prophecy" surfaces from time to time in the Pentateuch, it is not until later, in the books of Kings, that the notion gains increasing importance to the kingdom's religious vitality. Moreover, the adverb "yet" signals that the writer is expecting a Moses-like prophet to arise. His description that "the LORD knew him face to face" echoes Exod. 33:11: "The LORD spoke to Moses face to face as a man speaks to his friend." One of the passages in which prophecy surfaces is Deut. 18, implying that prophecy is on the horizon. Sketching out laws that involve king, priest, and prophet in the land, Deut. 18:15 emphasizes, "It is a prophet from your midst, from your brothers, like me, that the LORD your God will raise up for you." Verse 16 looks back on the day at Sinai during the assembly when in fear they asked not to hear God's voice or see the fire again lest they die. In Exod. 20:19, they said, "You speak with us and we will listen. Do not let God speak with us lest we die." God told Moses that this was a good thing because "I will raise up a prophet for them from the midst of their brothers like you, and I will put my words in his mouth, and he will speak to them all that I command him" (Deut. 18:18). Just as the LORD was "with Moses's mouth" (Exod. 4:11, 15), so would he be with this prophet. But this prophet's work will involve more than just words. Deuteronomy 34:11 declares that this future prophet will do the signs and wonders that Moses did to Pharaoh and Egypt before the eyes of Israel.

By the Pentateuch's conclusion, Moses has become a type of the one the reader should be expecting: a law-giving prophet. Deuteronomy 33:4 says, "Moses commanded us *Torah*, a possession for the assembly of Jacob," but in the end, the lion king is portrayed as one like Moses. He is the one who "made rules" (Gen. 49:10) and "came with the heads of the people, doing the righteousness of the LORD, and his judgments are with Israel" (Deut. 33:21).

Scripture Index

Subject Index

Aaron
  approaching God 149–51, 154–55
  death of 145 (fig. 10.3)
  the exodus and 129–32, 134
  garments and jewelry of 151
  genealogy of 131–32
  golden calf and 152, 176
  Levites and 156–57
  as priest 151, 154–55
  sin of 145 (fig. 10.4), 152, 154, 176
  sons of 145 (fig. 10.4), 150–51, 154–55
Abel 91, 97–99, 108n11
abominations. See idolatry of Israelites
Abraham. See also patriarchs; Sarai/Sarah
  builds altar 108
  election of 180
  genealogy of 115–17, 119, 120
  Melchizedek and 47
  name change of 111n13
  obedience of 56, 119
  slavery and exodus foretold to 128, 142
  walked with God 100
Abrahamic covenant
  Abraham's seed in 51–53, 56, 60, 117–20,
    122–25, 166
  blessings of 40, 51, 56, 115, 117–23, 147, 166
  circumcision as sign of 166
  curses of 46n2, 117, 121–22
  promised land in 34, 57, 68, 125, 128, 131
  unconditional 147
'acharit (end) 36, 38–39, 45, 61. See also end
Adam. See also Eden, garden of; Eve/woman
  authority of 65, 79
  counterpart for 85–86

garments of 81, 92
genealogy of 99–100
God speaks to 77
image/likeness of 100, 102
sin of 89, 91–93, 118, 120
as son of God 103
'adam (humankind) 76, 79, 88–89, 92–93, 100,
  102–3, 120
'adamah (ground) 93
adultery/harlotry 95, 157, 174–75, 177. See also
  idolatry of Israelites
Agag (king of Amalekites) 48
Almighty, the (Shadday) 47–48, 51–52, 60–61,
  74n12, 96
altars to the Lord 77, 108, 150–52, 154
Amalekites 48, 145 (fig. 10.3)
'amar (said) 149
Amorites 46
angels 47, 74n12, 152
animals/beasts. See also serpent/snake
  creation of 71 (fig.), 72, 75–76, 78, 85
  the flood and 106–7, 109
  impact of sin on 93
  naming of 85–86, 94
  sacrificing 108, 157, 177
Apocrypha, Old Testament 7n5
'arar (curse) 121–22
ark
  of the covenant 168
  of Moses 127
  of Noah 105–9, 111, 114n1
'asah (make/do) 70, 129, 131
assonance 39n12

191